WOMEN AND WELFARE CONDITIONALITY

Welfare Conditionality series

Series Editor: **Peter Dwyer**, University of York, UK

This series explores whether welfare conditionality works and asks how and why it might work differently for different people in diverse circumstances. It aims to develop an empirically and theoretically informed understanding of the role of welfare conditionality in promoting behaviour change among welfare recipients over time.

Also available

Dealing with Welfare Conditionality
Implementation and Effects
Edited by **Peter Dwyer**

The Impacts of Welfare Conditionality
Sanctions, Support and Behaviour Change
By **Peter Dwyer, Lisa Scullion, Katy Jones, Jenny McNeill** and
Alasdair B.R. Stewart

Find out more
policy.bristoluniversitypress.co.uk/
welfare-conditionality

WOMEN AND WELFARE CONDITIONALITY

Lived Experiences of Benefit Sanctions, Work and Welfare

Sharon Wright

Welfare Conditionality
SANCTIONS, SUPPORT AND BEHAVIOUR CHANGE

P

First published in Great Britain in 2023 by

Policy Press, an imprint of
Bristol University Press
University of Bristol
1–9 Old Park Hill
Bristol
BS2 8BB
UK
t: +44 (0)117 374 6645
e: bup-info@bristol.ac.uk

Details of international sales and distribution partners are available at policy.bristoluniversitypress.co.uk

© Bristol University Press 2023

British Library Cataloguing in Publication Data
A catalogue record for this book is available from the British Library

ISBN 978-1-4473-4773-6 Hardcover
ISBN 978-1-4473-4774-3 Paperback
ISBN 978-1-4473-4777-4 ePub
ISBN 978-1-4473-4776-7 ePdf

Cover design: Andrew Corbett
Front cover image: Andrew Corbett

Content warning

This book contains material that may be difficult to read. It includes women's accounts of experiences that may be upsetting or triggering, including sexual violence, domestic abuse, racism, extreme financial hardship, mental health problems and suicidal thoughts.

If you are affected by any of the issues, support is available from:

Samaritans
www.samaritans.org
116 123

National Domestic Abuse Helpline
www.nationaldahelpline.org.uk
080 82000 247

Citizens Advice
www.citizensadvice.org.uk

Contents

List of figure, tables and charts

List of abbreviations

DWP	Department for Work and Pensions
ESA	Employment and Support Allowance
ESA WRAG	Employment and Support Allowance Work-Related Activity Group
GSR	Government Social Research
HoC	House of Commons
IS	Income Support
JRF	Joseph Rowntree Foundation
JSA	Jobseeker's Allowance
NAO	National Audit Office
NHS	National Health Service
OECD	Organisation for Economic Cooperation and Development
ONS	Office for National Statistics
PIP	Personal Independence Payment
SMC	Social Mobility Commission
TST	The Sutton Trust
TUC	Trades Union Congress
UC	Universal Credit

Acknowledgements

I am hugely grateful to all the women who agreed to take part in the study and shared their often difficult and sometimes traumatic experiences of work and welfare during lengthy in-depth research interviews over up to three years of their lives.

It was an enormous challenge to find so many people to take part in the study and I very much appreciate the efforts of the many local and national support organisations who helped us make contact.

The 'Welfare Conditionality: Sanctions, Support and Behaviour Change' (ES/K002163) project would not have been possible without funding and support from the Economic and Social Research Council and the universities of Glasgow, Heriot-Watt, Salford, Sheffield, Sheffield Hallam and York.

Massive thanks are due to project leader Peter Dwyer and the whole Welfare Conditionality team, who put enormous energy into this mammoth qualitative research project: www.welfareconditionality.ac.uk/who-we-are/

Feedback from the anonymous reviewer and supportive discussions with Jane Millar and Jackie Gulland have improved the book greatly. My writing buddy Vikki McCall helped keep progress on-track with regular encouragement and dedicated writing time; our practice is inspired by Rowena Murray's social-writing model.

The team at Policy Press have been brilliant throughout the commissioning, writing and production process. Special thanks to Jay Allan, Zoe Forbes and Laura Vickers-Rendall. Huge thanks to Annie Rose from Newgen Publishing UK, who managed the production of the book.

I am very lucky to be surrounded professionally and personally by talented and caring people who help me to thrive through adversity, the greatest of all is my husband, Marcus. Thank you.

ONE

What does work-based welfare reform mean for women?

It's February 2015 and I've travelled north by train between snowy mountains to speak to Michelle, a 23-year-old single woman getting Universal Credit. We settle down in a confusingly repurposed room – recording studio in one corner, desk and chairs in the other – in a hidden corner of an anonymous community centre. Seagulls squawk through the skylight. Michelle is animated. Her pale eyes sparkle as she tells me of her enchantment with the new payment, which is "much better" than Jobseeker's Allowance. She's out of work now but boasts an impressive array of vocational qualifications for realistic-sounding job options – hairdressing, interior decorating – and has recent supermarket and call-centre work experience. Michelle is worried about "being sanctioned, basically not having any money". She recently got a letter from the Jobcentre asking why she missed an appointment. It left her "a bit confused because I honestly cannot remember having an appointment at that time and that date", which was during a period when she was doing a full-time employability training course. Once she explained, she wasn't sanctioned. She says: "I really want to find a job, because I'm so sick of not working; I really am."

In 2016, a soaked train rushes me back to meet Michelle again. We're in a bigger room, in the same complex. Since we last met, Michelle got a cleaning job at a supermarket, 16–20 hours per week, but it didn't last. A psychiatrist was assessing her during that time:

> 'I told my boss – I opened up to him, told him everything, that I thought I may have been schizophrenic or something. ... It came to an end partly because of the way I was feeling, but also because he actually – he was discriminative of me. And I resigned in the end because I just couldn't cope.'

Michelle's mental health problems are now diagnosed. She now has a zero-hours contract with a community centre but hasn't had any shifts yet and she volunteers at a charity shop. She wants to get a nursing degree. "That's the only thing that prevents me from working sometimes. I've got borderline personality disorder. And I suffer with anxiety and depression, so it makes things really, really hard. Sometimes unbearable. ... Medicines can't take it away; they can only manage it."

Before we know it, it's 2017 and our third and final meeting. Michelle asks if I can spare some change and if she can charge her phone while we're talking. She can't get the counselling support she needs for her borderline personality disorder, which "envelops my life. It controls me. I can't get away from it". With an incurable mental health problem, and little understanding from employers in multiple precarious jobs, Universal Credit seems like a life sentence of conditionality. I find it hard to imagine how things can turn around.

Introduction

Michelle was one of the first women to claim Universal Credit in the UK. Her experience exposes the truth that work-based welfare reforms are ineffective at securing sustainable jobs for those with long-term health problems. Despite Michelle's wholehearted dedication to job seeking, she finished the study where she started it – in poverty, disabled and out of work. She was never sanctioned in the three years we had contact with her. Like many women in the Welfare Conditionality study, the underlying threat of sanctions formed a perpetual feature in the backdrop of Michelle's life. Fear and foreboding are no accident – it is the intention of UK government policy that women feel economically unstable. Benefit sanctions[1] and making disabled women and mothers look for full-time work are part of a long-term strategy to cut social security spending. It started in the 1980s when there was mass unemployment. The Conservative government of the time changed the rules for unemployment benefit so that fewer and fewer people were eligible. Surprisingly, when 'New' Labour came to power in 1997, they continued the Conservative reforms during a decade of low unemployment (1997–2010). Then, from 2010–22, during good economic times as well as bad, Conservative-led governments ransacked the social security system. Cut after cut, on a previously unimaginable scale, went hand in hand with arbitrary limits like the benefits freeze, household benefit cap and the two-child limit to reduce women's incomes (Women's Budget Group, 2020, 1). Cruelty was dressed up as 'incentives' in policies like the spare-bedroom subsidy (the 'bedroom tax'), to take money away from women who need it during a government-induced social-housing shortage. Claimants were pressurised to renounce disability and declare their faith in job search. Blatant punishment shot Britain to silver place in the global rankings for overall strictness of benefits (Immervoll and Knotz, 2018), with open-ended and three-year maximum sanctions. Those worst affected are 'lone parents, survivors of domestic abuse, disabled women, BAME women and migrant women' (Women's Budget Group, 2020, 1).

Over my lifetime, social attitudes and policy requirements about women's work have changed unrecognisably. The welfare system that previously aspired to meet needs 'from the cradle to the grave' was not perfect, but it did offer working-class women an alternative to destitution in predictable circumstances that conspire against earning a living. The twenty-first century UK welfare system has moved the goalposts out of the park. Universal Credit (UC) treats women much the same as men – as if they are errant healthy workers who need to be coerced into full-time jobs. Women claimants are now legally required to seek work, even as sole carers for young children. There is no equivalent legal requirement for men to care. This leaves women in a strange position. Work requirements have been degendered but care obligations have not. Despite decades of gains towards equality, the onus of unpaid care is still on women. Childcare is extremely expensive in the UK, costing more than a third of female earnings and much higher than most OECD countries (Organisation for Economic Cooperation and Development [OECD], 2020, 2). Although Universal Credit covers 85 per cent of childcare costs, claimants must pay up-front first and then claim back, which is unaffordable for many mothers (Garnham, 2018).

This book investigates how women live through the new work-based system of social security over time. It reveals the hidden gendered nature of conditional social security reforms in the context of deeply embedded labour market inequalities. The standpoint of this book is that: 'one must take account of the very real gender differences in productive and reproductive labour and access to civil and political rights and how these differences influence the ways in which men and women struggle for and claim benefits from the state as citizens' (Orloff, 1993, 309).

The aim of this chapter is to establish the importance of understanding how welfare conditionality impacts on women. First, welfare conditionality is defined and the rise in work-related social security policy is set out. Second, I explain how Canadian sociologist, Dorothy Smith's ideas can help to cast light on gendered experiences of work related conditionality. Smith's (1987) starting point is to compare women's actual lived experiences, situated within their local contexts, with the policy-related texts that mediate their lives. These concepts are used to interpret conditional welfare reforms and their impacts throughout the book. Third, the research on which this book is based will be outlined, exploring experiences of a subset of 138 women, claiming working-age social security benefits, who took part in three waves of qualitative longitudinal research. Fourth, the structure of the book is outlined.

What is welfare conditionality?

This book is about how fundamental change to social security impacts on real women. The main concept is welfare conditionality, by which I mean the formal behavioural requirements for women to engage with employment-related meetings at Jobcentre Plus and contracted-out employability programmes, work-related training and job-seeking activities, including digital systems. Welfare conditionality also encompasses a set of discretionary work-coach expectations, which are variable, unpredictable and difficult to challenge (Dwyer, 2018). Work-related conditionality is at the heart of social security reforms in many developed welfare systems in the 21st century (Welfare Conditionality, 2018). While many European and Scandinavian countries – starting from a much more generous position – have reduced or reformed benefit entitlements and moved more toward 'work first' forms of support, the UK is at the forefront of downgrading workers' social citizenship rights (van Berkel et al, 2017). Work-related conditionality in the UK applies to an unusually broad range of claimants, including groups usually exempt in other countries, like disabled people and those already working, and is backed by the threat of remarkably tough financial sanctions (Wright and Dwyer, 2022).

Benefit sanctions

The sanctions system was reformed in 2012 to 'act as a more effective deterrent to non-compliance' (Department for Work and Pensions [DWP], 2011b, 9). Change to the sanction system was an era-defining event. For much of the 20th century (1911 to 1986), benefit sanctions in the UK had a maximum period of six weeks loss of benefit (Adler, 2018: 22). There was some tightening up of the system for unemployed people in the late 1980s (Adler, 2018), but it was in 2010 when an obvious 'punitive turn' (Fletcher and Wright, 2018) began. According to official discourse, sanctions exist 'to encourage claimants to take reasonable steps to find employment or move closer to the labour market' (DWP, 2011b, 13). Research shows that heavy harm was inflicted first via managerial methods. Jobcentre Plus offices were issued with 'benefit off-flow targets' that functioned in effect – where there were insufficient suitable jobs in local labour markets – as sanctioning targets (see Redman and Fletcher, 2021). Jobseeker's Allowance sanctions rates shot up in response to the 'great sanctions drive' (National Audit Office (NAO), 2016; Webster, 2016) two years *before* harsher penalties were legislated for in 2012. At the height of the sanctions frenzy (2010–15), almost a quarter of all Jobseeker's Allowance (JSA) claimants were sanctioned (NAO, 2016). The regime has been described as 'cruel, inhuman, and degrading' (Adler, 2018). The 2012 system means that benefit claimants can easily trigger a substantial sanction with a momentary lapse in compliance, for example payments are reduced or removed for 28 days if one Jobcentre appointment is missed. Sanctions ramp up quickly, with repeat mistakes resulting in longer periods without income, for example the penalty for three missed appointments is 91 days. Open-ended sanctions were introduced and the maximum sanction was increased to three years (although in 2019 the government announced that three-year sanctions would be abolished). This toughening up of the system was designed to accelerate movements into employment (DWP, 2011a, 1) but removed 'financial protection entirely and threatens long-term penalties of extreme poverty and destitution whilst offering almost no support or escape via paid employment (since job search requirements continue for low-paid workers)' (Wright and Patrick, 2019, 597). The penalties far outweigh the transgressions, without equivalent support (Pattaro et al, 2022). Recent studies have shown that Jobcentre Plus offers little practical support to job seekers (Dwyer, 2018; Wright and Patrick, 2019; Wright et al, 2020). Despite promising those preparing for work 'the right support' (DWP, 2012, 42), Jobcentre Plus offers only cursory appointments with work coaches, framed by conditionality (Wright and Patrick, 2019). The main support instrument is an online job vacancy portal that also enables a high degree of surveillance over job search activities and is laced with compulsion, doubling as a digital panopticon and 'sanctions evidence-maker' (Fletcher and Wright, 2018; Wright et al, 2020). Benefit sanctions have been found to 'routinely trigger a range of profoundly negative outcomes that do not enhance the likelihood of people moving into paid work' (Dwyer, 2018, 142).

Punitive British welfare conditionality sits within a broad retrenchment strategy that is interconnected with the care crisis, reflecting 'decades of organised neglect suffered by our caring infrastructures and economies' (The Care Collective, 2020, 2). Welfare conditionality reinforces the 'near-ubiquitous positioning of profit-making as the organising principle of life' (The Care Collective, 2020, 3). Care is gendered. Globally, unpaid care prevents 42 per cent of working-age women from participating in the paid labour market, compared with only 6 per cent of men (Coffey et al, 2020, 14). The neglect of care, when care services are withdrawn and social protection is downgraded, is also gendered. By 'systematically prioritising the interests and flows of financial capital' (The Care Collective, 2020, 3), governments arrange societies around male-defined priorities that both depend on and disguise the unpaid care-work of women.

From conditionality 'creep' to 'ubiquity'

In 2013, Universal Credit fundamentally changed the UK social security system, from the 'creeping conditionality' (Dwyer, 2004) of the New Labour era to a new type of 'ubiquitous conditionality' (Dwyer and Wright, 2014). Universal Credit (UC) is gender 'discrimination by design' (Garnham, 2018, 1). UC is based on a full-time model of paid work, with claimants expected to comply with a default 35 hour working week, filled by either paid work or job search. Partners must decide who is the 'main earner' and 'main carer'. In fact, the design of work incentives and payment to only one person in a household supports a male breadwinner model of earning that is out of step with the fact that three-quarters of mothers now work (Garnham, 2018). Second earners, usually women, do not have a separate earnings allowance, so couples can be worse off financially if both work. For women, who traditionally balance unpaid care with reduced hours of paid employment, this is an incredibly significant change that has received less attention in public, policy or academic debates than it deserves (see Bennett, 2011, 2012; Bennett and Sung, 2013a; Ingold and Etherington, 2013; Ariss et al, 2015; Cain, 2016; De Henau, 2017; Reis, 2018; Gulland, 2019a; Harding, 2020; Andersen, 2020; for important exceptions). In May 2021, 53 per cent of the 5.9 million households on Universal Credit were women[2] (DWP, 2021e). Women consistently outnumber men as in-work Universal Credit recipients. In July 2021, there were 362,557 more women UC claimants in-work (1,347,355 in total), compared with 984,798 men (DWP Stat-Xplore, 2021g). As working lone parents transition from Working Tax Credit onto Universal Credit during the 2020s, it is anticipated that most in-work UC claimants will be women (77 per cent) and parents (70 per cent), with lone mothers making up 51 per cent of all in-work claimants.

Switching work expectations for lone parents: from protected status to androgynous workers

The complete turnaround in expectations for women to work is exemplified in the development of welfare conditionality for lone parents. This switch occurred over three phases. First, in the post-war welfare settlement, lone motherhood was designated as a special carer status in a needs-based category of benefit recipient exempt from job-seeking requirements and without service provision. This position was long-lasting and, unlike many comparable countries, lone parents in Britain were not subject to any job-search conditions until the late 1990s (Finn and Casebourne, 2012). Then, the second phase of reform happened, between 1997 and 2010, when consecutive New Labour governments began to redefine cohorts of lone parents as job seekers. Dedicated employment service interventions were introduced for lone parents as a group – primarily via the voluntary New Deal for Lone Parents. Most recently, the third phase of redefining lone parents as job seekers occurred when the Conservative-Liberal coalition government applied 'conditions of conduct' (Clasen and Clegg, 2007) to almost all lone parents. Since 1997, there has been a remarkable degree of consistency between all governing UK political parties in the direction of policy travel, the combined force of which has recategorised increasing proportions of lone parents primarily as workers.

Behavioural conditionality has gone too far too fast in applying minimal mandatory support and sanctions, originally designed for unemployed men, to lone mothers[3] (Davies, 2012; Whitworth and Griggs, 2013; Fletcher and Wright, 2018). These changes have occurred within a broad international trend of 'risk re-categorisation' (Clasen and Clegg, 2011), which, in the British case, has meant the conflation of previously separate states of unemployment, disability and lone parenthood for income-maintenance purposes (Clasen, 2011). Lone parent households, which by definition include children, are now subject to a harsh sanctions regime that includes withdrawal of benefit income, for periods of one month to indefinitely, until 're-compliance' (Johnsen, 2014; Rabindrakumar, 2017). Previous labour market and conditionality exemptions and protections have now been removed. Special statutory service provisions are no longer available. However, lone parents are positioned uniquely in relation to both the labour market inequalities and caring roles because they embody sole breadwinner and carer roles (Speak, 2000; Berthoud, 2003; Lewis and Giullari, 2005; Ridge and Millar, 2010; Graham and McQuaid, 2014).

Applying Dorothy Smith's ideas to interpreting welfare conditionality from a feminist perspective

This book applies insights from Dorothy Smith's body of sociological work to reveal how the texts of supposedly 'gender-neutral' (DWP, 2011b, 5) social security reforms both exclude and discipline women's voices and experiences. Welfare reform texts since 2010 include legislation (most notably the Welfare Reform Act 2012 and the Welfare Reform and Work Act 2016); official discourse (describing benefit cuts as 'fair and affordable', aiming to 'simplify the benefit system', 'improve incentives to work' and 'find savings' (Hobson, 2020, 5); policy documents (DWP, 2010a/b; 2013); guidance materials for front-line workers; and policy instruments (like claimant commitments, online job-search tools etc.). These texts structure women's everyday interactions with the social security system and reveal underlying power processes of the 'ruling relations' (Smith, 1987, 4). Male-dominated ruling relations underpin many textual representations of reality, presenting a partial perspective that appears as rational 'objectified, impersonal, claiming universality', but containing a 'gender subtext [that] has been invisible' (Smith, 1987, 4). For example, the male subtext of welfare reform legislation prioritises full-time paid work for all. This is evident in legislation such as the Welfare Reform Act 2012, which introduced Universal Credit and Personal Independence Payment (PIP), and the Welfare Reform and Work Act 2016 that was designed to reduce social security spending. A whole raft of austerity reforms follow the male-orientated assumptions of the legislation by: freezing the value of benefits for four years (resulting in rising poverty for both out-of-work and in-work claimants (Joseph Rowntree Foundation [JRF], 2017); lowering the benefit cap; limiting Child Tax Credits/Universal

Credit, abolishing the Employment and Support Allowance Work-Related Activity component reducing the financial value of the benefit by about a third; changing conditionality for 'responsible carers' and reducing housing support. The burden of austerity cuts (85 per cent) fell on women, removing twice as much income from women than from men (Sodha, 2016).

The study

This book is about women's lived experiences of social security work requirements. It is based on data from the first major qualitative longitudinal research (QLR) on Welfare Conditionality (ESRC-funded 2013–19, see Appendix 1). I was a co-investigator on the original study, which had a wider remit than this book and included investigating interventions for antisocial behaviour, families, offenders and social tenants. Women, 213 in total, participated in three waves[4] (A–C) of the study, between 2014 and 2018. For this book, I subsampled the data from 138 women who currently or recently received working-age benefits (Employment Support Allowance,[5] Jobseeker's Allowance[6] or Universal Credit) at the first interview. I re-analysed transcripts drawn from across the pre-existing selection categories (see Table 1.1 and Appendix 1). My approach is a form of original investigator 'supplementary analysis' (rather than 'secondary analysis') that sought new insights about women's experiences of welfare conditionality that were not 'fully addressed in the primary study' (Heaton, 2004, 38). Supplementary analysis is a rarity for complex qualitative longitudinal datasets and almost unheard of on the supersized 'Big Qual' (Brower et al, 2019) scale of the Welfare Conditionality study. The analysis explores overarching themes through individual cases and tells women's stories about what work-based welfare conditionality means to them in the context of their intersubjective lives and over time. Women's cases are used to animate key points and to illustrate the richness of the data.

Sanctioning patterns

The study included diverse samples of women in different circumstances (see Table 1.1). About half of the subsample had been sanctioned and just over half had not (see Chart 1.1). In the book subsample, 66 women had been sanctioned,[7] two-thirds of whom had only ever been sanctioned once at the start of the study. Seventy-one women had never been sanctioned. Chart 1.1 shows the number of sanctions each woman had received; one woman is excluded because she did not know if she had been sanctioned. Around a third of the women in the subsample had only been sanctioned once. Thirteen per cent were sanctioned two to five times and 3 per cent were sanctioned six times or more. Study participants were recruited using

Table 1.1: Women and welfare conditionality book subsample (n = 138)

Selection category	Benefit received Wave A			No benefits Wave A	Total
	JSA	ESA	UC		
Antisocial behaviour	2	4	0		6
Disabled person	1	19	0		20
Ex-offender	3	5	0		8
Family intervention project	0	1	0		1
Homeless person	4	6	0		10
Job seeker	21	1	0		22
Lone parent	18	11	0	5	34
Migrant	10	1	0	3[8]	14
Social tenant	1	4	0		5
Universal Credit	0	0	18		18
Total	60	52	18	8	138

Chart 1.1: Women and welfare conditionality subsample (n = 137), number of times sanctioned

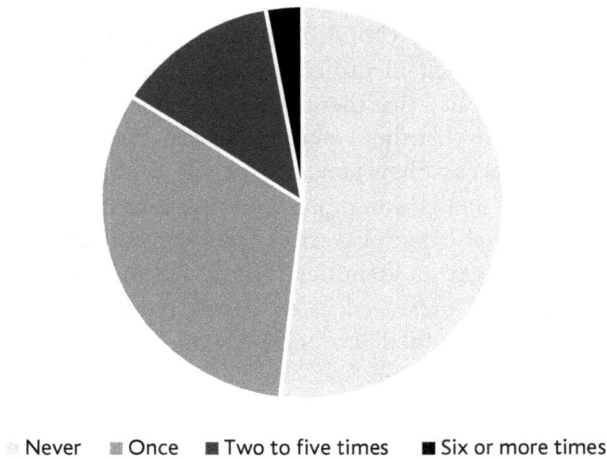

 Never Once Two to five times Six or more times

convenience sampling methods, so these proportions are stated for descriptive purposes and are not generalisable to the claimant population. Job seekers were the sample with the highest proportion of female study-participants who had been sanctioned at Wave A (10 women). More than half of the women we sampled as disabled, homeless, migrant and lone parent had been sanctioned. Smaller proportions of women had been sanctioned in the Universal Credit and family-intervention project samples. It was only the social-tenant sample that included no sanctioned women. The threat of sanctions and fear of being sanctioned was widespread and experienced in many different circumstances, affecting many more women than those who appear in the official statistics. There were few new sanctions over the course of the study for female participants. At Wave B, there was only one fewer of those who said they had never been sanctioned and 11 women who reported being sanctioned within the last year (three within the last 1–3 months, one 4–6 months ago and seven between 7–12 months). By Wave C, only two women reported a recent sanction (in the last 1–3 months). This fits with national sanctioning rates during the period of the fieldwork (2014–17). The next section focuses on the women subject to the most intensive sanctioning.

Defining gender

Interviewees selected their gender identity in response to the question 'how would you describe your gender?', as part of a post-interview questionnaire. The question was asked openly and recorded by the interviewer using the census 2011 categories of 'male', 'female' and 'other', with open space for description. There was only one question on gender. On reflection, it would have been beneficial to distinguish (as the UK 2021 census does, Office for National Statistics [ONS], 2021a) between sex at birth and gender identity. All participants self-identified as binary female or male. Subsequent qualitative analysis revealed that there was at least one transgender person in the study. It is possible that there were other non-binary participants who did not disclose or discuss their gender expression. My decision to use the terms 'women' and 'men' throughout the book matches participants' self-identification and is not intended to oversimply, exclude or homogenise transgender experiences or identities (Hines, 2006). The policy analysis and empirical material presented in this book reflects a 'gendered social order [that] is deeply ingrained' (Lorber, 2022, 4), to the detriment of many women and non-binary people.

Gender, 'race' and intersectionality

Kimberle Crenshaw (1989, 139) coined the term 'intersectionality' as part of her sociolegal Black feminist critique of the: 'tendency to treat race and gender as mutually exclusive categories of experience and analysis … perpetuated by a single-axis framework that is dominant in antidiscrimination law and that is also reflected in feminist theory and antiracist politics'. Crenshaw (1989) emphasises the importance of beginning with Black women's experiences of gender and class to appreciate the multidimensional processes of disadvantage and discrimination. She draws attention to the 'implicit grounding of white female experiences in the doctrinal conceptualization of sex discrimination' (1989, 144). It is therefore important to acknowledge that I am a middle-aged childless heterosexual White cis woman from a working-class background with a middle-class lifestyle. In writing this book, I strive to appreciate and represent multidimensional aspects of other women's lives that are largely dissimilar to my own. I try to do this respectfully, by recognising difference and agency to 'embrace the complexities of compoundedness' in discrimination and disadvantage (Crenshaw, 1989, 169). I am prone to implicit assumptions that confirm what my own lived experiences have taught me and that my current privileges afford. It is difficult to strip-off subconscious preconceptions, so I attempt better awareness by listening, through discussion and by reflecting on my thought processes in the context of wide reading, to access diverse experiences and perspectives including LGBTQIA+, minoritised ethnicities, different age groups and disability.

I have chosen 'gender' as the main category for analysis with an awareness that gender identities are varied and multifaceted, rather than essential, biologically-determined or homogenous (Lorber, 2022). I have also chosen to analyse welfare conditionality from a feminist standpoint – 'by women, for women'. In doing so, I have neglected in-depth analysis of the discrimination and disadvantage faced by men in the study, which is no less important but qualitatively different. Scope remains to explore the Welfare Conditionality data on male experiences of care and conditionality. However, for practical (time did not allow for in-depth analysis of all 1082 interviews in the study) and conceptual purposes, the focus for this book is on how women are disadvantaged in relation to work-based welfare policies and includes important experiences of intersectionality between structural disadvantages of gender and race/ethnicity, disability, age and class (Williams, 2018, 2021). I have adopted the approach that: 'Gender shapes identities and perception, interactional practices, and the very forms of social institutions, and it does so in race- and class- specific ways' (Howard et al, 2005, ix–x). Although the welfare system is designed to – and often does – tackle inequalities it also 'institutionalises, class, gender and racial divisions and inequalities' (Ginsburg, 1992, 2). Black feminism is crucial in establishing the need to understand how processes of racism and gender can combine as 'double-discrimination' (Crenshaw, 1989, 149). Black and minoritised ethnic women, LGBTQIA+ people, disabled women and those from different age groups may experience the social security system in many different ways. Little is known about the ethnicity of social security recipients in the UK. Since the change to Universal Credit, equality data is collected via a voluntary survey during the claims process. The response rate is too low to meaningfully estimate ethnicity across the claimant population (DWP, 2021d).

Structure of the book

Chapter Two provides a conceptual discussion of women and work-based social security. It establishes Dorothy Smith's feminist ideas as the main framework for understanding welfare conditionality in this book, which combines perspectives on gendered lived experience, constituted via intersubjective street-level practices. There are three main conceptual threads, which are closely related to the methodological approach, combining feminist analysis with interpretivist theory applied to develop street-level bureaucracy analysis. This gendered analysis of welfare conditionality builds on existing literature that focuses on particular groups (for example, lone parents, see Rafferty and Wiggan, 2011; Haux, 2012; Millar and Ridge, 2013) and specific policies (such as Universal Credit) (Millar and Bennett, 2017). The analytical framework begins from the interpretivist feminist stance of 'where we are actually located, embodied, in the local historicity and particularities of our lived worlds' (Smith, 1987, 8) in order to assemble authentic and differentiated accounts of the multiple ways in which experiences of conditionality are gendered in practice. The advantage of this approach is to 'interrogat[e] taken for granted practices of knowing' (Campbell, 2003, 7) about the meanings of social security and its associated systems of sanction and support. This theoretical position allows for the identification and appreciation of multiple insider accounts from different perspectives.

This conceptual approach combines insights from two distinct bodies of literature, feminist analysis and interpretivism, which are aligned only in a specialist niche in the field (see Smith, 1987; Kruks, 2014). Both feminism and interpretivism have distinct roots and traditions and within each, critiques of the other can be found (see Scott, 1992; Prus, 1996). Despite debate, for example over the risks of essentialising female experiences or giving voice only to privileged women, feminist phenomenologists (Fisher and Embree, 2000; Kruks, 2001; Olkowski and Weiss, 2006; Heinämaa and Rodemeyer, 2010) have continued to: 'suspend our already conceptualised accounts of human experiences in order to describe how phenomena appear to us as they are "lived": ... as we engage with them as embodied agents in the world' (Kruks, 2014, 75). It is particularly in the engagement of feminist phenomenology with analysis of institutional practices (Smith, 1987; 2005; Griffith and Smith, 2014a) where existing literature offers most fertile ground for original analysis of welfare conditionality. Application of Smith's (1987) concepts of 'relations of ruling' also offers scope to develop the study of street-level implementation. Although the concept of street-level bureaucracy (Lipsky, 1980/2010) is widely known and is currently enjoying a revival (Brodkin and Marston, 2013; van Berkel, 2020), it is less commonly acknowledged as an expression of rational choice theory from a positivist-leaning political science tradition (Brodkin, 2012). This body of literature provides very valuable insights into how policies are brought into being through the work of front-line officials, who balance organisational goals with client needs to mediate both policy (Lipsky, 1980) and politics (Brodkin, 2013b). This book reconceptualises street level analysis from an interpretivist perspective (as detailed previously) to view welfare conditionality implementation practices as gendered social processes of interactive intersubjective accomplishment.

Chapter Three sets out how work requirements for women claiming working-age benefits have changed over time. Post-World War II, the social security system was based on principles of gender difference. Married women were expected to be full-time mothers and housewives, dependent on their working husbands. Entitlements to social security mirrored this 'male breadwinner' model (Lewis, 2001). In the 1950s, the marriage bar prevented women in certain professions from continuing their jobs after marrying. It was perfectly legal to pay women less than men. Pregnant women could be dismissed without recourse. Attitudes began to change over time and in the 1970s equal opportunities and equal pay legislation were introduced. In 1996 – a late stage by international standards – job-seeking obligations were put on lone parents receiving benefits. These were gentle at first but ramped up through the 2000s. In 2010, welfare reforms turned ugly (Fletcher and Wright, 2018; Wright et al, 2020) and in 2013 Universal Credit sealed the deal that social security would treat women on seemingly equal terms to men. The degendered 21st-century benefits system operates on an 'adult worker model' (Lewis and Giullari, 2005) that squeezes out the capacity to care.

Next, there are three findings chapters that draw directly from the interviews to explore different aspects of welfare conditionality. Existing literature tends to explore women's encounters with welfare conditionality either together with men's (see Dwyer, 2018; Dwyer et al, 2018; Dwyer, 2019) or from the perspectives of specific groups like Universal Credit recipients as mothers (Andersen, 2020; 2023) or couples (Griffiths et al, 2020; 2022). This book does things differently in three ways. First, it looks directly at a how a range of benefits (Universal Credit, Jobseeker's Allowance, Employment and Support Allowance and Income Support) mediate women's lives in relation to care, work and welfare. Second, it shifts the focus away from family structures and onto the lifecourse, highlighting the impacts of conditionality on a cohort of women aged 55+. Third, it compares the intense experiences of those who were hammered by repeat sanctions (Chapter Five) with those who were sanctioned only once or not at all (Chapter Six).

Chapter Four shows how 22 women aged in their late 50s and 60s encountered the alien system of job-search requirements at a late stage in their working lives. For a cohort of women born in the 1950s, societal expectations and legal mandates about women's roles in care and employment have reversed over their lifetime. Some were discriminated against in their early forays into the labour market in the 1970s and given a clear message that they were not welcome in the world of work. Now, 40–50 years later, they face an extended phase of employment when they had expected to retire. Instead of easing out of paid work or providing grandmother care to help their daughter's work, this cohort of women are compelled to seek full-time work and undergo patronising work-preparation training as conditions of receiving financial support from the state. Karen, Anne, June, Jane and Donna's experiences show how 'ubiquitous conditionality' (Dwyer and Wright, 2014) has expanded to fill the gap where their pensions were to be.

Chapter Five identifies women's experiences of crushing conditionality, highlighting the lived experiences of heavily enforced work-related conditionality. It tells the stories of the most-sanctioned women in the study, representing 16 women who were sanctioned multiple times. Sarah, Helen and Jo are three of the women who received six or more sanctions in the 12 months leading up to participating in the research. Mira experienced racism at work that was reinforced by sanctions via the social security system. She is part of a wider cohort of lone parents who were shifted off Income Support and onto Jobseeker's Allowance. Shaneta was also sanctioned for leaving work 'voluntarily' despite the job having hours incompatible with her childcare responsibilities. These women's stories show the unrelenting punishment that the sanction system can mete out, regardless of heavy unpaid caring responsibilities. The disproportionately harsh financial penalties for missed appointments were experienced while dealing with severe ill health, disability and distress. Women were left with a strong sense of injustice at how they had been treated.

Chapter Six investigates the long shadows cast by the sanction system. It explores the majority experience of sanctioning for women in the study – the threat of sanctions – and the impacts of one-off sanctions. At first glance, these may seem like lesser forms of punishment than those endured by the women in Chapter Five. However, single sanctions often involved very upsetting experiences and intense emotional responses, including anger, shame and despair, which were long-lasting. This chapter is difficult to read because of the horrific situations that some of the women found themselves in and the contrast between their pain and the blithe way their benefit income was reduced or removed. Twenty-seven women were sanctioned only once, including Javeria, Lisette, Anja, Grace, Amira and Bilyana. Almost all of the reasons given for sanctions were unjust and included disregard of female health conditions and pregnancy. Angela, Anastasia, Kerry and Terri were sanctioned because of their children's health and well-being needs. This chapter also shows how sanctioning mothers has an amplified impact on children. Fifty-eight children were impacted by 25 mothers being sanctioned. Amy, Jordan and Yastika's experiences show how conditionality can reinforce gender-based violence and domestic abuse.

Chapter Seven concludes by summarising and synthesising the main arguments of the book. It highlights the original contributions to knowledge and the research, policy and street-level practice implications of the findings.

Re-theorising conditional welfare as gendered lived experience and street-level practice

Bridget is living a "nightmare". She is 36 years old, White British and lives with her 18-year-old son. She left her stressful social care management job three years ago, for her "own sanity", after being bullied. She spun "into a complete and utter downward spiral". Unable to work she withdrew "from everyone". Without any income, she used a credit card to pay her mortgage. 'I bought right at the height of the housing price, and my dad had given me a big deposit, so even with that I'm still in negative equity, so I was kind of stuck in the house.' Bridget stopped opening her post. The debts mounted up. With severe depression and on the brink of eviction, a friend and former colleague stepped in. Bridget's mortgage provider suggested applying for benefits. At the medical assessment, Bridget was deemed 'fit to work', despite her debilitating mental health condition. She qualified for Employment and Support Allowance (ESA) but was put in the Work-Related Activity Group instead of the Support Group. This meant she was required to do regular work-related activities. The Work Programme was "just horrendous" and heaped "sanction upon sanction upon sanction upon sanction" for missing appointments that she knew nothing about.

"Long periods of time … without money" felt "impossible". Being sanctioned nearly every month for a year "delayed my recovery and it exacerbated a situation that was already at a breaking point of going further and further into a black hole". At Bridget's "lowest point" she was reassessed. This time she was placed appropriately in the ESA Support Group, without any work-related conditionality, which put an end to "catastrophe after catastrophe".

Freed from conditionality, Bridget "instantly had relief". She started to recover, changed medication and got counselling support. Then she took on "a real battle" to successfully appeal her original Work Capability Assessment outcome and got a small pot of backdated benefits. She appealed her sanctions. Bridget started doing voluntary support work a few hours a week as 'permitted work'. Over the next year, a local support agency "helped me get back into my normal, full-time professional job". Another year later, Bridget passed her six-month probation period as a full-time social worker. She is "still struggling a bit" with her mental health but "definitely better off financially". She is looking forward to a surfing holiday for her son's 21st birthday. The last time we speak to her, Bridget is 39, still working full-time, no longer on benefits and "getting better and better".

Introduction

Bridget's experience of being wrongly categorised as 'fit for work' and then sanctioned for being unable to comply with inappropriate intensive work conditionality was shared by many other women in the study. The abstract principles of welfare conditionality were entirely inappropriate for her situation. This chapter begins from the perspective of Bridget and women like her – where she is 'actually located, embodied, in the local historicity and particularities of … lived worlds' (Smith, 1987, 8). This chapter recognises the gendered nature of policy makers' conceptualisations of the 'the problem' (Bacchi, 1999) that welfare conditionality is designed to fix and starts to reveal how gender is woven through the fabric of street-level practices. The aim is to apply Dorothy Smith's ideas to show how gender shapes the legal framework, policy documents and intersubjective and interactive practices that bring welfare conditionality into being. This chapter offers a feminist analysis of welfare conditionality in practice that builds on existing literature, which focuses on particular groups (for example lone parents, see Rafferty and Wiggan, 2011; Haux, 2012; Millar and Ridge, 2013) and specific policies (for example Universal Credit) (Millar and Bennett, 2017). These literatures combine to 'interrogat[e] taken for granted practices of knowing' (Campbell, 2003, 7) about the meanings of social security and its associated systems of sanction and support. First, the gendering of academic conceptualisations of conditionality is considered. Second, the ethics of care literature is discussed to propose a central focus on interdependency and care of self and others. Third, the focus changes to understanding how women's lives are mediated by welfare conditionality, drawing first on feminist interpretivism, then the street-level bureaucracy literature and developments in profit-based outsourcing of services and front-line discretion. Fourth, Smith's approach is outlined to view social security in terms of textually-mediated relations of ruling. This section highlights the gendered hierarchy of 'facts', 'boss texts', ideology, the disjuncture between institutional categories and women's lived experiences, and institutional circuits. I then propose that UK welfare conditionality can be understood as involving four textual layers: layer one consists of the domain assumptions and origin stories of policy texts; layer two is the legal and policy boss texts; layer three is the hidden institutional texts that preconfigure front-line practice; and layer four is comprised of the many policy instruments that operate at street-level.

Gendering the concept of conditionality

The scholarly concept of welfare conditionality – and its associated dominant thought traditions – suffer from the same weaknesses as the field of policy itself, in that the masculinist 'domain assumptions' (Stanley, 2018, 15) are falsely universalised in androcentric ways. Female concerns have not traditionally been central to the study of employment, welfare-to-work, activation or welfare conditionality, although this is changing (see Andersen, 2023). Women's everyday lives have tended to be neglected in an multidisciplinary academic field where 'the mainstream still resists the deeper implications of feminist work, and has difficulties assimilating concepts of care, gendered power, dependency, and interdependency' (Orloff, 2009, 317). While there are many examples of important academic literature that analyses the gendered impacts of welfare reforms and conditionality, these are mainly *post hoc* critiques of the disjuncture between policy design and women's lives *in response to* male-orientated reforms. The closest academic voices whispering into the ears of UK-level powerholders tend to be White male elites whose own values match the establishment (Jones, 2015). An elite male gaze on human endeavour produces the *a priori* 'knowledge' from which fiscal and economic concerns have grown and behavioural science has thrived, to build a sophisticatedly punitive 21st-century policy architecture that impoverishes women and children.

Broadly, 'modern welfare states have shaped needs and rights of caregivers and care receivers and have done so in ways that contribute to gender inequality in citizenship rights' (Knijn and Kremer, 1997, 330). Work-based welfare conditionality magnifies existing gender inequalities by colonising citizenship with a 'male sub-text' of paid employment. The academic conceptualisation of welfare conditionality has developed in response to policy reforms across the globe, which have been led by rich English-speaking countries. Work-first welfare reforms (Lindsay, 2007; Kowalewska, 2017) are ideologically driven (Newman, 2011), largely from a neoliberal paternalistic and individual behaviour perspective (Wright, 2016; Monaghan and Ingold, 2019). For decades, academic literature has been dominated by critiques and analysis of welfare conditionality policies that focusses on their impacts and outcomes. Unwittingly, researchers evaluate policy success *in its own terms* – repeating and reinforcing the male-biased viewpoint of policy makers. For example, a lot of scholarly energy has gone into testing the extent to which benefit sanctions influence job outcomes (Abbring et al, 2005; Lalive et al, 2005; Arni et al, 2013; Boockmann et al, 2014) without questioning whether that is something a system of social support for carers has any business doing. Subsequent work has evaluated the philosophical and ethical rationales of conditionality (Watts and Fitzpatrick, 2018). Academic responses to welfare conditionality often either restate or reinforce the familiar male subtexts that 'textually-mediate' (Smith, 1987) women's lives, even when the aim is to critique them. There are three arenas of textual mediation that are important to unpack: first the policy process itself (which involves multiple layers, see discussion following); second the academic texts that assess the policy; and third the public debate.

Surprisingly little of the mainstream literature on welfare conditionality highlights gender, beyond the extent to which it helps or hinders women's engagement in paid work. However, important exceptions are worth mentioning. Ingold and Etherington demonstrate how social security systems in the UK, Denmark and Australia have been restructured to fit the new expectation that partnered 'women will normally be in paid work' (2013, 637). This shift values paid work over unpaid care (Ingold and Etherington, 2013). In Australia, for example, childcare is a reframed by ParentsNext policy as a problem that mothers should individually overcome so they can get a job (Klein, 2021). Mothers are in effect *'expropriated'* from their role in bringing up their own children (Klein, 2021, 1475). Separating mothers from their children has a particular potency in Australia as a colonial territory because punitive welfare conditionality is applied to First Nations women as part of an ongoing process of settler domination that includes the forced removal of land, languages and cultural practices. Most poignantly, it follows a century of government policy that physically removed 'Stolen Generations' of Aboriginal and Torres Strait Islander children from their families (Klein, 2021).

Hidden structures reinforce women's enduring disadvantaged labour market position and vulnerability to poverty. As Smith argued, academia, like policy making, is seemingly genderless: 'its apparent lack of center was indeed centered. It was structured by its gender subtext. Interests, perspectives, relevances leaked from communities of male experience into the externalised and objectified forms of discourse. Within the discourses embedded in the relations of ruling, women were Other' (1987, 13). Although much has changed in academia since Smith was writing in the 1980s, White male-dominated traditions of thought continue to shape the ways in which social and economic problems like unemployment, and policy interventions to address them, are framed and analysed. Because theories, explanations and measurements of unemployment originate from a time when women's labour market participation was severely limited (see Chapter Three), unemployment studies is a field that struggles to fully appreciate women's working lives. It is therefore essential to reorientate the analysis of welfare conditionality from a feminist perspective to highlight the ways in which unpaid care and interdependency influence the definitions of conditionality and its impacts and outcomes. Rather than viewing work and welfare as purely individual concerns, it is crucial to consider how conditionality impacts *interdependencies* for families, communities and wider societies. A better place to begin is with care – and the ethics of care – rather than employment and the work ethic.

The ethics of care

Feminists have argued that the work ethic has been mistakenly established as the only legitimate route for social citizenship. Paid work is constructed within welfare systems as the route to independence and economic self-sufficiency, providing an escape from poverty and the core connection between individuals and society (Williams, 2001, 474). Paid work has been described as a role model to offer children and the glue that binds society together (Williams, 2001). This preoccupation with paid work ignores the extent to which many women operate within a moral framework of care (Gilligan, 1982). Feminists have argued that care has a specific meaning for women and is crucial to how they construct their identities and worldview (Graham, 1991). It is important to note that there are tensions between the multiple perspectives of feminist thought and not all feminists agree that family or care are essentially female concerns. Finch (1989) presents family obligations as social obligations with normative structures. This highlights the underlying assumptions about heteronormative gender categories and reveals the power relations between carers and those who are cared for. These ideas inspired the development of a body of work on the 'ethics of care' to rival the dominant pre-existing work ethic that many social policies are based on across the globe. Importantly, Tronto (1993) and Sevenhuijsen (1998) position care as a universal concern for all humans: 'Care is not a parochial concern of women, a type of secondary moral question, or the work of the least well off in society. Care is a central concern of human life. It is time we began to change our political and social institutions to reflect this truth' (Tronto, 1993, 180).

The ethics of care positions interdependency and the care for others and of self as moral qualities that are essential for contemporary societies and include attentiveness, caring about and noticing the needs of others; responsibility for taking care of others; competence in terms of care giving as an activity; and responsiveness in care receiving (Tronto 1993, 127–13). Williams takes this further to argue that care is the rightful basis of citizenship. 'Care provides an important lens through which to make situated judgments about collective commitments and individual responsibilities' (Williams, 2001, 478). Williams (2001) and Held (2006) propose reorientating welfare systems to support a new ethic of care, recognising that interdependence is the basis of all human interaction. This allows us to reframe how we value caring for ourselves and others as the civic responsibility that 'binds us all together'. Such a reconceptualisation highlights the moral worth of caring relationships and empathy (Slote, 2007). This allows us to think about time and space differently. Rather than fitting care around work, which is an obsession, work and life need to be interconnected through consideration of time and space for personal care needs and care activities. Time and space for paid work that enables economic self-sufficiency could become the final, rather than the first, concern. Work could fit around care for self and others, rather than vice versa. A care-centred social welfare system could become possible by building service and policy architecture to support increased maternity, paternity and carer leaves, shorter working hours, part-time and flexible working arrangements on employees' terms. Care-centric reforms could emphasise the gendered nature of social citizenship, rights and responsibilities (see Lister, 1997). Care-orientated social security could better support new family formations and encourage men to increase their care efforts. Such reforms could support the connections between love, intimacy and care, which are not straight forward. Establishing an ethic of care could rebalance the pre-existing overemphasis on the work ethic that warps the design of social security for working-age adults.

Conceptualising how women's real lives are mediated by welfare conditionality

Understanding how policies are made and what policies do in practice, that is, the policy process and implementation studies, is a field of academic study that barely mentions women. This is surprising since women are more likely to experience poverty than men, are often the targets of social policies and may outnumber men in the front-line jobs of welfare services (see Chapter Three). While there are many studies of how policies impact detrimentally on women, few challenge male-dominated theoretical assumptions. The English-language international literatures on the policy process, implementation and street-level bureaucracy are interdisciplinary but established thought-traditions have been influenced more by an impersonal, objective, rational choice style of political science than interpretive sociology. Even in the 2020s, core policy process textbooks do not reflect basic sociological insights about how social structures like gender are related to intersubjective social interactions in the construction of policy texts and the accomplishment of front-line services. The focus of street-level bureaucracy research is usually on the micro-level interactions between front-line workers and service users. While this style of research is important and meaningful, the analytical project sees policy as 'indeterminate' and discretion arising from conflicting organisational goals or ambiguity (Brodkin, 2012, 940), which deflects attention from the extent to which gender ideology preconfigures all layers of the policy process. Although some studies explore how 'racial and gender identities shape street-level interactions and how social status is negotiated' (Brodkin, 2012, 946) the full extent of gendered power relations is obscured by a blank rationality towards the wider social relations within which policies are written. For example, the 'founding father' of street-level bureaucracy studies, Lipsky (2010) does not use interpretivist sociology, institutional ethnography or feminist thought. Disciplinary silos work both ways. Dorothy Smith's feminist sociology, with institutional ethnography at its heart, does not reference Lipsky (1980) or apply insights from street-level bureaucracy studies. In this chapter, I aim to connect these disparate realms of thought to better understand how welfare conditionality mediates women's lives.

Feminising interpretivism and street-level bureaucracy

Feminist analysis and interpretivism are aligned only in a specialist niche in a subfield (see Smith, 1987; Kruks, 2014). Both feminism and interpretivism have distinct roots and traditions and within each, critiques of the other can be found (see Scott, 1992; Prus, 1996). Despite debate, for example over the risks of essentialising female experiences or giving voice only to privileged women, feminist phenomenologists (Fisher and Embree, 2000; Kruks, 2001; Olkowski and Weiss, 2006; Heinämaa and Rodemeyer, 2010) have continued to: 'suspend our already conceptualised accounts of human experiences in order to describe how phenomena appear to us as they are "lived": ... as we engage with them as embodied agents in the world' (Kruks, 2014, 75). Feminist phenomenology and analysis of institutional practices (Griffith and Smith, 2014b; Smith, 1987; 2005) offers fertile ground for the original analysis of welfare conditionality. Smith's (1987) sociological concept of the 'relations of ruling' chimes with (but has not previously been connected with) the field of street-level implementation studies. Although the concept of street-level bureaucracy (Lipsky, 2010/1980) is widely known, and enjoying a revival (Brodkin and Marston, 2013; van Berkel et al, 2017; van Berkel, 2020), it is less commonly acknowledged as an expression of rational choice theory from a positivist-leaning political-science tradition (Brodkin, 2012).

In this book, the aim is to adapt insights from street-level bureaucracy without these rational choice undertones. My contribution is to adopt something of an institutional ethnography (Smith, 2005) approach to understanding the field of social security and the social relations of the Jobcentre (and related call-centre and digital services). This means taking apart existing definitions of welfare conditionality to look at their constituent parts from the perspective of what they mean to women benefit recipients. Then, when the parts are put back together again, we can better understand what the texts of welfare conditionality mean in the everyday world. Instead of evaluating 'what policies do' from the perspective of distant policy makers or academics using idealised shorthand in place of real human behaviour, we can see welfare conditionality for what it means to those on the receiving end. This was my first conceptual instinct, in my own original ethnographic study of one Jobcentre (Wright, 2003), which began from an interpretivist stance and used methods of direct observation (which were unfortunately not possible for this book). Street-level ethnographies like Dubois' (2009) study of welfare control in France and Zacka's (2017) research in an urban anti-poverty agency in the US, share this urge to understand the interpersonal and moral aspects of the interaction between welfare officers and citizens. The street-level literature demonstrates how policies are brought into being through the work of front-line officials, who balance organisational goals with client needs to mediate both policy (Lipsky, 1980) and politics (Brodkin, 2013).

Street-level studies of contemporary welfare conditionality

Welfare conditionality practices are shaped both by the actions (and inactions, see Lipsky, 1980; Hupe et al, 2013) of front-line workers and the nature of the contexts within which they work. Van Berkel (2020, 194) argues that the 'street-level delivery of welfare conditionality is structured by policies, the governance context in which workers deliver welfare conditionality, the organization in which they work, and the occupation they are part of'. Examining the policy documents and formal guidance surrounding the application of conditionality only tells one part of the story. Front-line workers are 'sometimes harsher, sometimes more lenient than policies lead us to expect' (van Berkel, 2020, 194) and this can be influenced by factors like race, class (Watkins-Hayes, 2009) and gender (Kingfisher, 1996). There can be wide practice variations between workers in the same office and between offices even within standardised national policies (see NAO, 2016 for the UK). The picture of what happens during encounters between women and welfare agencies is complicated by the contracting-out of back-to-work support to private service providers.

Profit-making in Public Employment Services

Since the late 1990s, financial incentives have been used to structure the front-line work of outsourced employability services. This delivery model is based on a self-seeking profit motive that derives from privileged male traditions of value, which flourished originally within power systems controlled violently by wealthy White men who claimed land and resources from indigenous custodians. Fundamentally, the financial profit is based on reaping rewards for the labour of disempowered people – invariably the toil of working-class people, disproportionately women and Black and minoritised ethnic groups. Profit-making is one of the relations of ruling that largely excluded women for generations and changed over the 20th century, with many women in Europe and north America now amassing great wealth. In the welfare-to-work field, back-to-work services have been increasingly contracted out in many rich countries, especially from the late 1990s onwards. Payment by results is commonly used to influence the behaviour of street-level workers delivering public employment services.

During the period of the fieldwork for this book (2014–17), the Work Programme operated throughout the UK as the main mandatory back-to-work programme for long-term unemployed people and disabled people. The Work Programme was contracted out on a payment-by-results model, mainly to large for-profit providers, with the voluntary sector holding a minority of prime contracts and being subcontracted by profit-making agencies to deliver services. Work Programme providers were required contractually to report participants for non-attendance, even when they knew individuals were engaging in other ways. Webster (2016) charts a huge rise in sanctioning because of this requirement. There are three sets of ethical issues. First, the level of sanctioning far exceeded successful job outcomes for participants, meaning the system punished more than it enabled (see Fletcher, 2011; Fletcher and Wright, 2018; Wright et al, 2020). Attendance requirements were unyielding for a caseload exclusively made up of multiply-disadvantaged and potentially vulnerable benefit claimants, with many likely reasons for non-attendance, including health problems. Second, the administrative arrangements were inadequate. Evidence has subsequently shown that many claimants were sanctioned unfairly when they were not informed of meetings. This was problematic at the point of referral to the programme. There was no reliable system for rearranging mandatory appointments with subcontractors. Claimants did not necessarily have phone numbers for services/advisers and there was no easy method for making contact. Third, enormous profits were amassed by underperforming private providers, including multimillion-pound bonuses for company directors – some of whom were prosecuted for fraud (see Larsen and Wright, 2014). The whole 'relations of ruling' of outsourced employment services in the UK (and in countries like Australia, Denmark and the USA, Marston et al, 2005; Brodkin, 2013b; Brodkin and Larsen, 2013; Ingold and Etherington, 2013) is based on a punitive version of productivity that squeezes out care. Claimants are pushed at all costs towards applying for jobs, which they are, for the most part, unlikely to get. At the slightest slip up, they have their essential income withdrawn or reduced, without warning and with little recourse. Financial incentives for subcontracted employment services are mediated by texts in the form of contracts. Delivery contracts 'shape relationships between manager and line staff and their treatment of clients' (Johnson Dias and Maynard-Moody, 2007, 189). Rees et al (2014) show how known limitations of outsourced employment services were repeated under the Work Programme, including creaming and parking. American research also shows 'that contract design, coupled with bottom-level management efforts to meet contractual obligations, leads to a performance paradox – the same actions taken to achieve contractual results ironically produce negative program practice and poor client outcomes' (Johnson Dias and Maynard-Moody, 2007, 189).

Discretion

Debates about discretion are central to understanding how services are delivered and experienced at street-level (Lipsky, 1980; van Berkel and Valkenburg, 2007; Sainsbury, 2008; Zacka, 2017). Internationally, it has been argued that increasingly 'work-first' active labour market policies (Lindsay, 2007; Wiggan, 2015) implemented via outcome-based performance targets for subcontracted employability services have reduced discretion at street-level (Brodkin, 2011; Fuertes and Lindsay, 2016). Kaufman (2020, 205) shows that in contracted back-to-work programmes in the UK (2008–15) 'behavioural conditionality provided street-level workers with the means to intensify or moderate activation' within reduced scope for discretionary action. Kaufman demonstrates how front-line workers used a 'street-level calculus of choice' to decide 'how, on whom, and to what extent' (2020, 205) sanctions were used. Soss et al (2011a, b; 2013) show how performance management operates to punish claimants in practice, with differential impacts on Black people and women. However, there is also Norwegian evidence of reverse discrimination in frontline sanctioning (Terum et al, 2018). Front-line workers navigate a complex 'moral ecosystem' (Zacka, 2017), within which official policy is only one of multiple contexts (van Berkel et al, 2017; van Berkel, 2020) of influence. How workers reconcile their own 'dispositions' (Zacka, 2017) with competing frames of reference (Eikenaar et al, 2016) in their interactions with service users influences 'who gets what when and how' (Brodkin, 2012). 'Context configurations send diverse and often conflicting signals to workers on what to do and how to do it' (van Berkel, 2020, 193). This book uses Dorothy Smith's work (discussed next) to reconceptualise street-level analysis from a feminist interpretivist perspective, to view welfare conditionality implementation practices as gendered social processes of intersubjective accomplishment.

Applying Dorothy Smith: social security as 'textually mediated relations of ruling'

The bridge between the street-level literature and feminist scholarship is in 'creating a way of seeing, from where we actually live, into the powers, processes, and relations that organise and determine the everyday context of that seeing' (Smith, 1987, 13). This section establishes how Smith's ideas can help us to understand social security policy and practices. The emphasis is on understanding how official texts (law, policy, guidance and implementation instruments) are accomplished through everyday interactions and reveal a hidden gendered subtext. Analysing policy texts, organisational action and the interaction of front-line workers with citizens, makes it possible to see how women's lives are 'put together by relations and forces that are not fully available to her experiencing' (Smith, 1990a, 3). Social security presents a case study of 'a gender organisation of the apparently neutral and impersonal rationality of the ruling apparatus' (Smith, 1987, 10). Dorothy Smith's ideas are very useful for understanding how women's experiences of work, welfare and care are *textually* mediated by welfare conditionality. Smith's (1987) approach has an important advantage over Nancy Fraser's (2009) more frequently cited feminist framework for understanding injustice (in terms of redistribution, recognition and representation). Although Fraser's (2009) framework is exceptionally useful, it 'seems unable to capture law as an important site and medium of injustice' (Lepianka and Knijn, 2020, 5). Smith's (1987, 10) focus on 'textually mediated relations of ruling' offers a better alternative for viewing written forms of social security (law, documents, formal regulations, guidance materials and implementation mechanisms), through a feminist lens. Smith's approach is incredibly useful for understanding 'the social organisation of textual reality' to make sense of formal texts as 'conceptual practices of power' (1990b, 68).

Gendered hierarchy of 'facts'

Smith's sociology begins from the position that knowledge is produced and interpreted within hierarchical social relationships. Knowledge is socially structured and 'facts mediate relations' (Smith, 1990b, 69). 'The socially organised practices of fact and the relations in which they are embedded go beyond the intersubjective world known tacitly among those sharing a here and now' (1990b, 68–69). Facts, in a sense, have a life of their own 'external to the particular subjectivities of the knowers' (Smith, 1990b, 69). What is interesting from a policy-analysis perspective is the role of public (and quasi-public) services in producing 'factual' accounts of women's lives that are used as the basis for official decision-making and intervention. In the case of the UK social security system, since 2010, the purpose of people-processing is less to do with helping and more to do with punishing (see Redman and Fletcher, 2021). Official decisions about benefit sanctions are routinely about whether to impose severe financial penalties with potentially life-changing, or life-threatening, consequences. Organisational action is of great consequence for women and their families. *How* facts are constructed matters within welfare organisations because they 'warrant the treatment of given statements not merely as true but as factual' (Smith, 1990b, 73). Front-line workers actively negotiate the gap between service users' accounts of their experiences and the 'institutionally approved procedures' (Smith, 1990b, 73) that screen out 'irrelevant' contextual details to select only the approved information that 'counts' for the organisation. Interactions between front-line workers and clients are shaped by 'the conceptual structure already in place … [to] determine the relevancies selecting and assembling further detail' (Smith, 1990b, 78). Facts are used within the institutional context of social security to determine benefit entitlement and categories for action, like 'fit for work' to apply 'intensive work conditionality', or 'did not attend' to trigger a sanction. Institutions like Jobcentre Plus assert conceptual categories onto women's actual's lives.

Boss texts

It is no accident that policies with thoroughly gendered effects are presented impersonally in policy documents (Smith, 1987, 10). The production of policy texts – like laws, policy papers, guidance for front-line workers and communications with benefit claimants – are part of a long tradition of male power, which excludes the concerns and voices of most women. Policy making and institutional texts objectify people through an ideological process: 'an aspect of actuality is written up into a text; this is then taken as a stand-in for actuality by being used by institutions and is then imposed back onto actuality; and then actual persons and behaviours are framed by and subordinated to this textual reality' Stanley (2018, 42).

Organisational texts have a life of their own that influences the possibilities for current and future action for women service users. Textual realities are crucial to how organisations operate within society (Smith, 1990b). The textual realities of the British social security system for working age people is dominated by an 'androcentric stereotype of productivity' (Taylor et al, 2021, 7), which prioritises paid work over unpaid care. Welfare conditionality pressurises women to shoehorn complex interconnected relations of family life to fit idealised impersonal male constructions of full-time labour market participation. Female-dominated roles in child and adult care within the family and local communities have been recast in male terms. Taking time out of employment to raise children, for example, which was once classified as economic inactivity, is now seen simply as 'worklessness', which in policy discourse serves as a functional equivalent term for 'unemployment'. This is achieved in practice using organisational 'textual surfaces' that record a one-sided version of service users' lived experiences. Selected snapshots of women's lives are displaced by a version of events that is rewritten according to organisation's frames. In this way, knowledge is recorded and 'defines the objects of its power' (Smith, 1990b, 84). Organisational records are powerful in establishing altered 'textual realities' that 'constitute shared, identical and perspectiveless objects and environments, locked into decision processes through the schemata, categories and concepts that organise them' (Smith, 1990b, 84). Organisational processes, including short appointment times and computer systems that require front-line workers to follow scripts or preformulated prompts combine in the 'discarding of women as authoritative speakers in public textually mediated discourse' (Smith, 1990b, 84). Women's actual, local, experiences are squeezed into predefined moulds.

There can be a high degree of conflict between different renderings of the same actuality. There can also be multiple claimant accounts of actuality, so it is a messy business within which it is difficult to pinpoint 'the facts' or 'the truth'. Facts are 'abstracted from the events as they actually happened' (Smith, 1990b, 90) and the 'mediating procedures directly enter into the constitution of the object as it becomes known' (Smith, 1990b, 91). Organisational records, like case histories, are structured by the organisation and administered by front line workers, with claimants having little influence about how their lives are reformed. Crucially, 'some have authority to contribute to the making of textual realities and others do not' (Smith, 1990b, 91).

Ideology and disjuncture

UK welfare reforms are ideologically driven (see Chapter Three) and Smith argues that: 'Ideological organisation creates a disjuncture between the world as it is known within the relations of ruling and the lived and experienced actualities its textual realities represent as 'what actually happened/what is' (1990b, 96). The texts of welfare reform and associated discourse create 'an objectified knowledge of happenings and states of affairs that have been or are lived by actual individuals' (Smith, 1990b, 96), which has a 'peculiar power ... to subdue and displace the perspectives of particular subjects' (Smith, 1990b, 97). This process disarms service users and disempowers frontline workers, whose experiences are suppressed (Smith, 1990b, 97–98). Although frontline workers and clients are excluded from the textual realities of the organisation, their complicity is essential to 'repair the disjuncture between the categories and the world so that the cogency of the policies and the schemata embedded in them were confirmed continually at the top in their capacity to make sense of the information received' (Smith, 1990b, 99). These processes reinforce the authority of the 'boss texts' and their ideological categories and operate within 'historically established gender relations' of 'super- and sub-ordination' (Smith, 1990b). The policy text and the underlying relations of ruling reinforce each other to further disadvantage those who are already excluded. The exclusion of working-class women, who are 'discounted speakers in public discourse' determines 'the textual surfaces of objective knowledge in public contexts' (Smith, 1990b, 101). Women's local experiences are supressed in public accounts of what is going on, for example, in parliamentary debates. This is a circular process that reinforces structural disadvantages. It is frontline workers who plaster over the ideological ruptures as they 'work hard to reproduce the sense of the enforced and enforceable categories in which they are to be made accountable' (Smith, 1990b, 104).

Ultimately, the local lived experiences of women subject to social security policy are subordinated via organisational practices to boss texts that enshrine falsehoods that they then must adapt their behaviour to, regardless of their 'bodily being' (Smith, 2005, 228). The potency of the policy text is not abstract, it is in its ability to 'enter into and coordinate people's doings, and, as activated in the text-reader conversation, they *are* people's doings' (Smith, 2005, 228). Social security and welfare conditionality are part of 'an object world assembled in textually mediated discourses and from the standpoint of men occupying the apparatuses of ruling' (Smith, 1990a, 1). Institutional texts govern the behaviour of policy subjects as well as 'the relations that organise front-line work in the public sector' (Stanley, 2018, 50). 'The activities encompassed by institutional circuits are what enable organisational objectives to be realised at the front-line' (Stanley, 2018, 51). These institutional circuits make workers accountable (Stanley, 2018, 51) and service users 'institutionally actionable' Griffith and Smith, 2014b, 3). Griffith and Smith highlight the significance of new managerialism as a context for institutional circuits that make 'visible changes in the front-line work of organisations delivering services to people ... behind our backs' (2014b, 3).

Four layers of welfare conditionality text – mediating relations of ruling

Social security is a very powerful field where women's lives are mediated by texts. There are multiple relationships between claimants and the texts that shape their lives. The 'boss texts' – the welfare reform legislation and policy documents – that set the parameters of organisational action and debate for the whole field of social security are usually remote. Women subject to welfare conditionality may not be aware of the detail of the text of these documents, but the contents of the 'boss texts' have a major influence on their everyday experiences of (for example) job search expectations and sanctions. Some of the texts that mediate welfare conditionality are hidden from public view, for example, performance-management arrangements, work–coach targets and expectations. I suggest here that UK welfare conditionality mediates women's lives in four interconnected layers of texts: 1) domain assumptions; 2) the policy 'boss texts' in the form of publicly available social security laws and guidance documents; 3) hidden internal organisational texts (for example performance-management systems, including targets, and tendering documents for contracted-out services); and 4) the policy instruments used to directly engage with citizens (application forms, formal communications like letters, emails, web-based information, claimant commitments, online systems for job search). Each of these textually-mediated layers are more heavily influenced by the values and mindsets of men who are far removed from the realities of the text subjects – women benefit recipients in their locally-situated everyday lives. I consider each layer of text in turn.

Layer one: tracing the origins of policy texts to domain assumptions

The top layer of textual mediation consists of the domain assumptions that underpin the 'boss texts' (see layer two, following). The whole British welfare reform fleet is commanded by privileged elite politicians and senior civil servants who set the coordinates for changes during closed discussions in exclusive spaces (Jones, 2015). The British ruling establishment, including politics, the civil service, law and journalism, is dominated by wealthy White men, who tend to be privately educated[1] (The Sutton Trust [TST] and Social Mobility Commission [SMC], 2019). These privileged agenda-setters are influenced by 'traditions as a set of understandings someone received during socialisation' (Rhodes, 2011, 4). Many influential lawmakers in the judiciary, Westminster and Whitehall were cloistered by elite education, including the 'absurd sexual apartheid' (King, 2020, 1) of single-sex[2] boarding schools – a world apart from the majority experiences of women and everyday family life. Although there is some evidence of diversity, only seven per cent of all MPs are 'working class', compared with 34 per cent of the population (Quilter-Pinner et al, 2022). Arguably, long-standing traditions, systems and institutions continue to reward the atypical values of White male elites (Jones, 2015). For example, Lord David Freud went to an all-boys private school and Oxford University before becoming an investment banker. Lord Freud was commissioned by the Labour Government in 2006 to recommend welfare-to-work reforms and was Conservative Minister for Welfare Reform (2010–16). Sir Robert Devereux, Department for Work and Pensions Permanent Secretary 2011–18, was knighted in 2016 in recognition of achievements including 'services to … welfare' (University of Oxford, 2023). During his tenure, welfare reforms included increasing the pensions age, benefit cuts, the benefit cap, payment-by-results outsourcing of the Work Programme, disability benefit reforms (replacement of Disability Living Allowance with Personal Independence Payment), Universal Credit, introducing the sanctions regime and applying work obligations to lone parents. The knighthood of military-educated Sir Iain Duncan Smith, Secretary of State for Work and Pensions (2010–16) caused controversy in 2020. A petition opposing the honour on the grounds that he was 'responsible for some of the cruellest, most extreme welfare reforms this country has ever seen' was signed by 284,177 people (Change, 2023, 1; Pidd, 2020).

In my view, the priorities of UK welfare conditionality originate from 'domain assumptions' (Stanley, 2018, 15) set by rich White men and rewarded by the establishment. During the decades when welfare conditionality was conceived, only approximately 10–18 per cent of UK Members of Parliament were women (Uberoi et al, 2021), which is about a quarter to a half of the proportion in countries such as Sweden (Bonoli, 2005, 437). Even in 2021, only around a third of MPs and 28 per cent of peers were female (Uberoi et al, 2021). Elite policy makers in the British state operate within a privileged heritage of 'practices of power' (Smith, 1987, 10) that have developed over centuries of oppression and exclusion of women, Black and minoritised ethnic groups and working-class people. Those who 'do' social security policy almost never have it 'done to them'. The setting of the policy paradigm (see Hall, 1993[3]) is the core 'practice of power' that routinely excludes women who are likely to be most impacted by it. This process is inherently political. It is not primarily designed with the needs of policy recipients in mind. The inner sanctum of UK political decision-making is motivated by a range of factors beyond the ideals of impartial rational problem-solving for the public interest. High-level policy makers are moral beings, who are shaped by 'the power structure' and have personal and shared 'selective response to interests' (Levin, 1997, 29–65). Elite politicians and civil servants have 'beliefs and practices [that] are embedded in traditions in webs of routines, rituals and languages' (Rhodes, 2011, 1), which bias how 'boss texts' are written.

Layer two: 'boss texts' in law and policy

'Boss texts' (Smith, 1987) are the second layer of textual mediation and crucial in determining the relations of ruling for welfare conditionality. Boss texts include formal government statements of policy intent, ministerial statements, green and white papers, legislation and formal policy-guidance documents. Boss texts also include documents that set the conditions for service delivery like the marketisation of employment services, including, for example, calls to tender for contracted-out back-to-work programmes (New Deal programmes, the Work Programme, the Work and Health Programme, the Universal Credit Support Line), formal evaluations of these services, and service agreements. These are produced within the Westminster/Whitehall machine (see Table 2.1). Policy is understood here also as discourse 'as a conversation mediated by texts that is not a matter of statement alone but of actual ongoing practices and sites of practices' (Smith, 1987, 166).

Labour market and claimant count statistics are an interesting example of a public form of boss text. Smith argues that the 'textual realities of labour statistics and the like are integral to state management of a labour force' (1990b, 89). Post 2010 UK welfare reform involves a conscious manipulation of labour market statistics that seeks to erase categories that were formerly legitimate alternatives to paid work: lone parenthood, disability and mental health. The label of 'worklessness' is applied to these states to justify mothers, carers, disabled women and those with long-term health conditions being

Table 2.1: Key UK welfare conditionality boss texts 2010–18[4]

Title	Year	Type of document	Author
Universal Credit: welfare that works	2010	Policy paper	DWP
21st Century Welfare	2010	White paper	DWP
Welfare Reform Act	2012	Primary legislation	UK Government
Jobseeker's Allowance (Sanctions) (Amendment) Regulations	2012	Statutory instrument	UK Government
DWP Explanatory Memorandum to The Jobseeker's Allowance (Sanctions) (Amendment) Regulations 2012	2012	Guidance Memorandum	DWP
The Work Programme	2012	Policy	DWP
The disability and health employment strategy: the discussion so far	2013	Policy	DWP
Jobseeker's Allowance: overview of revised sanctions regime	2013	Guidance	DWP
Work Programme Provider Guidance	2013 2018	Guidance	DWP
Universal Credit at work	2014	Policy paper	DWP
2010 to 2015 government policy: welfare reform	2015	Policy paper	DWP
Welfare Reform and Work Act	2016	Primary legislation	UK Government
Universal Credit and You	2017	Guidance	UK Government
Improving Lives: the future of work, health and disability	2017	Policy paper	DWP
Universal Credit programme full business case summary	2018	Business case	DWP

treated as if they were unemployed. The process delegitimises common forms of non-work and unpaid work. In this way a 'distinctive organisation of ruling is entered into a specific textual form' (Smith, 1990b, 89). Mothers become sanctionable cases first and foremost as organisational priority.

Layer three: hidden institutional texts that shape front-line practice

There is an exclusive hidden world of texts that mediate women's lives in the world of social security. These are the internal Jobcentre Plus organisational policy and practice guidance documents and communications that inform and implement managerial methods. These include the setting of performance indicators, targets (which are unusually prominent in the UK system in comparison with other countries, Considine et al, 2015), performance-management techniques and organisational systems that shape the design of Jobcentre Plus back offices (service centres, anti-fraud services, benefit-assessment practices, compliance decision-making) and front offices (Jobcentres) that ensure compliance with politicised policy goals. This third layer of male-dominated textual mediation includes tendering processes for outsourcing employability services, medical assessments for disability benefits, IT-system procurement, digital-delivery services and their underlying algorithms. Digital systems are interesting to consider here. Since 2013, the era of digital welfare has begun to dominate interactions between citizens and the social security system. The design of the IT architecture has a powerful influence over how claimants experience the system – having an individualising and dehumanising effect (Robertson et al, 2020). IT systems were designed behind the scenes by for-profit subcontractors. The design of digital systems is almost exclusively a male endeavour. For example, only 15 per cent of software authors are female (for common software programmes like R, OECD, 2018, 16). The UK, like other rich nations, has a tiny proportion of women working in information and communication technologies (OECD, 2018, 63; Criado-Perez, 2019). The situation is not on course to change either since 82 per cent of computer science and 80 per cent of engineering and technology university students are male (Government Equalities Office, 2019, 18). Only 9 per cent of STEM apprenticeships went to women (Government Equalities Office, 2019, 19). It seems safe to infer, therefore, that the digital systems used by Jobcentre Plus to administer social security and enforce welfare conditionality are unlikely to have been designed by women or to be centrally concerned with the everyday realities of working-class women's lives. Male writing structures the algorithms, digital systems and software programmes that preconfigure (see following) women's options for accessing financial support, the chances of being sanctioned and the parameters of human interactions with call centres and in Jobcentre Plus.

Another controversial example of this level of textual mediation is sanctions targets, which were officially called 'benefit off-flow targets' and are associated with the phenomenon of mass impoverishment from 2010 onwards (Redman and Fletcher, 2021; Webster, 2016). Behind the scenes, hidden from view and accountability, the whole UK-wide system for working-age benefits was politically manipulated towards an aggressive 'disentitlement strategy' (Fletcher and Wright, 2018; Redman and Fletcher, 2021). Sanctions targets were introduced secretly to Jobcentre Plus in 2010 and were used to radically alter the behaviour of front-line workers, pushing sanctioning rates up two years ahead of the formal legislative change that introduced a harsher sanctions regime in 2012. After the new tougher sanctions regime was introduced, benefit sanction rates continued to rise to a peak in 2013, when a quarter of all Jobseeker's Allowance claimants were being sanctioned (NAO, 2016).

The use of 'benefit off-flow targets' (WPC, 2016) can be understood using Smith's concept of the 'institutional circuit' because they were instituted within 'managerial routines ... reporting processes for front-line work' with 'textual technologies translating local work into standardised and measurable representations' (Griffith and Smith, 2014b, 23). This process reconceptualised the practices of work coaches in local Jobcentres and back-office decision-makers. Jobcentre Plus has gone through a dramatic organisational transformation in response to this political rewriting of the 'boss texts' that govern its activities and priorities. Jobcentre Plus was formed in 2002 in a hopeful Employment Service mould, connecting with nearly a century of history stretching back to the 1909 labour exchanges. The purpose of the organisation, and the front-line work within it, was explicitly to get unemployed people jobs. Jobcentre Plus had another, equally important, aim to 'help employers fill their vacancies'. Job matching was emphasised so much at its inception that former Department of Social Security employees were in uproar about being co-opted into the organisation. The merger of the two arms of benefit administration and job matching was intended to stimulate job entry among benefit recipients of all types (not just unemployed people as before) as part of a 'work first' activation strategy that was been interpreted as a global 'workfare project' (Wacquant, 2009; Brodkin, 2013b). It is hard to imagine that the organisation became so derailed that by 2014 some users no longer recognised the Jobcentre as a place to get a job: 'It's not a Jobcentre; it's a sanction centre.' (Universal Credit claimant quoted in Dwyer and Wright, 2020, 10).

Behind the scenes performance management has played a key role in bringing about this transformation, using the categories of 'job' and 'sanction' to recast the intention of front-line work to fit a punitive 'political project' (Brodkin, 2013b). 'As front-line workers coordinate their work with the managerial routines, a new conceptual framing of their work is established' (Griffith and Smith, 2014b, 251). Those front-line workers involved in the transformation 'engage actively in controlling their new work situations' and use 'self-governance as a feature of how redesigned managerial practices shape front-line work' (Griffith and Smith, 2014b, 251). In this way, 'texts coordinate what people do' (Griffith and Smith, 2014b, 339). The sudden change in sanctioning practices in 2010 involved 'reorganising work being done at the front line' (Griffith and Smith, 2014b, 17). Performance targets, as a feature of new public managerialism brought 'changes in how workers relate to the clients they are working with, but also how the new textual modes of management themselves are forms of work to be done' (Griffith and Smith, 2014b, 10).

Layer four: how the encounter is shaped by the text of policy instruments

The fourth layer of 'textually mediated relations of ruling' (Smith, 1987, 10) can be observed in the 'male subtext' of 'apparently impersonal forms' that constitute the everyday policy instruments that claimants use in their interactions with the social security system. This includes digital and human interactions of many types, including interaction with street-level workers (in Jobcentres, service centres and subcontracted arenas, for example, the Universal Credit phone support line, medical assessments, employment services such as the Work and Health Programme) and digital-delivery systems (such as the Universal Credit claim system). These include: information on government webpages, the claimant commitment, Universal Jobmatch (its replacement the 'Find a job' system) and the Journal. Women – as benefit applicants/claimants – are excluded from the 'male subtext' that underpins all of these routinised engagements with the social security system. Matarese and Caswell (2017, 715) show, similarly, how naturally occurring conversations in an American homeless shelter are accomplished in practice through 'standardisation, routinisation, time and documentation'. This type of documentation-driven approach limits the extent to which homeless people can express their needs, preferences and concerns in their own voice. From the outset, case workers *pre-construct*, rather than co-construct client plans (Matarese and Caswell, 2017). Pre-existing administrative requirements can structure talk to such an extent that the form itself can be considered as an active participant in the conversation (Matarese and Caswell, 2017, 730). At the front line where 'the state meets the street' (Zacka, 2017), claimants have a direct relationship with the texts of policy instruments. They may read these in formal agreements like the 'claimant commitment' (used for Jobseeker's Allowance and Universal Credit) and hear their work coach read or paraphrase the content of their agreement. However, even when policy texts are at close proximity to claimants, their power is not necessarily experienced fully. Not only are the women subject to policies largely or entirely excluded from the processes of forming the most influential policy texts, but they have little or no experience of what is written (or omitted) about women in their position and how they must be treated.

UK welfare conditionality not only severely restricts the claimant's ability to define their textual realities (in claimant commitments, online claim forms and so on), but also discards forms of textual reality compiled by GPs and medical specialists. Smith observed that the service user is 'a resource, but not an agent' (Smith, 1990b, 91) in formal accounts of her behaviour. For example, benefit recipients with mental health problems face a continuous fight for factual legitimacy with their formal records. Individuals have multiple records generated in parallel fields. This includes medical evidence generated in interactions with professionals such as doctors, community psychiatric nurses, psychiatrists and therapists. Housing is another arena within which conflicting records and forms of evidence about a claimant can be generated and held. Interactions with Jobcentre Plus generate multiple records, including those created in back-office processing, accounts from online activities and phone calls with the Service Centre, relating to benefit processing. Records are also constructed in contracted-out employability programmes like the Work Programme. These different records compete for legitimacy as facts or factual accounts. The judgement of work capability assessors, using a process skewed towards finding people fit for work so that they can be subjected to intensive work conditionality, can override these other forms of evidence and account. In silencing women's accounts of their own experiences and discounting ways of knowing about care commitments and health impairments, 'a deep disjuncture is created between the lived experience ... and the social organisation producing their representation within the order of textual reality' (Smith, 1990b, 92). Anything that does not fit the framework is excluded from the process.

The male subtext of the 'claimant commitment'

A primary point at which work-conditionality is negotiated and enforced is when new claimants agree their claimant commitment (for Universal Credit and Jobseeker's Allowance) and the online Universal Jobmatch job vacancy site. The claimant commitment is a standardised written agreement that preconfigures the tone of Jobcentre encounters and elicits responses only within tight parameters. Its impersonal design appears to appeal to bureaucratic values of impartiality and fairness but the claimant commitment operates to further exclude women from the 'practices of power' (Smith, 1990a) that shaped it. It consists of a series of statements that enforce a male-defined work ethic, specifying regular required daily steps that claimants will take to seek paid employment. The penalties of non-compliance are written in the document – removal of income essential for survival. The potentially devasting consequences of non-compliance are repeatedly stated and remain on view for claimants and their work coach within the online Journal for Universal Credit claimants.

The claimant commitment can also be understood as involving institutional circuits that strip real activities down to institutional categories 'readable and interpretable within the frame established by the boss text' (Griffith and Smith, 2014b, 14). The global rationale for welfare conditionality takes what Smith calls the 'extralocal' as the primary reference point. The enlargement of formal work requirements directly encroaches on the space for care. For example, explicit written requirements mean that job searches must be conducted over large geographical areas and that jobs must be accepted, up to one-and-a-half hours away from home. This further diminishes and dilutes the private sphere, drawing women into the public sphere, on male-defined terms: money, financial transactions, written documents. Female-orientated concerns of giving and receiving care are squeezed out of the claimant commitment. The main concession, which is described as 'individually tailored conditionality', is to reduce the number of weekly hours that should be spent job seeking. There is no standard national amount of protected time for 'personal care' or 'caring for others' (see Williams, 2001).

Universal Credit full service made an important change by giving claimants direct access to the texts of their claimant commitments online within their digital claim. Claimants can view their job-search obligations, for example, and the 'To Do List', where their work coach can allocate them tasks. However, there are many soft barriers between claimants and the text within 'The Journal'. For example, instructions or agreements may be written there, but claimants must also have the knowledge, skills and resources to access this text and to interpret what it means. If, for example, a work coach uses their discretion to advise a claimant verbally that they do not need to take certain action, there can be gaps between the verbal agreement and the written text of the claimant commitment. In these circumstances there can be ambiguity around what to do and the potential consequences. Some claimants may use smart phones to access their online claim, where the text is very small. They may not be able to see it very well or may not remember login details. These practicalities can mean that they are not able to experience the text of their claimant commitment or 'Journal', so in a sense it may not exist to them.

Conclusion

This chapter has offered insights from three distinct bodies of literature: feminist analysis, interpretivist theory and street-level bureaucracy. It explores Dorothy Smith's (1987) approach for understanding textually-mediated relations of ruling in social security systems. In this book, Smith's ideas are applied to develop a new conceptualisation of conditionality that emphasises the gendered dimensions of welfare reform for working-age recipients. Key concepts include the gendered hierarchy of 'facts', the influence of 'boss texts' and the ideologies they represent, front-line workers efforts to repair the disjuncture between institutional categories and women service users' everyday lives. I identify four layers of text in UK welfare conditionality: the origins of policies and domain assumptions; the 'boss texts' of law and policy, the hidden institutional texts that shape font-line interactions and the policy instruments. The findings chapters (Chapters Four, Five and Six) apply Smith's ideas to reveal the male subtext of work-first welfare conditionality in practice. The analysis demonstrates how women's experiences of work, welfare and care are mediated by policy 'boss texts' (Griffith and Smith, 2014b, 12). The findings examine how reforms that are formally overlooked or presented as impersonal or 'gender-neutral' (DWP, 2011b, 5), impact in highly gendered ways to compound women's disadvantaged economic and social position and to constrain family life. The contrast between institutional texts and the local everyday lived experiences of women subject to welfare conditionality are investigated. This analysis aims to 'make visible the forms of ruling that are largely not observable' (Smith, 2005, 226). Next, Chapter Three outlines how welfare conditionality has developed and intensified over recent decades of reform and how it has increasingly interfered with women's lives in harmful and potentially abusive ways.

THREE

Policy context: the hidden gendered impacts of conditional welfare reforms

Margaret cares. Her pebble-dash council house on the outskirts of Glasgow reminds me of my gran's. It's sparse-side modest and scrupulously clean. It's quiet and still. It feels a bit empty, as if she doesn't quite fill the room. Something, and I soon realise someone, is missing. We drink hot thin tea in floral mugs and she tells me about losing her mum. Margaret lives her life caring for others – bringing up her children, then looking after mum until she died.

In 2014, at the age of 59, Margaret (White Scottish) is near the end of her 'working life'. She's up against unfamiliar expectations: claiming for Universal Credit digitally when she has never used a computer before; chasing proof of her rental agreement for the home she's lived in all her adult life; asking her daughter for food over her six weeks without income, while she waits for her first payment; looking for work 35 hours a week.

These policy realities are alien to Margaret's lifelong expectations about her role as a mother, a wife and a daughter. Finally, without anyone to care for, Margaret's identity is abruptly rewritten as an unemployed benefit claimant – a giver who feels like a taker. The hours that had been filled by serving the personal needs of her family were suddenly requisitioned for online job search, indistinguishable from the expectations of the young able-bodied men we spoke to. Margaret was required to adapt immediately to welfare conditionality as if she were unencumbered by grief and ill-health, as if she were fully at ease with IT. Her private caring life is rewritten as a public work responsibility and it is the culture shock of a lifetime.

Introduction

Margaret's life is a life lived caring – a biography of family-orientated interdependence that is familiar to many working-class women of her age and a far cry from the individualistic economic rationales of welfare reform. Margaret's story epitomises the consequences of the policy shift from viewing women primarily as carers to workers. Women in Margaret's position have their lives mediated textually by employment and social security law. This chapter begins by reflecting on enduring gender inequalities in the paid labour market and persistent patterns of unpaid care. It then sets out how work-related conditionality has ramped up to the point where women are treated 'as if' their orientations towards work and care are identical to men's. This chapter explores parallel changes in the world of work and in social security policy. However, the relationship between the two is far from straightforward. The overarching trend is to recategorise disabled women and mothers in male-defined terms using punitive policies designed for able-bodied men (Fletcher and Wright, 2018; Wright et al, 2020), particularly from 2010 onwards. Policy changes are related to gender-neutral narratives that have been used by politicians from all three of the UK ruling parties to justify enforcement of an 'adult worker model' (Lewis and Giullari, 2005) that squeezes out the capacity to care.

First, gendered labour market inequalities are discussed in historical context. Ongoing vertical and horizontal occupational segregation is highlighted alongside women's need for part-time work during care-dominated phases of the life course, like childrearing and elder care. Second, women's orientations towards work-related social policies are set out in relation to early interventions and the post-war development of social security based on gender differences. Women's changing employment patterns and welfare rights are discussed. Third, New Labour's (1997–2010) 'creeping conditionality' (Dwyer, 2004) and the start of the process of redefining lone parents as workers is highlighted. Measures to address low pay, child poverty and childcare shortages are acknowledged. Fourth, post-2010 Conservative-led cuts and reforms within an 'austerity' narrative are set out. Welfare conditionality and benefit sanctions are explored. Fifth, the heavy impact of Universal Credit in the era of 'ubiquitous conditionality' (Dwyer and Wright, 2014) is considered. Sixth, older women workers and the implications of changes to the state retirement age are discussed. Seventh, devolved social security arrangements in Scotland are outlined. Finally, the conclusion summarises how changes in the labour market relate to enduring care concerns for women, mediated by expansive and punitive welfare conditionality.

Women face deep labour market inequalities despite obvious gains

Deep inequalities endure for women in the world of work, despite many radical improvements over the last century. Women's employment in the UK is at an all-time high.[1] About three-quarters[2] of women of working age have a job, which is 15.6 million women, about two-thirds of whom have dependent children (Devine and Foley, 2020; ONS, 2022). However, in-work poverty is peaking too (JRF, 2018; Bourquin et al, 2019; McNeil et al, 2021). Real wages are falling while the cost of living rises (Harari et al, 2022). Poverty is feminised (Millar, 2003) and paid work offers women less protection from poverty than men because women are more likely to balance employment with unpaid care and may take maternity leave periods and change their patterns of work while caring for young children or older parents. In the UK 1.7 million women look after family or home to the extent that they cannot be economically active (Devine and Foley, 2020, 8). Unpaid care impacts directly on the amount of time available for paid work, which constrains earnings and the related extent to which women can pay into social-insurance schemes, increasing risks of poverty throughout the life course (Criado-Perez, 2019; Coffee et al, 2020). Many women are structurally disadvantaged in the UK's 'toxic employment mix' (Warhurst, 2016). Poor-quality jobs are common in the UK (Osterman, 2013). There is a polarisation between 'lovely' and 'lousy' jobs (Goos and Manning, 2007). Precarity has increased, including zero-hours contracts and platform work in the gig economy (Standing, 2009; Vosko, 2010; Kessler, 2018; Wood et al, 2019; Kaine and Josserand, 2019). Part-time work and self-employment are increasing and there is a 'bad jobs trap' (Warhurst, 2016). Underemployment affects three million workers in the UK (Newsome and Vorley, 2020). Women are more likely than men to be underemployed and one in eight Black and minoritised ethnic women are underemployed (Trades Union Congress [TUC], 2020, 2). This section puts contemporary experiences of employment inequalities in historical context and charts trends in women's employment over time, then highlights ongoing disadvantages related to occupational segregation, low pay and part-time work.

Historical context of unequal employment for women

Women 'have worked, constantly, continuously, always and everywhere, in every type of society in every part of the world since the beginning of human time' (Cremonesi, in Lewenhak, 1980, 9). Industrialisation disrupted the family as the productive unit (Yeandle, 1984) and combined with dominant Victorian ideals in Britain to construct a moral boundary between the female private domain of the home and male control of the public sphere that proves difficult to shake off two centuries later. By the mid-19th century, textile factories employed women and girls on a huge scale (Todd, 2005), with 'marked sexual division of labour and sharp irregularity in rates of pay' (Yeandle, 1984, 2). Unequal pay has prevailed in one form or another since then (see following). However, even in the 19th century, there were regional differences and exceptions to the rule that challenge taken-for-granted assumptions about gendered hierarchies of earnings, work roles and home duties. For example, in Lancashire, it was common for wives to work and fathers contributed to childcare (McCarthy, 2021). In Dundee, many women jute workers were the main breadwinners, which upended 'conventional family structures and authority relations' (Gordon, 1987, 29).

At the turn of the 20th century, there was open hostility towards working wives and mothers (McCarthy, 2021). Most women workers were working class and professions were largely closed to middle-class women (Todd, 2004). Women were mainly employed in domestic service, often as live-in servants, not permitted to marry, doing the types of tasks they would usually do in the home; and textile work also continued to be an important source of employment (Breitenbach, 1982). During the First World War, large numbers of women took on a range of classically 'male' professions like engineering and munitions, which they were subsequently ejected from in peacetime (Yeandle, 1984, 6). In the 1920s and 30s, 'political changes … slowly and unevenly improved their security and physical welfare' (McCarthy, 2021, 386). Women were increasingly being employed in office jobs and as shop assistants (Breitenbach, 1982).

Recession in the late 1920s and 1930s caused widespread unemployment and industrial unrest. In the late 1930s, only a tiny proportion of women had post-school qualifications, female professionals commanded lower salaries than men and were almost unheard of in senior roles (McCarthy, 2021). Marriage undoubtedly limited women's employment options and legal marriage bars allowed public services and private employers to dismiss women when they got married. Unsurprisingly, while almost 80 per cent of young, single women had regular jobs recorded in the 1931 census, less than 10 per cent of married women had paid jobs (McCarthy, 2021).

In the 1940s, women were called upon again in large numbers to fill wartime labour shortages in seemingly 'male' roles (Breitenbach, 1982). Wartime nurseries were set up to facilitate female employment. After World War II, partnered women were actively discouraged from jobs that could be filled by men. In a positive move, the marriage bar was lifted for parts of the public sector, starting with teachers in 1944 and the civil service in 1946. However, some private companies continued to bar married women. Overall, married women increased their labour market participation during the 1950s, with strong regional and sectoral patterns. A positive shift in attitudes about women's work happened in the 1950s and 1960s. For example, the state intervened to enable mothers to work, by subsidising nursery places for teachers in the 1960s. There were increasing calls for childcare in the 1970s. Greater control over fertility from the 1960s onwards enabled women to have more economic independence. These developments were reinforced by second-wave feminism and supported by equal opportunities legislation in the 1970s (McCarthy, 2021, 386). Marriage rates rose until the 1970s and returning to work after having children gradually became normalised. Mothers gained a 'greater foothold in the labour market' but not an equal one (McCarthy, 2021). The beneficial effects of equalities legislation in the 1970s did not change everything consistently or straight away. Gradually, over the 1980s and markedly from the late 1990s, women increased their labour market participation and the shift from manufacturing to service sector indicated a feminisation of paid work (Gerodetti and McNaught-Davis, 2017). Improved prospects for education and progression to well-paid jobs opened up middle management and elite professions in ways that were unimaginable a century before (Worth, 2022). 'For much of the 19th and 20th centuries, women's worlds were shaped by a labour market founded on sexual difference, a welfare state which institutionalised the dependency of wives and a wider culture which prized devoted mothering and housewifery as the apotheosis of femininity' (McCarthy, 2021, 390).

In the 21st century female leaders are in the public eye and it is common to encounter high-earning professional women, regardless of their marital status, in everyday life as teachers, doctors, managers or civil servants. However, the knowledge that some women now get big salaries distracts from the majority experience of low pay. Over a century of change, women have populated the labour market and it has become socially acceptable to combine motherhood with earning, but 'without seriously disturbing men's monopoly on the highest-paid jobs or reversing their exemption from domestic labour in the home' (McCarthy, 2021, 388). These inequalities are replicated across the globe and there is no country in the world where women have equal lifetime earning capacity to men. There are still 178 countries that have laws that restrict women's jobs or pay, limiting 2.4 billion women (World Bank, 2022, 2). While governments legislate to control or incentivise women's fertility and engagement with paid employment, not a single country legally requires men to do unpaid care. Lopsided change masquerades as equality. Next, the ongoing constraints of occupational segregation and low pay are outlined.

Limited options: occupational segregation and low pay

Universal truths are hard to come by in social science, but the fundamental difference between women and men in their capacity to meet their needs through earnings alone comes close (see World Bank, 2020). 'Women everywhere are over-represented in low-paying jobs and men in high-paying jobs' (Mandel and Shalev, 2009, 1874).

Many countries have taken leaps forwards in recent decades, but there is still a long way to go. In the UK, women earn on average 17.3 per cent less than men[3] (Devine and Foley, 2020, 3). Gender pay gaps are nearly double the average in some large companies like easyJet, where women earn 69p for every £1 men earn (Gov.uk, 2022, 1). Highly-educated women are not immune (Andrew et al, 2021), but the real problem is at the lower end of the income distribution, where women and children experience the worst impacts of poverty (Women's Budget Group, 2019). Women's earning potential is curbed by highly resilient vertical and horizontal occupational segregation (Crompton and Harris, 1998). Women still face both a glass ceiling that limits upward progression and a 'sticky floor' that keeps wages low in female-dominated roles. Horizontally, women and men are concentrated in different sectors with women tending to dominate lower-status occupations. Women are concentrated in health and social work, where 79 per cent of jobs are held by women, and the education sector, where 70 per cent of workers are women (Devine and Foley, 2020, 3). About a quarter of women are low paid, which is hard to escape because their jobs are 'concentrated in a handful of large firms' (Resolution Foundation, 2018, 7). One study showed that nearly three-quarters of low-paid workers in 2002 were still in low-paid jobs a decade later (Whittaker and Hurrell, 2013). Women are more likely than men to work in minimum-wage jobs (Low Pay Commission, 2020, 51). Low pay also increases the chances that women will need to take on multiple jobs (Smith and McBride, 2021).

Since 'class inequality inflates the gender wage gap' (Mandel and Shalev, 2009, 1901), working-class women fare badly. In the UK, the top jobs are dominated by privileged White men, who out-earn women, Black people, most minoritised ethnic groups and people from working-class backgrounds – even when they are doing the same elite jobs (Friedman and Laurison, 2020). Class pay inequalities in the UK are extreme, but they also exist in other countries like the US, Australia, France, Sweden and even Norway (Torche, 2011; Hällsten, 2013; Flemmen et al, 2017; Friedman and Laurison, 2020, 47). Gender pay gaps intersect with class pay gaps to limit maximum earnings and compound labour market disadvantage (O'Connor et al, 1999; Friedman and Laurison, 2020). Even among elite occupations, those from working-class backgrounds earn £6400 less a year than those from privileged backgrounds, who earn 16 per cent more on average (Friedman and Laurison, 2020, 47). Substantial disability and ethnicity pay gaps also interact with gender and class (Friedman and Laurison, 2020) to limit access to segments of the labour market, progression and pay. Disabled people in the UK face a significant disability employment penalty that limits their job prospect probabilities by 40 percentage points (Barnes and Mercer, 2005; Berthoud, 2008, 141). Disabled people's employment rates vary 'according to the medical conditions they report, according to the types of impairment they experience, and according to the overall severity of those impairments' (Berthoud, 2008, 143). Overall, 'disabled people's employment prospects are lower than those of non-disabled people, even if the comparison is with non-disabled people with similar family and economic characteristics' (Berthoud, 2008, 143). Generally, disability has a greater impact on employment prospects than gender. 'The average penalty for disabled people is less than the penalty for mothers of young children, but substantially greater than for all women taken as a group.' (Berthoud, 2008, 144).

Part-time work

Women's earning capacity is impacted by part-time work, including short-hours or 'mini jobs', which is the dominant strategy for reconciling family life with paid work. In the UK, 40 per cent of women work part-time, compared with only 13 per cent of men (Devine and Foley, 2020, 3). However, part-time work is also valued less than full-time work and often associated with lower job-quality, poverty pay and insecurity. Part-time work is interpreted by some academics as inherently precarious and marginal, conferring 'labour market outsider' status (Nicolaisen et al, 2019, 1; Vosko, 2010). In some disciplines 'standard work' (Bosch, 2006) remains the bar against which all forms of paid work are measured. Although women's part-time work is the global norm during care-intensive phases of the life course (during child rearing and elder care years), working less than full-time is categorised officially as 'deviant' (see Eurofound, 2021). The 'gendered division of paid and unpaid work is deeply rooted in national cultures and traditions' (Nicolaisen et al, 2019, 8). Unlike the Nordic countries, women in the UK are historically unlikely to transfer from part-time to full-time work (Nicolaisen et al, 2019). Part-time work 'only provides, at best, a very narrow bridge back into full-time work' and 'ghettos of low-skilled, sexually segregated employment act as barriers' to labour market integration (O'Reilly and Bothfeld, 2002, 435). About a quarter of the UK workforce works part-time,[4] which is high compared with other rich nations – the OECD average is 17 per cent, varying between the Netherlands with the highest at 38 per cent and Romania with the lowest at 4 per cent (Nicolaisen et al, 2019, 17).

There are heated debates about the extent to which mothers choose part-time employment and related lower wages. Hakim (2000; 2006) argues that women's work and care patterns are determined by their choices, according to 'preference theory'. Pfau-Effinger (2012) shows that women's choices are culturally and institutionally embedded. The idea that women are free to make individual choices has been heavily contested by sociologists like McRae (2003) and social policy academics, most notably Lewis (2006). Work-family preferences are presented by Hakim (2000) as 'types', whereas McRae (2003, 317) demonstrates that women's orientations towards paid employment are better understood as a continuum, meaning 'that women with similar preferences (but differing capacities for overcoming constraints) will have very different labour market careers'. Research shows that whole 'family strategies' (Tobio and Trifiletti, 2005) are negotiated between adult family members within powerful policy constraints (Lewis, 2006). Millar and Ridge (2008) found that it is not only adults, but also children who actively influence mothers' decision-making processes and develop their own contributions to family strategies within lone parent households. The next section demonstrates how changes to social security policy have increasingly required women to engage in paid work, regardless of unfavourable labour-market conditions.

Women and work-related welfare policies

This section charts the development of work-related social security policies over the last century to show how legal requirements about paid employment and unpaid domestic obligations have structured women's lives in changing ways (Pascall, 2012). At the beginning, and for most of the 20th century, women were treated as fundamentally different from men for social security purposes. In the early 20th century, major territories of the labour market were off limits to women (McCarthy, 2021) and unemployment interventions excluded women even further by denying access to female workers in large number. When the welfare state was established after the Second World War, women were written into social security law mainly as dependents of male partners with few rights to state income protection beyond maternity and family allowances. Gender difference continued as a basic principle of social security during the following decades when women flooded into the labour market. Policies began to change drastically in the late 1990s. More and more women were earning, but social security was being reformed to offer less and less in return. Between 1997 and 2010, Labour governments pursued work-first welfare-to-work policies that were explicitly designed to increase the proportion of lone parents in any job. Although this type of strategy has been found to hinder mothers' employment (Kowalewska, 2017) and impede unpaid care (Klein, 2021), Conservative-led governments from the 2010s onwards were undeterred. A pack of extreme reforms kicked enormous holes in the social safety net and work-related welfare conditionality along with punitive sanctions were introduced across working-age benefits. In the 21st century, women lost their social protection as mothers and carers to the extent that unpaid obligations are routinely denied in part or full (see Chapters Four, Five and Six). In a complete turnaround over the course of a century, social security law has been outwardly degendered but pushes women towards an unequal labour market without adequate compensation for unpaid caring activities.

Early state intervention: excluding women as 'different'

In the early 20th century, the first British unemployment benefit schemes gave preference to male jobs and excluded many women's occupations from protection (Whiteside, 1991). Trades unions resisted recognition of women's earnings, which were regarded as supplementary to those of male breadwinners. When mass unemployment broke out in the 1920s and 30s, many women who had established unemployment benefit entitlements were controversially denied payments because they were judged as 'not genuinely seeking work' on account of their domestic duties (Lewenhak, 1980). As increasing numbers of women moved into employment, it remained difficult to shed domestic identities. A century later, partnered women are still often viewed as dependents within male-headed households, for social security purposes. There is a lingering tendency to assume that unemployment is mainly a male problem, which can be traced back to this early era of intervention.

After World War II, the post-war welfare state provided for women based on difference, rather than equality, primarily in terms of motherhood, domesticity and nurturing roles. Famously, Beveridge said: 'The attitude of the housewife to gainful employment outside the home is not and should not be the same as that of the single woman. She has other duties' (1942, para. 6, 1).

Women 'were not only enabled to take care, but were also condemned to do so' (Knijn and Kremer, 1997, 329). Paid employment was firmly written into policy as the domain of men, with the expectation that working women would usually be single. The post-war welfare state was predicated on full male employment and men were therefore the main beneficiaries of insurance-based unemployment benefits (Beveridge, 1944). Instead, women were mainly constructed for social security purposes in relation to motherhood and state maternity benefits were offered at a higher rate than unemployment benefits. The message was clear – men and women had different roles in relation to employment and care, but both were vital to rebuilding the economy and society. Marriage was held as synonymous with homemaking and child-rearing, supplemented by family allowances. Retrospectively, Beveridge's writing about the roles of men and women in relation to work and care seem sexist (Sainsbury, 1996; Daly and Rake, 2003). However, Beveridge's (1944) impression of women's work was not a thoughtless stereotype. He based his analysis on the labour market data available at the time, which showed that most employed women stopped working when they got married and had children. Beveridge concluded that 'married women of working age, made marriage their sole occupation' (1942, para. 6, 108) and did not predict the radical changes that were to come. The post-war social security system proceeded on the assumption that:

> During marriage most women will not be gainfully occupied. ... Such paid work in many cases will be intermittent; it should be open to any married woman to undertake it as an exempt person, paying no contributions of her own and acquiring no claim to benefit in un-employment or sickness. If she prefers to contribute and to re-qualify

for unemployment and disability benefit she may do so, but will receive those benefits at a reduced rate. (Beveridge, 1942, para. 111)

In the 1940s, many women were considered as a 'reserve army of labour' (Rubery and Rafferty, 2013) outside the paid-labour market in an equivalent way to retired people (Beveridge, 1944, 130). The post-war national-insurance scheme excluded most women because of their marital status, expecting that wives 'would be dependent on their husband's contributions for their retirement pension, while not having any entitlement to unemployment or sickness benefits' (Gulland, 2019a, 119). Between 1945 and 1975 the 'widows' pension' remained the only major social transfer explicitly aimed at women in western welfare states (Bonoli, 2005, 432). The British welfare state was not, therefore, well equipped to deal with large-scale female unemployment, following the influx of married women to employment during the 1960s and 70s, when recession hit again in the 1980s. The policy response was to change the definition of unemployment to hide large numbers of non-claimants and to tighten the system up to reduce eligibility (Fletcher and Wright, 2018). Divorce rates were also rising, after divorce reform in 1969 and there were more lone parent families (Office for National Statistics [ONS], 2021b). Marriage no longer offered the lifelong financial protection in the private sphere that Beveridge assumed it would. The situation came to a head in the late 1990s when economic conditions supported high employment rates and the numbers of disability benefit recipients exceeded those claiming unemployment benefits for the first time. A major phase of welfare reform followed, with important consequences for different groups of women. First, a Conservative government introduced Jobseeker's Allowance in 1996, which reduced insurance-based entitlements for all unemployed people. This was a loss for women who had worked long enough to contribute into the National Insurance scheme. Then, when 'New' Labour came to power in 1997, they were determined to increase the employment rates of disabled people and lone parents. This mission pressurised many women social security claimants and was the thin end of the conditionality wedge.

New Labour: putting lone parents to work

Blair's first government in 1997 immediately instigated a strong reform agenda that began to cut back women's social rights by abolishing the Lone Parent Premium of Income Support. This signalling an end to the special carer status of lone parenthood. For lone parents, 90 per cent of whom are women (Office for National Statistics, 2016a), their role as sole carer/earner creates unique tensions in relation to welfare conditionality. Children in lone parent families face much higher risks of poverty and deprivation than those in coupled households (Chzhen and Bradshaw, 2012, 487), so they are more likely to need to claim means-tested benefits and wage top-ups. Lone parents in the UK are more exposed to changes in welfare conditionality because lone parenthood is much more prevalent in the UK than other European countries (Chzhen and Bradshaw, 2012, 498). In 1998, the Labour government introduced the New Deal for Lone Parents (NDLP) as the first national welfare-to-work programme for lone parents claiming means-tested Income Support, the main social-assistance benefit at that time. UK lone parent employment rates were historically similar to those of partnered mothers, until the early 1980s when they began to diverge to the point where, by the mid-1990s, lone parent employment rates were 20 per cent lower (Evans et al, 2003, 8–9). The NDLP was unapologetically 'work first', building to the 'challenging' ambition announced in 2000 to increase lone parent employment rates from 46 per cent in 1997 to 70 per cent by 2010 (House of Commons [HoC], 2004, para. 142–6). This employment strategy would mean moving from one of the lowest lone parent employment rates in Europe up to the level of the highest (Bradshaw et al, 1996). Considerable progress was made towards the target and in 2010 57 per cent of lone parents were in employment. However, it was not until 2017 that the target came into sight, with 68 per cent of lone parents employed, peaking at 69.9 per cent in 2019 (ONS, 2019).

New Deal intervention was directed at lone parents as a distinct group, offering support (initially on a voluntary basis, later mandatory) via a series of interviews with dedicated lone parent Personal Advisers. Gradually, lone parents with younger and younger children were moved onto the New Deal for Lone Parents (NDLP). The scheme was relatively well-funded, by frugal British standards. About 10 per cent of lone parents on Income Support participated in NDLP and 'employment chances were roughly doubled for those who took part in the programme' (Evans et al, 2003, xi). Keeping a job proved a much greater challenge than finding one and about a third of those who found work subsequently moved back onto Income Support again (Evans et al, 2003, xii). This policy move was very important symbolically in flagging the withdrawal of financial support free of behavioural conditions. Although the UK was a latecomer to lone parent work obligations compared with many other OECD countries (Wright, 2011), from the late 1990s onwards that situation changed rapidly over the course of two decades (Whitworth and Griggs, 2013) as conditionality crept in (Dwyer, 2004) and ramped up. Lone parents became subject to mandatory Work Focussed Interviews in pilot areas (Johnsen, 2014) and then, after Jobcentre Plus was established in 2002, these were universalised. Target-driven subcontracted Employment Zones included lone parents from 2003.

Lone parents' loss of conditionality-free Income Support

Another blow to women's caring rights came when lone parents were reclassified from mothers eligible for means-tested state support to unemployed workers. Traditionally, lone parents' eligibility for means-tested social-assistance benefits was established categorically by parenthood status and financial need. This long-standing arrangement recognised that lone parents had a legitimate role in the care of their children that was demanding of time to the exclusion of paid work and thus warranted financial support. However, there was little support on offer to assist those who did want, or need, to earn income and traditional provision reflected sexist labour market and family assumptions. In the early 2000s, lone parents could claim means-tested social assistance in the form of Income Support without any job-search obligations until their youngest child left school (Finn and Gloster, 2010). In 2008, this started to change when Lone Parent Obligations applied full job-search requirements to those whose youngest child was aged under 12. In 2009, this reduced to the age of under 10. Lone parents with older children lost entitlement to Income Support and had to claim Jobseeker's Allowance instead (Johnsen, 2014). Lone parents with younger children are also expected to engage in 'work preparation' activities. This policy required lone parents to engage with paid work, on threat of sanction, meaning: 'the right to work has become a requirement to work without a complementary right to care' (Rubery and Rafferty, 2013, 429). In 2009, the Flexible New Deal replaced all New Deal programmes and specialist support for lone parents was subsumed within generic work-first employability interventions. The Lone Parent Advisor role was abolished, meaning that the group status of lone parents as a special type of job seeker was substantially weakened.

Addressing low pay, child poverty and childcare shortages

New Labour significantly redefined lone parents as workers, but there were also meaningful steps to improve mothers' employment conditions. Importantly, the policy making frenzy included measures to tackle child poverty and expand childcare provision, particularly in deprived areas, via the National Childcare Strategy in 1998. Childcare became more readily available and nursery places for three- and four-year-olds were subsidised. A dedicated Minister for Women and a Women's Unit were established, along with an Equal Pay Taskforce. The UK's first National Minimum Wage was introduced in 1999, which benefitted women, who were much more likely than men to work part-time or be stuck in low-waged jobs. At the same time, the basic rate of Income Support was raised and Working Families Tax Credit (WFTC) replaced Family Credit. WFTC, and from 2003, Child Tax Credit and Working Tax Credit, were beneficial to many mothers because payments included help with a high proportion of the costs of formal childcare. There seemed to be a genuine intention to *enable* employment by making it financially viable and practically possible, on the assumption that many mothers wanted to work but were prevented by lack of affordable high-quality childcare and by low wages (Millar, 2008). The policy environment became much more hostile when Labour lost power.

'Austerity' and the Conservative-led punitive turn from 2010

In some respects, Conservative-led governments, from 2010 to the time of writing, continued the task that Labour began, by applying full job-search requirements to as many women as possible. However, the Conservative-Liberal coalition government in 2010 had a much more aggressive agenda. The context for punitive welfare conditionality was the aftermath of the 2007–08 global financial crisis. Deep cuts were made to public spending generally and social security specifically. These cuts were anchored to an indoctrinating 'austerity' narrative (Wiggan, 2016) that preconfigured national interests according to androcentric 'fiscal consolidation' priorities. This amounted to 'the reduction or withdrawal of welfare entitlements through appeals to frugality, self-sufficiency and fiscal prudence' (MacLeavy, 2011, 355). Repaying the national debt was likened by politicians to household belt-tightening that was needed, seemingly irrefutably, to 'balance the books' (Wiggan, 2016). Seventy-seven per cent of the money was to come from cutting back and only 23 per cent from bringing in additional funds from taxation (Elson, 2012, 177). Just like in the home, it was women who were more likely to go without, in this time of national need (see Goode et al, 1998; Pahl, 2002; Bennett, 2013; Main and Bradshaw, 2016). Social security cuts between 2010 and 2020 were estimated at a cumulative real-term £59bn, 57 per cent of which was 'from women's purses' (De Henau, 2017, 2). Since 2015, 75 per cent of the price of changes to tax and benefits has been paid by women (De Henau, 2017). The benefits freeze had the biggest direct impact, with the household-benefit cap, 'bedroom tax' and two-child limit also driving poverty (De Henau, 2017).

> the retrenchment in support for working parents is aimed at re-establishing women as a flexible and family-dependent labour supply, women are declaring themselves as unemployed rather than inactive and are beginning to use the in-work benefit system to facilitate becoming the sole or the joint breadwinner in recession-hit families. Part-time and temporary work is increasing but the share of women who would prefer a full-time or permanent job is increasing even faster. (Rubery and Rafferty, 2013, 428)

Ostensibly neutral cost savings impacted unduly on women, especially Black and minoritised ethnic women, via the '"triple jeopardy" of cuts to jobs, benefits and vital services' (Fawcett Society, 2020, 1). By the 2010s, in the UK, like many European and English-speaking countries, women's paid work was crucial to the economy. Women could no longer be seen predominantly as labour market 'outsiders' or a disposable 'reserve army of labour' (Rubery and Rafferty, 2013). Female-dominated sectors were hit hard by job losses (Rubery and Rafferty, 2013, 428). Women were impacted by 'austerity' cuts to a greater extent than men because they are more likely to use public services and to receive social security benefits, which is related to caring roles, longer lives and lower earning power (MacLeavy, 2011; De Henau, 2017; Reis, 2018, 1). Instead of offering 'a source of protection, the public sector is poised to be a source of women's vulnerability to both job loss and employment downgrading' (Rubery and Rafferty, 2013, 428). Reductions to social protection were made in line with neoliberal values, which impacted detrimentally on the social rights of women in many countries (Meneses et al, 2020).

Neutered discourse disguises the loss of part-time work strategies

The UK Conservative-Liberal government's white paper 21st Century Welfare (2010a) demonstrates that assumptions about who is 'normally in the labour market' have changed to such an extent that there is not a single mention of either 'women' or 'men'. Instead, genderless disembodied welfare subjects are held individually responsible for 'worklessness [that] blights the life chances of parents and children and diminishes the country's productive potential' (2010b, 3). Ideology has eclipsed the data-based strategies evident in Beveridge's proposals (described previously). There is no recognition that gender continues to shape lifetime earnings and opportunities for work and orientations towards time-consuming unpaid personal care duties. Expectations about paid employment apply to all 'people' and even include 'reforms to obligations placed on out-of-work lone parents' (DWP, 2010a, 5). All adults are now treated as non-disabled men previously were, that is, 'normally in the labour market' (Beveridge, 1944, 130). Lone parents are a named target for 'a strong system of conditionality' (DWP, 2010a, 5), intended to raise employment rates beyond 60 per cent (DWP, 2010b, 3). Not only are women carers, mothers of young children and disabled women now expected to work, but they are directed to full-time hours: 'whilst the majority should move into full-time work, for some people there may be temporary periods when part-time work is appropriate (for example, for some lone parents)' (DWP, 2010b, 4).

Part-time work, which (as shown) is a common strategy for women balancing irreducible care obligations, has been written out of the citizenship agreement, now only acceptable as a possibility which could potentially be negotiated in exceptional circumstances. Whereas countries with high rates of lone parents in employment usually have state-supported childcare systems, the UK makes it mandatory for mothers on a low income to work without guaranteeing the necessary childcare to make it possible.

Welfare conditionality

In the UK, the Liberal-Conservative government (2010–15) took a distinctly punitive turn when they redesigned the social security system to create hard-hitting disincentives, using tough financial sanctions (Fletcher and Wright, 2018; Wright et al, 2020). Conservative-led governments abandoned the goal of eradicating child poverty and relied on coercion and threats of destitution within a hostile environment of cuts. Political discourse towards benefit recipients became more antagonistic (Wiggan 2012; Jensen and Tyler, 2015). In contrast to the differentiated approach of Labour, Conservative policy makers sought to amalgamate the target groups for work-first intervention, giving everyone the same policy medicine, regardless of their condition. Disabled women were badly impacted by this disentitlement strategy (DWP, 2013), which reassesses all disability benefit recipients in a failed attempt (Beatty and Fothergill, 2018) to reduce social security spending (Garthwaite, 2011; 2014; Baumberg-Geiger, 2017).

Work obligations were applied more forcefully than before to lone parents claiming Income Support, Jobseeker's Allowance, Universal Credit and the Employment and Support Allowance Work-Related Activity Group, when their youngest child turned seven years old in 2010, then five years old in 2012 and three years old in 2017 (Johnsen and Blenkinsopp, 2018). Since 98 per cent of lone parents claiming Income Support were female (DWP, 2011b, 17), this has been interpreted as 'misogynistic' (Alston, cited in Buchanan, 2018). In 2011, the Work Programme was introduced as the main welfare-to-work programme, continuing the trend for generic support for uniform job seekers and increasing the conditions that are placed on job seekers irrespective of their circumstances. Little dedicated provision then existed for lone parents and benefit sanctions were applied for non-compliance with Work Programme attendance and instructions, as well as under Jobseeker's Allowance regulations. The shift from Income Support to Jobseeker's Allowance meant that lone parents were expected to produce back-to-work plans via generic tools (for example, the claimant commitment and Universal Jobmatch), without protection from sanctions. Lone parent easements for Jobseeker's Allowance are formal regulations that reduce the expected job seeking or working hours and distance to travel for work.

Benefit sanctions

Sanctions are the most blatantly punishing aspect of post-2010 reforms. The 2012 sanctions regime has severely detrimental impacts (Dwyer, 2018) for homeless people (Beatty et al, 2015), disabled people and those with mental-health problems (Dwyer et al, 2020). Sanctions are correlated with adverse effects for depression (E. Williams, 2021a) and anxiety (E. Williams, 2021b). The impacts of sanctions are gendered. Many structurally disadvantaged lone parents and disabled women (Barnes and Mercer, 2005) become newly subject to welfare conditionality and sanctions. An independent enquiry found that the 'work-first' push of social security towards 'any job' drove: 'a growing pattern of women being over represented in low paid jobs with poor prospects from which they will struggle to progress. This is not just a waste of women's potential economic contribution. It also makes it more likely that they will need other forms of state support to survive and that their children will grow up in poverty' (Ariss et al, 2015, 78).

The same inquiry expressed grave concern at the 'misapplication' of sanctions (Ariss et al, 2015, 81), particularly to large numbers of lone parents 'sanctioned unreasonably' (Ariss et al, 2015, 78). Alongside lone parents, women with language and literacy issues and those facing sexual and domestic abuse were identified as 'exceptionally vulnerable' to sanctions, affecting 'their mental and physical health, and the health and wellbeing of their children' (Ariss et al, 2015, 78). Care, especially motherhood, which was once valorised, is now barely acknowledged. 'The primary duty of citizenship has long been viewed as paid work and the citizen is perceived in masculine terms: as an economically independent wage earner unrestricted by caring responsibilities. ... Despite women's increasing participation in the paid labour market, women's citizenship status remains precarious' (Andersen, 2020, 434).

Universal Credit, ubiquitous conditionality and a hard push into unequal work

Universal Credit, introduced in 2013, was presented as 'the most far-reaching programme of change that the welfare system has witnessed in generations' (Iain Duncan Smith, then Secretary of State for Work and Pensions, DWP, 2010b, 1). It is designed to inculcate 'cultural change and behavioural shift for claimants ... requires them to be responsible' and is delivered 'online self-service'[5] (DWP, 2019, 1). The male subtext of Universal Credit pushes 'a working life' of paid employment over the many and varied formerly-legitimate states of economic inactivity, in a stigmatised overgeneralisation of 'worklessness' (DWP, 2019). Routine forms of gendered unpaid care have evaporated from the policy discussion and are replaced by degendered commodified forms of care, which are narrowly conceived. Although these reforms are beneficial to many women in some regards, it is crucial to acknowledge that the changes are not justified in relation to interdependency or care, but solely on depersonalised 'extralocal' (Smith, 1987) economic grounds as 'unsustainably expensive' (DWP, 2010b). The Universal Credit policy narrative and core assumptions are degendered to favour male-defined forms of productive activity. Universal Credit incorporates elements of New Labour's enabling policies that are credited with increasing employment rates among young people, lone parents and working families (DWP, 2010b, 59). However, the balance of policy design is firmly in favour of punitive welfare conditionality, intensifying starkly for those out of work and expanding ubiquitously to apply work expectations to partners of claimants (Dwyer and Wright, 2014). The globally unique decision to apply sanctions for job search expectations to UC claimants who already have a job (and may have previously claimed Working Tax Credit) produces a new 'coerced worker claimant' (Dywer and Wright, 2020). What has not been previously highlighted in academic or public debate is the extent to which the new target claimants are women (DWP, 2021b). When the policy establishes that 'claimants will be more open to short-term work or flexible hours' (DWP, 2018), this means many women, especially lone mothers, will be required to engage in short-term and flexible forms of employment. Universal Credit ends the long-standing social security protection for many carers, which legitimately excused them from job-seeking requirements. This is important because the: 'exemption from the obligation to work for parents and caregivers on social security should be considered as a citizenship right to time for care' (Knijn and Kremer, 1997, 332).

Universal Credit mainly removes *the right to time for care* by individualising the claimant commitment so that each woman must personally negotiate time for care, which is no longer protected by standard rights (Johnsen and Blenkinsopp, 2018). In fact, Universal Credit applies sanctions-backed conditionality to women by reinterpreting responsible carers as irresponsible workers, which 'devalues unpaid childcare and subjects mothers to conflicting responsibilities of mandatory work related requirements and unpaid childcare' (Andersen, 2020, 430). This is significant in two regards. First, it is a watershed moment in the underlying principles determining how women's unpaid caring roles are valued. Second, the scale of the change is enormous – half of all children in the UK are projected to be in Universal Credit claimant households by the time it is fully rolled out (Finch, 2015; NAO, 2018). Rewriting women's citizenship rights and responsibilities via Universal Credit has huge implications for women in a range of different circumstances and for children (Andersen, 2023). In practical terms, women's revised citizenship rights are rewritten at street level via policy instruments. The claimant commitment exists to 'incentivise claimants to meet their responsibilities' (DWP, 2011b, 13), defined purely economically as 'to take reasonable steps to find employment or move closer to the labour market' (DWP, 2011b). Caring activities are invisible. Successful negotiation of part-time job-search hours depends on the discretion of each work coach (2015). However, Andersen (2020, 439) demonstrates that in practice mothers feel pressure to agree to onerous job-search expectations, within their claimant commitments, that do not adequately accommodate their childcare obligations and could conflict with them. Similarly, the default 35-hour full-time work expectations enshrined in Universal Credit regulations delegitimise part-time working. This also undermines the citizenship right to care: 'Part-time work, which enables citizens to synchronize work and care responsibilities, is another translation of the citizenship right to time to care' (Knijn and Kremer, 1997, 333).

Universal Credit enshrines contradictory requirements for women's work. On the one hand, lone parents have almost entirely lost the right to care, and can be required to work full-time. On the other hand, partnered women face financial disincentives to engage in paid work as second earners because of the design of the household earning taper (Bennett, 2012). UC therefore acts 'to reduce active support for working mothers in couple households' (Rubery and Rafferty, 2013, 429).

Women are also impacted by sanctions incurred by lead claimants, where they are the designated 'responsible carer' – a situation calculated by DWP to characterise many households (DWP, 2015; WPC, 2018; Andersen, 2020). Since Universal Credit is a household benefit, paid at below-poverty rates, any reduction to an adult standard allowance – such as a sanction – will impact on the whole household (Millar and Bennett, 2017). Payments are made to one nominated person in the household, rather than being split between partners (Bennett, 2012). These aspects of UC design, independently and in combination with policies like the household benefit cap, make women experiencing domestic abuse more financially vulnerable than they might have been in the legacy system where child elements were paid by default to the main carer, who was assumed to be the mother (Women's Aid, 2017).

The Universal Credit impact assessment for conditionality and sanctions only considers gender with reference to the lower existing rates of sanctions for women, compared with men, for Jobseeker's Allowance. This misses the point that many women who will claim Universal Credit are working claimants (for whom there is no meaningful statistical comparator because in the legacy system there were no sanctions for Working Tax Credits), have health problems or are lone parents (who would previously have claimed Income Support rather than JSA). Superficially, the 2012 sanctions regime complies with equal-opportunities legislation because it does not overtly aim to discriminate between men and women. However, it does discriminate against women implicitly in at least the following four ways:

1. Women are more likely to have unpaid family care obligations than men, which limit the time they have available to meet work-related conditionality and can create complex circumstances where motivations and behaviour are interdependent, rather than purely individual (as the sanctioning rationale implies). The most obvious group of women this affects are lone mothers because they are main carer to dependent children and sole potential worker. However, other groups of women, such as grandmothers are impacted in more hidden ways.

2. Women are much more likely than men to work in low-paid or part-time jobs and sectors (see Chapter Three). This makes women more likely to be claiming Universal Credit while in work (DWP, 2021b).

3. Women are more likely to become secondary welfare subjects in their role as partners of claimants. Under Universal Credit, they are a new group of sanctionable subject.

4. Women will be more likely to end up on Universal Credit than insurance-based JSA or ESA because their reproductive and caring roles interrupt or limit their National Insurance contributions. The official Universal Credit[6] impact assessment does acknowledge that for some claimants, including lone parents, some forms of non-compliance, such as missing appointments 'can often be due to challenging circumstances rather than wilful evasion of the rules' (DWP, 2011b, 10). However, there is no system for identifying compliant claimants who are facing 'challenging circumstances' and very little protection even for lone parents to ensure they will 'only be subject to work-focused interview requirements' (DWP, 2011b, 10). The main provision is to cap the sanctionable amount at 40 per cent, which is a hefty financial penalty for those sanctioned through no fault of their own.

Shutting off options for lone parents

Under Universal Credit, lone parent easements were downgraded from rights-based regulations to guidance for discretionary practice (Cain, 2016; Andersen, 2020), reducing the protection of parental activities and pushing the boundaries of expectations for working/job seeking time and travel distance. Legal challenge to protect caring time has become less transparent (because of the introduction of internal DWP mandatory reconsideration, before formal appeal stage) and more ambiguous. The current systems use a limited range of basic employability tools and rely on the threat of sanctions to prompt job seeking with the goal of leaving benefits – either via immediate job entry or disengagement. Promises of 'individually tailored support' are rarely realised in practice, with little or no adaptation of standard rules to individual circumstances (Torien et al, 2013). Under the UK Coalition (2010–15) and the Conservative (2015–present) administrations, the special characteristics of category-based provision have been eroded, leaving little recognition of the substantial unpaid work done by lone parents. For lone parents and other 'vulnerable people', Universal Credit involves a fundamental withdrawal of state protection. Instead of automatic reductions to conditionality expectations, the default is 35-hour job search. Disabled people, carers of young children and those in vulnerable situations, such as homeless people, are required under UC to negotiate discretionary easements, budgeting advances, hardship loans or alternative payment arrangements. Work coaches decide individually whether to grant easements and there is evidence that many vulnerable people do not request them because they are either unaware of the provision (which is not widely advertised) or they do not feel empowered to request them (Stinson, 2019).

Like all UC claimants, lone parents are increasingly being funnelled towards employment-orientated forms of social security (Johnsen, 2014), with much reduced recognition that their ability to meet conditionality requirements is different from single job seekers without children. The reconstruction of lone parents as 'workless' workers involved the application of individualised behavioural responsibility. This policy approach also assumes that claimants are motivated and act individually. This policy approach is based on minimal self-help and a high level of threat of harsh financial sanctions (Fletcher and Wright, 2017). However, this behavioural approach individualises responsibility to look for work and creates pressure (via mandatory meetings, the claimant commitment and associated conditions) to behave primarily as a potential worker, rather than primarily as a parent. Jobseeker's Allowance and Universal Credit systems are designed to engage on an individual basis with recipients, with minimal regard for their embodied personhood, or their defining interconnectivity with the needs of their children (Wright, 2011). The underlying model of agency is androgynous, a synthetic construction of the ideal worker, 'a fictional version of invincible humanity' (Wright, 2011, 322).

Symbolically, this package of change is of major significance to how lone parents are treated in the British system. The process of 're-categorising risk' (Clasen and Clegg, 2011) has involved a loss of recognition, even at group level, of the parenting role and identity. Instead, generalised 'conditions of conduct' (Clasen and Clegg, 2007) are now applied to lone parents with less protection of the necessary time, energy and financial resources for parenting without a partner to share the load of earning or caring. The design of the social security system, in particularly the heavy-handed threat of sanctions, appears to have closed the space available for recognising the non-individual aspects of lone parenthood. Lone parenthood is fundamentally an interconnected state of interdependency (Wright, 2011) and lone-parent care demands are irreducible, personal, relational and involve time commitments that are non-negotiable (Himmelweit and Plomien, 2014).

Multiple phases of welfare reform have established behavioural conditions that create tensions for lone parents because of these aspects of their caring role. Welfare conditionality engages only with one dimension of the individualised self and may diminish, devalue and discredit other important aspects of the parental self. To be clear, I am not arguing that lone parents should not engage in paid work. Paid work can be both necessary and desirable for many lone parents (Rafferty and Wiggan, 2011; Ridge and Millar, 2011) and can play an important role in developing multiple aspects of selfhood in constructive ways (Millar and Ridge, 2008). However, lone parents are not one homogenous group, but are positioned uniquely as sole earner–carers (Finch and Mason, 1993; Edwards and Duncan, 1997). Lone parents' decisions about paid work are also mediated by powerful social expectations about motherhood and 'gendered moral rationalities' (Duncan and Edwards, 1999) as well as financial concerns.

Impoverishment by design: the two-child limit

The 'morally odious' (Bradshaw, 2017, 1) 'two child limit' on Universal Credit[7] was introduced in 2017 to cut social security costs. The policy denies financial assistance in the form of the child element to all but the first two children in large families (see DWP, 2021c). It affects almost a third of families and breaks the fundamental link between need and the provision of minimum support and implies that some children, by virtue of their birth order, are less deserving of support. It is a very large direct cut to the living standards of the poorest families (Bradshaw, 2017, 1). The 'two child limit' implicitly discriminates against minoritised ethnic groups such as Pakistani and Bangladeshi families and religious groups including Orthodox Jews and Roman Catholics (Bradshaw, 2017, 1). The House of Lords Economic Affairs Committee deemed the policy 'unfair' (Economic Affairs Committee 2020, 47) and expressed concerns about the traumatic impacts of the so called 'rape clause' – an exception[8] that allows payments for subsequent children if there is written evidence from a professional they were conceived during non-consensual sex (Machin, 2017).

Financial subordination and economic abuse

Universal Credit implicitly normalises female-carer financial subordination within couples because of its payment design, the extension of conditionality to partners of claimants and new disincentives for second earners. Universal Credit reduces 'women's financial autonomy' (Howard, 2018, 1) within heterosexual couples because it lumps together payments for different purposes (children, child care, adults and housing) into one single payment for the whole household (HoC, 2018). This is paid into to a single nominated bank account and means 'main carers (usually in practice mothers) losing clearly-labelled child payments' (Howard, 2018, 1). This breaks the tradition of paying child-related allowances to the main carer, which has been the default since family allowances were introduced in 1946 and continues to be supported by research (Griffiths et al, 2020) as the best way to ensure that child payments are used for their intended purposes. Paying large monthly sums to one adult affords an unprecedented degree of control over the whole household's benefit income and can: 'facilitate domestic or economic abuse; by narrowing 'women's space for action', a single monthly payment could make it easier for men to establish or retain financial control, while making it harder for women and their children to leave an abusive relationship' (Griffiths et al, 2020, 148).

While temporary Alternative Payment Arrangements are possible for domestic abuse survivors, they deviate from standard practice and must be negotiated with work coaches (Griffiths et al, 2020, 2). Work coaches may be unaware of split payments (Serwotka, 2018) and 'often do not have the skills or knowledge to support survivors adequately' (HoC, 2018, 11). The 'male subtext' (Smith, 1987) of family finances is written in favour of male earners at the expense of female carers. Women experiencing economic abuse may find it 'highly dangerous' to disclose abuse (Women's Aid, 2018, 1) and are not guaranteed split payments even if they do. Universal Credit creates 'an additional barrier to their ability to escape abusive relationships' (Women's Aid, 2018, 1). Griffiths et al (2020, 16) found that many of the coupled women UC claimants they interviewed had experienced domestic violence, financial abuse or controlling behaviour in past or present relationships and some found lack of access to the household income contributed to relationship breakdown. Domestic abuse survivors may negotiate up to 13 weeks of 'easement' in their mandatory job search requirements only after they provide evidence of abuse within the preceding six months (Women's Aid, 2018, 1). They must also stop living with the perpetrator and provide written evidence that they are engaging with support for domestic abuse (Women's Aid, 2018; Serwotka, 2018).

The in-work conditionality trial

During the period of the study reported in this book, Universal Credit 'live service' was being rolled out throughout the UK. Recipients claiming UC as an earnings top-up (instead of the old system of Working Tax Credit) became subject to in-work conditionality (see Wright and Dwyer, 2021). During 2015–18 (a period that encompassed the study fieldwork), 42,452 in-work claimants[9] were automatically enrolled in a compulsory nationwide DWP 'In Work Progression' randomised control trial. The trail (DWP/Government Social Research (GSR), 2018) was designed to push claimants towards 'more work', which is referred to disingenuously as 'in-work progression' – to increase weekly working hours to full-time 35 hours and/or to increase pay. In-work claimants were randomly allocated to one of three conditionality groups, without their knowledge or permission. All three conditionality groups involved risks of sanctions for non-compliance. The option of exempting in-work claimants from conditionality was not tested. The 'Intense' group were called to fortnightly meetings at Jobcentre Plus and were required to undertake mandatory job-search actions at the discretion of their work coach. The 'Moderate' conditionality group had compulsory Work Search Reviews every eight weeks with mandatory actions. The 'Minimal' conditionality group had a mandatory phone call every eight weeks with their work coach and follow-up voluntary action. The trial did not find any evidence of increased pay and fewer participants were in work at Wave B than Wave A.

Easing work transitions and supporting childcare

Universal Credit expanded financial support for formal childcare by including a Childcare Element to help initially with up to 70 per cent of the costs of formal childcare[10] (DWP, 2010b, 21). In 2016, in response to lobbying, DWP increased financial support for up to 85 per cent of childcare costs. At the same time, tax-free childcare was expanded to offer young children 15 hours of free early-years education (DWP, 2014). This style of financial assistance for childcare, inherited from Working Tax Credit[11] for working parents, is very valuable in enabling women to work. This part of the design of Universal Credit enables labour market participation to a greater extent than the legacy system, which did not offer help with the costs of childcare for those working a small number of hours or 'mini jobs' (Millar and Bennett, 2017). Lone parent households lose out financially to a far greater extent than other household types under Universal Credit (Brewer et al, 2019, 13).

Older women workers

In many countries, older women workers, defined by the OECD as those aged between 55 and 64, have been increasing their rate of labour market participation over the last four decades (Taylor et al, 2021, 3). Before the onset of punitive conditionality, older women workers in the UK already had higher labour market participation rates than their counterparts in many comparable countries – tracking 5–13 per cent higher than the OECD average 1965–2010 (Taylor et al, 2021). Surprisingly, the UK even had higher rates of older women in employment than Sweden in 2010 – a country with historically higher rates of women in paid employment (aged 15–64; Taylor et al, 2021). This indicates a grey area where policies for working-age social security intersect with policies for early retirement and labour market exit. Many European and English-speaking countries consider older workers as early retirees. Universal Credit takes an extreme approach by redefining early retirement as unemployment and applying punitive conditionality to part-time workers (who in other countries would claim wage top-ups). The financial position of older workers is influenced by a combination of the employment, social security and pension policies that were in place in the preceding decades. The UK is unusual in its very limited coverage of insurance-based social security. This offers women advantages and disadvantages.

It is important to understand the impacts of ramping up conditionality for women aged 50+[12] because unpaid care is likely to have had a major impact on their current income, lifetime earnings and present commitments. Older women have diverse needs and obligations but are more likely than men to be primary carers for aging parents or other relatives and perhaps also grandchildren. Because women are more likely to experience poverty throughout their lifetime and in older age, they are more likely in older age to rely on financial assistance from the state. Since the post-war welfare state, expectations about older women's engagement in paid employment have varied. Shifting patterns of relationship formation and uncoupling have made marriage a less predictable route to income in older age than Beveridge (1942) imagined. Women who were born in the 1950s and 1960s are much more likely than previous generations to divorce. The parallel withdrawal of financial security from the state and the family has been integral to older women's changing attachment to paid employment.

While older workers have been increasingly targeted by punitive welfare conditionality, there is little recognition of the influence of gendered care obligations as a constraint on availability for paid work or the enduring horizonal and vertical labour market segregation of opportunities. A government-commissioned report on older workers recognised that:

> The cohort of women who are now reaching their 50s and 60s has been especially disadvantaged in terms of lifetime income and pensions, and faces particular workplace barriers. They are more likely than their male colleagues to be carers which can have an impact on how they manage work, and although both men and women can face various health challenges as they get older, women have a particular health issue which is largely ignored in workplace thinking – the menopause. (Altman, 2015, 12)

Older workers are generally 'more vulnerable to long-term unemployment upon losing their job and those over 60 are more likely to leave work early due to ill-health and caring responsibilities' (TUC, 2021; ONS,

2021; Fitzpatrick and Chapman, 2021, 2). Some older workers receiving earnings top-ups via Working Tax Credit and due to move onto Universal Credit wanted to combine part-time work with family life (Fitzpatrick and Chapman, 2021, 11). This fits with broader preferences across Europe: 'Part-time work facilitates a better work–life balance – particularly, it seems, for people aged 50+. Among people aged 50+, both in and out of employment, there is a preference for more part-time options' (Eurofound, 2014, 7).

However, Universal Credit does not offer dispensation for older workers to reduce their job-search/working hours below the 35-hour-per-week norm. Many governments have sought to extend working life to save on pensions expenditure. However, this strategy may involve a zero-sum gain: 'People aged 50+ often care for a partner or parent with health problems or disabilities. … If less informal care is provided, demand for formal care is likely to increase, implying greater public expenditure and potentially a lower quality of life for the person being cared for' (Eurofound, 2014, 6).

Because Universal Credit is based on an ill-fitting individualised notion of human behaviour, the interdependencies between adult women and their mothers have been overlooked. The pivotal relationship between mother's employment and grandmother childcare does not appear to have been well appreciated in the design on Universal Credit. Within 'conditionality discourse, unpaid childcare is viewed as a barrier to paid work', meaning 'the relational and affective orientation of care is unrecognised' (Andersen, 2020, 438). Universal Credit disrupts existing arrangements that facilitate mothers' employment because it draws new groups of older carers into their own individualised work-conditionality. Grandmothers, aged in their 50s and early to mid-60s, face new expectations to work in their capacity as UC claimants, both in and out of work, and partners of claimants. Previously, low-income grandmothers caring for their grandchildren would have remained eligible for other benefits, without the requirement to work 35 hours per week, if they claimed (for example) disability benefits, working tax credits, or were partners of Jobseeker's Allowance claimants.

It is important to understand the intensification of work expectations for older women in the context of the UK's exceptionally high levels of grandparent care. Sixty-three per cent of grandparents provide care for grandchildren aged under 16, compared with 40 per cent in a review of 11 European countries (Glaser et al, 2013). About 30 per cent of grandparents in the UK are in the sandwich generation, with grandchildren and parents still alive; 60 per cent are still working; and nearly 80 per cent care for grandchildren (Wellard, 2011; Glaser et al, 2013, 16). Grandmothers often care for their grandchildren to enable mothers to work.

Given that grandmothers aged 50 to 69 who are not in paid work are the most likely to provide childcare, the plans of European governments to extend retirement ages and increase female labour force participation at older ages are likely to conflict with grandparents' role in providing childcare. This will have significant implications for labour market participation by younger mothers, and for pension acquisition and the financial security of mid-life women. (Glaser et al, 2013, 3)

Two-thirds of women aged over 50 are grandmothers in the UK and have an average of 5.2 grandchildren (Glaser et al, 2013, 5–6). 'The pattern of female labour force participation in a country is associated with childcare by grandmothers, independently of the policy context. ... Use of formal childcare for young children is inversely related to intensive childcare by grandmothers' (Glaser et al, 2013, 11). In the UK, like Germany and the Netherlands, 'public support for families is varied but less universal, and childcare coverage is patchy and often provided by the market rather than the state, and the norm is that women work part-time. Here, grandparents generally play a middling role in both intensive childcare and occasional/less intensive childcare' (Glaser et al, 2013, 3).

The family and employment policy context for maternal employment is associated with the frequency of grandparent care in European countries (Bordone et al, 2017). In southern European countries like Italy, grandparent care is a main source of care because there are few part-time employment opportunities, so mothers usually work full-time or not at all, and state childcare is mainly absent (Bordone et al, 2017, 845). At the other end of the spectrum, in Nordic countries where subsidised state childcare is plentiful and maternity support is relatively generous, grandparent care is a reserve (Glaser et al 2013; Bordone et al, 2017). In between, much of Western Europe sees grandparent care as supplementary to state services (Glaser et al, 2013).

Universal Credit creates a conflict for low-income grandmothers, between fulfilling the new state responsibility to engage in 35 hours per week of paid employment and the old family obligation to care for grandchildren. Working-class women are more likely to claim Universal Credit than women from other socio-economic backgrounds because of their greater reliance on low-paid work. This raises the possibility that both mothers and grandmothers may become subject to new sanctions-backed work requirements under Universal Credit. Without affordable childcare available to all, the increased work expectations for grandmothers within Universal Credit risks driving 'a care gap for working parents, largely impacting on mothers' employment' (Glaser et al, 2013, 15).

Pensions reform: prolonging women's employment

Tighter conditionality also coincided with equalisation of the state-pension age for men and women in 2018 when women's retirement age increased from 60 to 65. This created new pressures for older women, who had lived their lives in the expectation of retiring at the age of 60. Not only did they have to adjust to staying in work for another half decade, but suddenly they were doing so under the harshest conditions that the post-war welfare system had ever known. This has greatest impact on women from areas of multiple deprivation, whose life expectancy is shorter than women from wealthy areas.

The post-war welfare state established the retirement ages of 60 for women and 65 for men, who would receive the state pension on those birthdays. The Pensions Act 1995 changed the state retirement age for women from 60 to 65 (implemented between 2010 and 2020). The changes were brought forward by the Pensions Act 2011 and for women born in the mid-1950s, retirement age was increased to 66 (Thurley and McInnes, 2020). The Pensions Act 2007 increased the retirement age for women born in the 1960s to 67 and for those born from the late 1970s onwards it went up to 68 (see DWP, 2021a). The Pensions Act 2014 accelerated these changes. Increases in state pension age for women are driven by a cost containment rationale and justified with reference to rising life expectancy (Thurley and McInnes, 2020). However, wide class differentials in life expectancy were not accounted for, which disproportionately disadvantages women from low-income backgrounds. This is an important example of intersectionality – where structures of gender and class interact to compound financial vulnerability (see Williams, 2021).

Scottish social security

Interviews for the project were conducted in Scotland as well as England. During the study there was a media buzz about Scotland's historic new devolved social security system, which is based on human rights and the principles of 'dignity, fairness and respect' (Scottish Government, 2019). At the time of the research interviews (2014–17) the 11 new devolved social security benefits (informed by User Experience Panels) were still in development phase (Social Security Scotland (SSS), 2021). Legislation was passed in 2018 and the delivery agency Social Security Scotland was set up the same year – both after fieldwork was completed.[13] Work First Scotland was introduced in April 2017 (near the end of our last wave of interviewing) as a transitional arrangement (Scottish Government, 2018a). This Scottish back-to-work programme was available for long-term unemployed and disabled people. In 2018, Fair Start Scotland replaced the transitional scheme, which was after the Welfare Conditionality fieldwork finished (Scottish Government, 2018b). Unlike the UK Work Programme, Scottish employment services are offered on a voluntary basis for claimants who opted in and the Scottish Parliament designed the system to be completely separate from the UK sanctions regime (Shaw, 2017). Additional financial support is available to claimants of UK benefits living in Scotland via the Scottish Welfare Fund, in the form of crisis grants and community-care grants.

The UK government has power over working-age social security for people living in Scotland (Shaw, 2017). This includes setting the rules and standardised processes for: eligibility, fitness for work, the rates of payment, the claimant interface, IT systems, performance management for work coaches, claimant expectations and penalties for non-compliance. The laws and implementation guidance for conditionality and the sanctions system are controlled by Westminster. Universal Credit is the main income benefit for people of working age (both in and out of work) in Scotland in much the same way as in England. UC claimants have choices[14] that their counterparts in England do not. Claimants can choose whether to receive their payments fortnightly or monthly; and whether the housing element is paid directly to claimants or to landlords. In practice, uptake of these 'Scottish choices' has not been as popular as expected, with under half opting in (Scottish Government, 2019). The Scottish Parliament decided to fund additional support for Universal Credit claimants in Scotland and to mitigate the 'bedroom tax'.

Conclusion

This chapter has shown how the expectations about women's work enshrined in social security legislation have turned around over the course of the last century. In the early 20th century, although many women were working, great chunks of the labour market were off limits (McCarthy, 2021) and unemployment insurance gave preference to male trades. In the post-war period, social security and employment law were designed on the assumption that most women would find financial security in marriage with a male breadwinner while performing an unpaid reproductive role themselves. Since the 1950s, much has changed. Women have increased their labour market participation, signalling greater economic independence. However, this has not been matched by an equal contribution in unpaid care from men. There has been a lag in policy development to support female employment and childcare in the UK remains expensive by international standards. Until the late 1990s, there were little or no work obligations for most lone parents or female partners of unemployed benefit claimants, which is unusual by cross-national comparison. From the late 1990s, all three main UK ruling political parties have pursued work-first welfare reforms that have extended and intensified welfare conditionality, impacting many women and children. New Labour mixed enabling and disciplinary policies. Since 2010, Conservative-led punitive policies and managerial reforms in the austerity era were justified using ideological assumptions and cost-cutting priorities that bear little or no resemblance to women's lived experiences of paid work and unpaid care.

'Gender-neutral' discourse has disguised the hidden harms to women. The 21st-century welfare settlement involves a radically different legal framework for work and welfare. Now, under Universal Credit, women are expected to work full-time whenever possible, with few protective rights. This degree of work-based conditionality marks a watershed for women's social citizenship and UK family policy, with a deep undercutting of maternal roles. Recently, the UK has started to develop the type of childcare infrastructure that is commonplace in many European and Scandinavian welfare systems, with state-subsidised nursery care. While this enables women with young children to engage in paid work to a greater extent than earlier eras, when state involvement in the provision of early-years childcare was very limited, it delegitimises motherhood for working-class women in favour of economic productivity, with very marginal financial gains.

The policies and practices of welfare conditionality have hidden gendered assumptions and impacts, which reinforce pre-existing structural disadvantages for women and men. Instead of being excluded from many parts of the labour market based on gender difference, women, including mothers, are now usually in paid work. However, neither their jobs nor their social security provision offer true equality. Amidst complex social and demographic shifts, policy makers changed formal expectations about women's citizenship rights and responsibilities towards a form of male-defined pseudo equality (Lister, 2003; Orloff, 1993; 2003). In the 21st century women face new expectations about when and how to combine unpaid care with paid work. Women, who in earlier eras were banned from some workplaces, gained mid-century rights as mothers and dependents, which were later expanded to incorporate large-scale labour market participation. Now, many women are compelled to work in circumstances constrained by care. The rise of punitive welfare conditionality has created a new sanctionable worker-mother subject to degendered work obligations.

FOUR

Rewriting retirement as 'work experience': older women's gendered encounters with the work ethic

Karen[1] was born in 1955 and "grew up before the human rights thing". She launched her Royal Navy career in the early 1970s but, two years later, it was over when it had barely begun. Karen was discharged for breaching her contract by becoming pregnant. Because it happened before the Sex Discrimination Act 1975, Karen was lawfully denied her job and her occupational pension for those years of service.

Like many married women at the time, Karen prioritised raising her children. When her marriage ended in the 1980s, she wanted to work but "there was no childcare and all that sort of stuff". She took part in a local authority initiative for women returners, got a diploma for office work and did a government training scheme working as an administrator with a benefit top-up of £15 per week.

Karen's "strong work pride" spurred her on and she had full-time and part-time employment continuously for 30 years. These were mainly administrative jobs and varied widely, including managing multimillion-pound contracts for a government department, legal work and support for female survivors of violence and sexual assault.

In 1995, half-way through her working life, the government rewrote state pension law. Instead of retiring at 60, Karen would have to wait until 66. Karen was 59 when we first interviewed her in 2015. She gets Universal Credit and is legally required to look for full-time work to receive financial support. At the second interview, Karen is 60 – the age she had expected to retire. She wishes she "could spend time ... with my grandchildren and if I wanted to work I could but then it would be choice rather than being forced. I still would".

Aged 61, the third time we speak to her, Karen has held a series of transitory jobs, volunteered and completed work placements. As for training courses, she has "done them all". Her generation was the last to be legally excluded from work because of pregnancy and the first to be legally mandated to work full-time beyond 60. Instead of retiring, Karen is stuck in a 'work preparation' holding pattern.

Introduction

The cohort of working-class women born in the UK in the 1950s began working in the 1960s or early 1970s when gender discrimination and unequal pay were legal. Their high risk of poverty during the 2010s and 2020s is both a hangover from their unprotected years of employment and due to the pension gap created when the state retirement age was raised. The prevailing social norm for that generation's working life involved career gaps for motherhood, periods of part-time employment and a secondary role for women's earnings in heterosexual households (McCarthy, 2021). Although women's attitudes and preferences about working and having children changed over the intervening decades (McCarthy, 2021), deeply embedded gender norms continue to constrain the earnings potential of younger generations of women, meaning they will be more likely than men to have to rely on Universal Credit – with its full-time work requirements – when they reach their 50s and 60s. The aim of this first empirical chapter is to demonstrate how welfare conditionality rewrites older women's lives according male-defined working norms. First, the focus is on the cohort of women born in the 1950s and sanctions for baby boomers. Anne's story demonstrates how shameful sanctions can be and shows how retirement has been rewritten as work experience. Second, Karen's story illustrates how changing legal expectations about work and care are experienced over a life course. Karen's lived experiences of Universal Credit and the Work Programme demonstrate how retirement is redefined as unemployment and punitive conditionality is applied in practice. Third, June's story illustrates how disability is redefined as unemployment for older women. Fourth, the interdependent nature of supporting family and being supported is considered in relation to meeting conditionality requirements. Fifth, tensions between work and care are discussed.

Sanctions for baby boomers

Twenty-two of the women in the study were aged 55–64 at the time of the first interview, generating a total of 56 interviews.[2] Almost all (20) were single. Most (18) were out of work, one was self-employed, one worked full-time and two worked short hours. In total, 11 of the older women were disabled.[3] Nine were grandmothers and likely to be providing caring support to enable their adult children, especially daughters, to work. Two interviewees talked about regularly caring for their grandchildren, including overnight stays and supporting disabled grandchildren. Five were on Universal Credit, four claimed Jobseeker's Allowance, two were migrants, one was homeless, one a lone parent (the main carer for her granddaughter) and one was recruited to the study as a social tenant. Although only five of the older women had experienced a sanction, almost all were worried that they could be sanctioned. Three had no income from any source at the time of their first interview.

These are the baby-boom generation who were born in the 1950s.[4] These were girls born to women who had lived through wartime, in the first flush of the post-war welfare state. Their mothers were among the first to receive state maternity allowance and family allowance. They were the first generation to grow up with a National Health Service. Textual expectations about their contributions to the economy were articulated in Beveridge's societal reconstruction plans (1942; 1944), based on data from the 1930s when the marriage bar prohibited married women from being employed in many sectors (including teaching, banking and the civil service). The social norm was for women to leave the labour market when they married to raise their own children and fulfil their responsibilities as wives and homemakers (McCarthy, 2021). These were not just prevailing cultural norms – these expectations were written into social security and employment law and they influenced the extent to which women were able to draw on financial support from the state throughout their lifetimes. For the cohort of women aged 55+ in the study, the policy expectation was that during their adult lives their husbands would provide for them financially and they would contribute to the home and to society mainly as unpaid carers in support of others.

When this cohort of women left school in the 1970s, equal pay legislation was brand new (1970).[5] For example, it was not until 1973 that married female civil servants could work for the Foreign Service. It was 1975 before sex discrimination in the workplace was outlawed.[6] Gender-based discrimination in the workplace was rife. Many women in this era continued to perform traditional gender roles in work and in the domestic sphere during the 1970s and the 1980s, when it was usual for mothers to prioritise their family over paid employment (Yeandle, 1984). For this reason, many women did not develop or advance in their careers. Their lifetime earnings were limited by the expectation that they would spend much of their time supporting their families rather than in paid employment. This generation of women is also affected by changes in expectations about retirement ages.

Anne's story: "it's not as though women really retire, do they?"

Anne is 60 the first time we speak to her. She claims Jobseeker's Allowance and receives a small private pension. She had to give up working as a carer because it was too physically demanding and stressful. She has high blood pressure and osteoarthritis in both knees. She felt too ashamed to tell some of her friends and family when she got sanctioned for insufficient job search, which felt like entrapment. Anne fulfilled the expectations of her usual work coach but got caught out when a replacement adviser had different demands. She found it "very harrowing" to have no income for a month. "I mean how is that helping somebody to find a job? It's just punishment, when sometimes people need that extra bit of help, the encouragement, but you certainly don't get it."

At Wave B, she is out of work and feels ready to retire. By Wave C, she is doing voluntary work, but still has not found paid employment. Anne feels frustrated:

> 'I've come to the point in my life, because I'm 63 now, where I don't really want a job. I should have retired three years ago, but they're not going to let you are they, so what can you do? I mean I'm still applying for jobs.
>
> 'They've changed the rules and we've missed out, us born in the 1950s, but there's not really a lot you can do. So, it's just like a waiting game because I will be a lot better off when I do retire.
>
> 'You're not having enough time to prepare. ... I've got about 40 [years'] National Insurance stamps; it's not as though I've never worked. I've had children, so with them in full time education you get Child Benefit, so it's not as though you haven't got enough National Insurance stamps to retire.'

Pre-retirement 'work experience' was required of Anne as part of an inappropriate Community Work Placement, as if she was a school leaver learning about entering the labour market for the first time. "I don't really need work experience because I've had that and I'm coming up to retirement, so why put me on it? It costs the government £2000 ... so why send me on it? Why not send younger people who have perhaps never worked and need that experience?"

Ultimately, Anne was busy enough with her existing unpaid domestic and family care work. "It's not as though women really retire, do they? I mean they've always got housework, grandchildren, you never really retire. Men might, but women don't."

Sanctioned between a rock and a hard place: elder care and disability

June is a 61-year-old White British woman. Eighteen months ago she stopped working as a secretary because of a chronic cough. June also has "some nerve damage, and I find it difficult to stand and lift heavy things". She received ESA for a year but lost entitlement after a Work Capability Assessment and claimed Jobseeker's Allowance instead. She previously did a range of jobs including babysitting, cleaning and supermarket packer. She lives with her octogenarian parents who are not in good health. Her father is "having tests for prostate cancer; he's in his mid–80s. He has severe osteoporosis". She was sanctioned twice for travelling 300 miles away to prepare her "very small holiday home" for sale or rent, which she informed her work coach about. She was "very shocked" to be sanctioned because she was still looking for work while there. June had "no idea there was no flexibility ... to deal with personal matters". She was distressed about the sanctions and had depression.

> 'I had reactive depression, really. The sudden loss of income, even with a huge financial cushion and lots of family support. I just felt overwhelmed with despair, because I had tried to get work, without success, and even sort of mediocre jobs that I knew I could do skill-wise, I just couldn't seem to get anywhere.'

At Wave B, she lost her JSA entitlement because of informal caring duties: "My aunty was having a series of blackouts, and she ended up with stitches in her face, and we were trying to help her and provide lunches and lifts and things like that. But unfortunately, from a Jobseeker's point of view, that was disallowed."

Although June also lives with and cares for her parents, her elder care is not extensive enough to qualify her for Carer's Allowance. Her own chronic undiagnosed cough constantly impacts on her quality of life and she is extremely tired. She feels stressed and not able to work. She has not had any income for many months. June now survives on modest savings.

Redefining retirement as unemployment: job seeking in the pension void

When we first met Karen (her story opens this chapter) in 2015, she had been on Universal Credit for eight months and was living alone in her home of 27 years – a former council house now owned by a housing association. This is where, first while married, then after separating from her partner, Karen raised her two children. Karen grew up in an orphanage. Like many of her contemporaries, she served her country in the armed forces after leaving 'care'. On completing her basic Royal Navy training, Karen was stationed 500 miles away from where she grew up. Right from the start of her working life, she was acutely aware of gender inequalities:

> 'I was only 17 then and I was seven and a half stone, like you are when you're young. I can remember asking them to lift something for me, one of these guys, 'You do it. You want equality, you want feminism; you bloody lift it. If you can't do the job, get out.'

Two years later, the awakening was ruder, when she was discriminated against because of her maternity. The timing had immediate and lifelong financial and career consequences for Karen. When her military career ended, she limited her societal contribution to the private sphere of her family in her role as a mother. Karen's choices about work and care were curtailed by the text of employment law and armed forces employment policy. She lived out the socially accepted gender roles of the time. In the 1980s, after her marriage ended, she claimed social security. At the time, there were no work obligations for lone parents (see Chapter Three), but Karen chose freely to return to work: "I was an unmarried mum at the time. My kids had gone to school and I thought 'I want to work.'"

In the 2000s, after 30 years of working and in her late 50s, Karen found herself out of work and claimed benefits. This time 21st-century punitive welfare conditionality was in place and social security law required her to look for 'any job' on a full-time basis. While on the Work Programme Karen found herself two different jobs, but neither was sustainable. The first was an administrative role for a lettings agency that proved too stressful because it was an impossible job – trying to make a failing business function. After finishing by mutual agreement ("lots of people were leaving"), Karen took on a full-time job in a bakery. The job was advertised as administrative, but it transpired that heavy warehouse work was involved:

'It was too physical for me. It might've been all right if I was 20 years younger. I just found it just not – I just didn't have it now. ... I loved it, I loved the staff, I loved the job. I just couldn't do the physical side of it. The person that had it before me – because I actually met him – he was about six foot. He was a bloke and he was quite physically strong. Now, I know about women's equality and all this sort of stuff but I am terribly sorry, a six-foot man and a five-foot-two and 60-year-old woman, really, there are some things that women can do and some things we physically need help for.' (Karen, Wave A)

On the verge of retirement, Karen faced opposing work requirements from those she encountered in her first job. Whist as a young woman, Karen had pushed herself to perform physical tasks at work, she found this was no longer possible in older age. She found her gendered physiological boundaries by testing them to the limit:

'I was having to climb stepladders and lift boxes down from shelves ... I couldn't do it. My blood pressure went "eee" and I just didn't have the physical strength. In the end I only managed about five weeks although I loved it, I knew I physically couldn't do it, not when

I couldn't get out of my son-in-law's car. I could not get out, I was like doubled over. ... Some of the things they were asking me to do, I just couldn't do them, do you know what I mean? I couldn't even open the great big gate things: you had to pull down on grate chains. I'm not actually a very strong person. My daughter said that. She said, "Mum, you're as weak as a church mouse". And because I'd had so much damage to my hands as well, things that I was doing were sort of affecting me.' (Wave B)

A year later, when we spoke to Karen for the second time, she was still unemployed, despite applying for "loads" of jobs. Following an unsuccessful interview for an office job with a housing association, Karen's work coach negotiated her a work-placement there instead. Although she very much enjoyed the work placement, which was going well and may have led to a sustainable job, Karen's conditionality requirements meant she had to leave the placement to take up a job in another bakery, serving take-away food. It was a busy workplace with high staff turn-over. There were multiple employer failures. In her first week, Karen was left to cash up the till without training and to lock up without keys. Supplies had not been ordered. By peak time, "it got really manic" but there was "no bacon, there was no butter, there were no sausage" (Wave B) and a broken coffee machine flooded the serving area with boiling water. There were long queues of irate customers, further provoked by the manager's retaliation, which created the feeling that violence could spark off. Rats were attracted because other staff "were putting all the old food into this big bag and leaving it there for the pig man to come and pick it up, but it was left inside the premises" (Wave C). Karen left:

'I just knew I couldn't do it. ... It left à bitter taste, yes, because it would have been an ideal job for me. It was 20 hours a week. With the money I got from my pension plus ... the Jobcentre ... and I was still ... contributing National Insurance. ... I had a little bit of pride back. I felt I was going outside and I was getting out and meeting people.'

Karen also realised her computer skills were 'obsolete' and started studying for a certified European Computer Driving Licence course and spent £150 updating her computer software. She continued applying for jobs with an open mind: "What I'd like to do now is just do anything." Throughout her life, Karen had experienced changing expectations like shifting sands. Instead of retiring with her husband, she had separated from him. Neither the family nor the state had held up their sides of the citizenship bargain. Karen herself had worked hard in both the paid-labour market and the domestic sphere, raising her children. Instead of benefitting from adequate state-pension income at the age of 60, as the post-war welfare state promised her in youth, Karen had to claim means-tested Universal Credit. She was denied her first occupational pension entirely and her second – from a decade of government employment – was minimal. Her UC was reduced because of her pension income. Nearing the end of her working life, Karen was not financially independent. 'I did get a gratuity and I've got a small pension which hasn't really made any difference because they take it off what I get anyway. I was getting £70 a week and I only get like £50 now because that comes into whatever it was, so there you are.'

Over the three years of the study, Karen's financial situation worsened. This was related to the relative decline in the value of UC due to the benefits freeze, while "obviously things have gone up in price" (Wave C). Universal Credit did not pay enough to cover the basic costs of living and Karen had to rely on her adult children to get by "they'll bung me a few quid here and there to buy groceries" (Wave C). Having some income from an occupational pension, albeit reduced, made it possible for Karen to keep her home:

> 'If I hadn't had the gratuity, I'd be struggling I think. I probably would have had to leave my home, yes, because I wouldn't be able to afford the bedroom tax. The problem being there are no one bedroom places in the area. ... When the government said they wanted us to move from three-bedroom houses to one-bedroom ones, there are none. So, they knew they'd got us between a rock and a hard place.'

Under Universal Credit, Karen could only continue to receive payments if she sought full-time hours:

> 'Punished if you work and you're punished if you don't work. I think that's wrong because I think sometimes, when you've worked all these years, I think you should get just a little bit more leeway maybe, I don't know. I've paid a lot of taxes in my life, but there you go.
>
> 'I don't want to sign on. I feel quite humiliated about me signing on. I don't like it. I don't think we realise for somebody who when you've worked full-time how it would actually feel that you're just one of the great unwashed as they call it.'

Karen faced triple intersectional disadvantages as a woman, aged in her 60s and unemployed. It was gender discrimination that denied her adequate lifetime earnings and occupational pensions to avoid relying on state support in older age. Now she was required to break barriers to take up work aged over 60 while redefined from 'retired' to 'unemployed'. Expectations about age and unemployment combined as barriers to finding work that could not be overcome with motivation, a cheerful attitude, upskilling or years of job applications.

'I'm quite a positive person. ... But even though the pension age has actually increased, people still think retirement's 60. They've got this mental thing about it. Now, I know there are people out there who are 80-odd and they're running the marathon, but they are few and far between. And there are people out there who are maybe – if you've got a job and you're older and you keep at it, then you can work longer. But if you're coming in from being unemployed, I think that's what makes the difference.' (Wave C)

Following a major health scare and six weeks of being signed off by her doctor – thereby becoming 'economically inactive', Karen had to reapply for Universal Credit as a new claimant, despite two years of receiving it. Again, she was subject to redefinition, from 'inactive due to ill-health' to 'unemployed'. This time she received Universal Credit Full Service. The new 'digital first' delivery felt to her less personal and more threatening. The last time we spoke to her she was weary of conditionality:

'I don't expect not to look for work. But I just wish they were a little bit less, like, almost threatening you that you will get sanctioned. ... I've worked all my life. And I feel – sometimes you just sort of feel so tired of it, being pushed as if you're a child, I suppose. I'm a grown adult. I feel I don't need to be told what to do in that way.'

Karen's work life was part of 'a world put together in ways in which we [she] had had very little say' (Smith, 1990a, 1). Universal Credit is falsely gender-neutral – appearing to treat all claimants without discrimination, while enshrining implicit discrimination that is impossible to challenge. Next, we turn to another older women in the study, Jane, whose broken-promise pension years were filled with 'work experience' and constant pain.

Redefining disability as unemployment: Universal Credit and full-time work expectations for those in constant pain

Jane is a 57-year-old White British chef who was made redundant twice in the lead up to claiming Universal Credit. The first time we spoke to Jane, she had been diagnosed with an incurable condition that affects seven times more women than men (National Health Service (NHS), 2019a). Despite recognised long-term symptoms of 'widespread pain', 'difficulty sleeping' and 'irritable bowel syndrome' (NHS, 2019a), Jane was still keen to work part-time. However, her work coach had different ideas:

'I just want a job. Even if I can only do 16 hours with my fibromyalgia – oh, that was another thing she [work coach] kept on about because I said to her that I've mainly been applying for part-time work. She said, 'Well, you really should be applying for full time.' (Wave A).

Jane's experience demonstrates how Universal Credit disregards women's bodily experiences and overwrites them with able-bodied male-standard work expectations. Jane faced intersectional disadvantages of gender, disability and age. Jane was 'doubly disadvantaged' (Crenshaw, 1989) by a hidden health condition – "no-one can see it" (Wave A) – that undermined her earning ability and a social security system that treats claimants indiscriminately with punitive conditionality. Jane was 'in a lot of pain all the time' (Wave A). She experienced fibromyalgia as

'a nightmare really because I'm used to being so active. I'm so stiff, I've really had to slow everything down. … It's never going to go, but this course I'm doing at the hospital [four hours per week] is to show us how to manage the pain and manage what we're doing and rest quite frequently.'

However, Universal Credit does not have an effective mechanism to protect her health, for example via reduced work expectations – Jane had to negotiate these individually herself with her work coach, while she was "still learning" (Wave A) about fibromyalgia and how it affected her.

'I said to my doctor: "Is this one of those things that I just need to kick myself up the backside?"
    "No, no," he said, "It's a proper syndrome."
'When I first started [as chef] at the Red Lion I was doing 30 hours and then they cut my hours after the Christmas because they were overstaffed. So, I was doing 15, 16 hours then and to be honest, I don't think I could do any more than that. Trying to get out of bed in the morning is a nightmare. … But it's weird, you just feel tired all the time. Sleeping at night, you have this; one minute you're hot, then you're cold.'

Part of the problem is that fibromyalgia is not well understood medically and treatments are limited (NHS, 2019a). In addition to debilitating pain, Jane experienced age discrimination when applying for a domestic vacancy as "a housekeeper – which I'd done before and which was on my CV": 'I applied for [it] online and she [employer] said I was too old. … I think my age is against me, to be honest, with applying for a lot of jobs. Well, especially in catering because it can be bang, bang, bang, pretty busy.'

Jane did not receive any training, advice or support from the Jobcentre, either to help her job search or to deal with age discrimination. All that was available was the 'mainstream offer' (DWP, 2013, 52) of self-help vacancy applications. By the second wave of the study, Jane "got fed up with applying for jobs and nothing happening". She took matters into her own hands and set up her own cleaning company. Jane was still claiming Universal Credit, but now enjoyed being self-employed because it was rewarding and she could work flexible hours at times when she was in less pain:

> 'I just need my little business to pick up a bit more and gradually get into that. I mean mornings are my worst time with the fibro. It seems to be when I'm in bed my legs are not so good. A couple of times I've had awful pains at night where I've been screaming with the pain.'

However, Jane was only doing two hours of paid cleaning per week, for an older neighbour whose husband has dementia. When she declared her earnings, her UC payments were stopped entirely – "no money went into my bank" (Wave B). It took three months and many phone calls to resolve the problem. Meanwhile, Jane was still required to continue to attend Jobcentre meetings every other month and was applying for jobs. Jane wanted to work around 25 hours per week because she felt that was manageable with her health condition. She did not want to continue on Universal Credit: 'Obviously, it [UC] is something I don't like to be on, but when you have no choice it's – I mean if my business picks up I might not be on it. You know, if I can earn enough without that, it would be nice.' By Wave C, Jane was aged 59, had recently got married and was no longer claiming Universal Credit because her new husband worked full-time and she was financially better off. Jane's escape from punitive conditionality came when she reverted to traditional gender expectations. It was marriage and female financial dependence on male wages, rather than the supposedly gender-neutral welfare system that brought her out of poverty. Jane continued as a self-employed cleaner and had increased from one to three private homes, with about 15 hours per week. The last time we spoke to Jane, she was looking forward to "a few holidays, hopefully" and her role as a grandmother – to "enjoy my grandchildren" (Wave C). The next section explores the interdependency of women's lives in relation to work-related conditionality and care.

Interdependency: digital reliance on adult children to fulfil conditionality requirements

Conditionality did not stay contained within the household of the claimant. Online requirements became a wider family chore for three of the research participants. In the UK, about a third of people in the lowest earning or out-of-work households and 27 per cent of those aged 55–64 were digitally excluded at the time when interviews were conducted (Ofcom, 2014, 14). Although most women in the UK (83 per cent[7], Green and Rossall, 2013) did use the internet and rates are generally rising, there are substantial gaps in skills and access according to age, class, education and gender (Ofcom, 2014; 2022). Three of the women in the study aged 55+, Joan, Margaret and Jane, struggled with computers and were flummoxed by the digital requirements of Universal Credit. Conditionality became a chore for their working family members. First, they needed their children for the one-off set up of their UC claim: "I'm not very good on computers so my daughter helped me do it" (Jane, Wave A).

Years later, after taking computer courses, Joan, Margaret and Jane remained unable to manage their online conditionality requirements and turned to their adult children for regular support:

'I'm not computer-literate, because I've never done that. I have to ask my son to help me, and my daughter. But they've got their own lives, with working and that, and I can't do it. They [Jobcentre] want me to do five hours every day. I can't do that.' (Joan, Wave B)

Conditionality was not, for these women, the 'individual behaviour change' tool envisaged by policy makers. Instead, it was a cooperative, *inter*dependent process, that formed a new type of informal exchange with family members. The time costs of digital conditionality took a heavy toll on those family members who already contributed to society productively via their own waged work and reproductively via their own rearing of children. It formed a new and distinct form of pseudo-productivity, sharing the psychological tyranny (Friedli and Stearn, 2015; Wright et al, 2020) of the task with others. This wider family conditionality burden seemed particularly futile in the case of working UC claimants on the brink of retirement. Joan, for example, was limited by multiple health problems (arthritis and depression) and already held 3–5 jobs at all three waves of the study and became a grandmother, which also meant her daughter could no longer help with online conditionality requirements. Nevertheless, Joan had to evidence daily online job searches while working (see Wright and Dwyer, 2021).

'I'm early 60 and I'm trying my best and I just feel as if you're [work coach] on my back all the time. When you get to 60, I was hoping I'd get the bus pass and I'd be able to not spend all this money on the bus going to places and that, but it's not worked out. I've got to wait until I'm 66 now so – … I think I'll have to carry on working when I do get to that age because the pension, only working part-time, I don't think it will be much of a pension.' (Joan, Wave C)

Similarly, eight of the women aged 55+ talked about how their adult children, especially their daughters, fill the gaps left by welfare cuts. Adult children helped with financial survival during periods with very low or no income from Universal Credit. Practical measures included cooking meals, doing grocery shopping, filling-out forms, changing utility companies, laundry and treats like going to the cinema. Next, we turn to Donna's experience of disability, a broken citizenship bargain and extensive informal grandchildren care.

Donna: a lifetime of good citizenship for a broken bargain – 'us pensioners should be left alone'

At 61 and disabled, Donna[8] is "at the end of my tether" yo-yoing on and off work-related conditionality between ESA and JSA. Disputes over the institutional rendering of facts (see Chapter Two) had life changing impacts on Donna: "It's driven me to suicidal tendencies before now. If it wasn't for a good friend of mine a few years back, I wouldn't be here. … There are times when I really seriously want to end it all because of all this hassle."

Beyond expected working life and ahead of retirement, Donna is struggling financially on Employment Support Allowance in the Support Group the first time we meet her. She stopped her office job six years ago because her mobility deteriorated to the point where "I couldn't get to work sometimes". She has arthritis, depression and is borderline diabetic. Once or twice a week "my legs go" and she is bed-ridden. Donna fears work capability reassessment because a few years ago things "started going downhill" when she was deemed 'fit for work', lost her ESA entitlement and had to claim JSA. Around the same time, she also lost her Disability Living Allowance.

> 'I went into the Jobcentre one day to sign on. I staggered in on my crutches and I looked like death warmed up according to one security guard. He thought I should go to hospital. "No, I've got to go and sign on". … I saw the woman where I should sign on and she said, "What on earth are you doing here signing on?" I said, "This is what I'm like 99 per cent of the time but you say I'm fit for work." "You're not fit for work; go home and go back on ESA".'

Each time Donna reapplied for benefit, she incurred more debt in the weeks in between income. She is now in deep poverty.

'I have to have my washing taken up to my son's to be dried because my tumble drier has broken down. I have continence issues, which means that I have more washing than the average person and I can't get a tumble drier. I haven't even got my cooker plumbed in because I cannot afford to pay a man to come and plumb it in. All I've got to cook with is a combination microwave.'

Like Karen (described previously), Donna feels suffering in her 60s is unjust because over her lifetime she fulfilled both the old *and* the new citizenship responsibilities of care and employment: "I've always worked low-wage jobs … always paid my tax and National Insurance and here I am struggling to scrape by. … I've worked four jobs at a time when I've had to and I have bent over backwards to bring my family up properly." She kept up her side of the citizenship bargain, but the state did not. Now she needs social security in older age, it falls short.

'I shouldn't have to rely on my children but I do. Not only do I rely on them because of my poor health; I'm having to rely on them because of my poor income. It's sick. When I think about all that tax money I've paid and National Insurance, it's just ridiculous.'

Now, in desperation she uses foodbanks and relies on her son for a phone and meals "four or five times a week". Otherwise,

'I live on cereal and sandwiches most of the time at home – and … noodles at 30p a pack, 20p a pack. If I can get them, I get them cheaper. I've not had a decent slice of bread in I couldn't tell you how long. … I have got 57 pence in my purse … I need bread, I need milk. I could do with some potatoes. I've not seen proper meat in my house for 18 months.'

Donna borrows money from her son, daughter and a doorstep lender. She cannot afford Christmas presents. "MPs and the people in the DWP … kick people who have paid taxes over the years and kick them when they're down and make sure they kick them down hard. It's totally unfair; why should we suffer?" At Wave B, Donna is 62 and still in the ESA Support Group. Overall, she is "more relaxed … more in charge and it's been a much better year all the way round". Although her "mobility has deteriorated" and "it's getting more and more difficult to get about … my medication has been upped". Donna's disability has been recognised accurately in the institutional text (see Chapter Two) and she has qualified for Personal Independence Payment (PIP). Although PIP is intended to help with the extra costs of disability, it functioned as the essential income maintenance that Donna was missing because of how an array of austerity welfare cuts and reforms reduced and removed her income, including the benefits freeze, the 'bedroom tax' and wrongly losing her disability benefits:

'I was very lucky. That lady was really nice, that did my PIP assessment. She was very thorough with how she did the assessment. ... She was very precise about making sure that she got the right kind of information from me. Whereas before the people I'd seen just wrote virtually anything down. ... She was a wonderful – she'd done really well for me. I mean she solved all my problems in one fell swoop, just by ticking the little box that said I was entitled.'

A surprise six-month benefit back-payment and a regular income increase, "from £120 a fortnight to £240 a fortnight", made an enormous difference to Donna's quality of life.

'My depression's lifted one heck of a lot. I'm still, I still have my down times but they're by no means as down as they were.'
'I received over £1,000 back money. I was like running round shouting "hooray" – if I could have done, you know. I was over the moon about that. But then the week after that there was another substantial amount of money went into my account, over £1,000. I knew it wasn't from PIP so I panicked. I rang my bank, I said, 'Where's this money come from? It can't be mine. Nobody has said they're giving me anything, where's it come from?' It came from DWP. So I got onto the phone, and I said, "Why have you sent this money? Is it really mine?" Because I had already spent the PIP back pay, paying off a lot my debts and that. They turned round and said, "You've been underpaid".'

Donna is on a mission to clear her debts and rent arrears incurred because of the 'bedroom tax'. She was even able to make a small donation to the food bank she used. However, the good fortune is tinged with injustice since Donna now knows that she was underpaid for a full two years, but was only reimbursed a maximum of six months. Full reparation would mean "I'd have cleared all my debts". To add insult to financial injury:

'Now they've started taking money off me again ... for previous loans. But I've not had any loans for three years. ... It just doesn't make any sense to me. They're now taking ... £40 a fortnight off me. ... I swore blind I'd never get into the situation where I was so low on food, ever again. But unfortunately if you looked in my cupboards now they're bare. Again. My freezer's empty.'

Donna experienced this as state-endorsed financial harassment.

> 'I haven't got a clue how much I owe or anything. And I've asked if I can sit down with somebody and discuss it, find out what it's all about, when I went to the Jobcentre with my sick note a few weeks ago. They turned around and said, "You'll have to phone up and discuss it over the phone with them". Well I can't afford it. ... £10 on one phone call.'[9]

Although Donna is recognised as mobility disabled, she travels two hours by bus (including a change) and then walks 30 minutes to a Jobcentre to submit a paper copy of a 'sick note': 'I was in there precisely five minutes, dead on my feet, gasping for breath and in absolute agony, and I had to come back and do the return journey. ... I cannot cope with that.' It is possible to post the medical certificate, but Donna prefers to go in person after a recent certificate ran out on the day her payment was due and she only received notification five days later. In the meantime, she had no income.

Donna's informal family commitments to her eight grandchildren have increased. She is estranged from one of her daughters but now, after 10 years, is reunited with one grandson, who is 'looked after' in local-authority care and comes to visit. Her adult daughter-in-law, who used to drive Donna places has now developed agoraphobia after a bereavement and the tables have turned. Donna is "providing her with support rather than she's providing me" and those three grandchildren live with Donna in an irregular informal arrangement. Donna now does her daughter-in-law's laundry and takes three buses to visit her other daughter. The extent of Donna's family care is large and unrecognised by the social security system because she is not a formal kinship carer.

At Wave C, Donna is 63 and claims ESA and Personal Independence Payment. Delays with benefit payments left her short for electricity. She recently received a back payment for both. She has a thyroid condition; her mobility has worsened and she has difficulty getting in and out of her home. She has problems with her knees and is still borderline diabetic. She is having memory problems. Her mental health has improved a lot and she rarely feels down. She gets no benefits for having her 16-year-old grandson live with her temporarily. He helps to look after her. She supports a friend that she visits. Donna worries that something might go wrong with her benefits and she would have nothing to rely on. She has three more years until her state pension (at age 66). Donna thinks it is unfair that the pension age has been changed. She thinks a lot of women are younger than their husbands, so they will not enjoy retirement together because men die younger.

Conclusion

This chapter has shown how older women's working lives have been shaped and constrained by enduring structures of gender, age and disability. This includes direct and indirect forms of discrimination in the worlds of work and welfare. Explicit laws forbade or restricted pregnant women and married mothers from pursuing careers they were qualified and trained for, even after they began their employment. In the worst instances, occupational pensions were denied. For most of the older women claiming Universal Credit, the long-term impacts of complying with the state-endorsed traditional expectations about the women's unpaid domestic priorities during the earlier decades of their potential working lives combined with many subtle forms of past discrimination to create financial vulnerability on the cusp of retirement. Lifetime constraints on earnings due to years of labour market absence for child rearing and long periods of part-time low-paid employment as worker-carers are entirely unrecognised in post-2010 welfare reforms. The very fulfilment of their post-war citizenship duties is what now leads them to require state support. While the state does offer financial support, it is based on a falsely individualist behavioural rationale. The pendulum has swung from gender discrimination that constrained or precluded paid work to male-defined work norms veiled as gender-neutrality that require full-time employment. This chapter has presented new empirical evidence of women's encounters with the work ethic. It demonstrates the contrast between women's lives and the assumptions of welfare conditionality. Social security is designed to focus on economic contribution in narrow male-defined terms of productivity, to mean only paid work. This draws attention away from women's unpaid work and devalues care activities and grandparenting roles.

Crushing conditionality: women living through heavily enforced work-related conditionality

Sarah[1] works as a security guard but was sanctioned repeatedly. She was told "I should be searching for work, not looking after my mum". Sarah is 30 and has "a lot to cope with". "Family matters" and being "quite poorly" – "in and out of hospital for operations" – meant she had to reduce her full-time job to part-time, which meant irregular hours. Sarah "absolutely loves" working at festivals, horse races and premiership football matches. Her job transports her to "places I've never seen, things I've never thought of going to". Universal Credit tops up her variable wages.

Sarah is "hands-on with my family" and "running around for them all the time". She cares for her mum, her nan, and her 18-year-old sister, who has high support needs.

> 'My mum has mental health issues and she's sectioned[2] every year. ... She's just been sectioned now two weeks ago but she's been poorly for six. ... My mum is poorly and my nan's been poorly and then we found out my sister's got diabetes.'

Relentless sanctions made matters worse. Sarah "didn't know what they were for". She submitted written evidence of her distressing and time-consuming family obligations to her work coach to explain her good cause for missing appointments, but: "They don't really understand it at the Jobcentre. ... They said it's not relevant."

Introduction

Sarah's experience reflects irreconcilable differences between welfare conditionality and the everyday realities of women's family lives. The lives of all three generations of women in Sarah's family are intertwined. Sarah does not have children and is not a designated carer, but nonetheless, the buck stops with her. The societal expectations of female kin care do not diminish, so Sarah is caught between the government insistence that she work full-time and her family identities – with all the private expectations of what it means to be a grand-daughter, daughter and "just big sister". Welfare conditionality is not designed to facilitate informal care or reflect family identities. Instead, rules and sanctions push women to fulfil male-defined working norms. This chapter focuses on the 16 women in the study who were sanctioned most often. Sanctions 'boss texts' mislead us to expect that those who are sanctioned repeatedly are intentional work evaders, facing rational consequences for conscious wrongdoing. This was absolutely not the case for any of the multiply-sanctioned women in the study. Instead, what we discover by looking at the actualities of women's lives is that their sanctions were almost always irrational, unjust and unrelated to work efforts.

This second empirical chapter begins with the stories of three[3] White women (all UK nationals) who were sanctioned six times or more for missed appointments or insufficient job search despite their current or recent paid work, care obligations and/or disability. These women describe a crushing form of conditionality, involving six or more sanctions within the 12-month period leading up to their first research interview. First, Sarah's experiences (related here) of being sanctioned as a disabled *in-work* Universal Credit claimant illustrate how conditionality displaces adult kin care. Second, Helen's story of being sanctioned as a disabled ESA Support Group claimant participating voluntarily in the Work Programme demonstrates some injustices of system design, the challenge of wanting to work while in pain and supporting her brother. Third, Jo fell foul of excessive job-search expectations on Jobseeker's Allowance. After losing her JSA, a support agency helped her reclaim and she got an empathetic work coach (himself disabled) who put reasonable adjustments in place that made all the difference to her. Finally, Arab lone parent Mira's experience of in-work racism and out-of-work sanctions reinforce the intersectionality between gender and race. She is caught between the needs of her five-year-old son and Jobcentre requirements to look for work, which are not always flexible enough to respect her mothering hours or recognise that leaving a job because of racism does not constitute 'voluntary unemployment'. Mira is part of the cohort of lone parents shifted from Income Support to Jobseeker's Allowance post-2010 (see Chapter Three). Within the study, eight lone mothers were hammered by sanctions as soon as they were exposed to job-search requirements. The actualities of these women's encounters with punitive welfare conditionality seem so extreme that it is easy to assume they must be the exception rather than the rule, but time and again, woman after woman spoke of how her caring duties and bodily realities were dismissed and overwritten with work-related welfare conditions. All the women in this chapter shared a strong and enduring sense of injustice at what sanctions had meant for them.

Sarah's story: Universal Credit – "how much more can you sanction me? ... I can't just leave my mum"

Welfare conditionality makes no concession for the time Sarah (described previously, also see Appendix 2) spends looking after her mum, nan and taking her sister shopping and to appointments. Sarah's conditionality expectations are not reduced (as they might be for the mother of a newborn baby). Sarah already has a job but is required to job search for up to 35 hours per week, depending on her working hours. Unexpected events, like having her sister come to stay when her nan (who is the legal carer for her sister) goes into hospital, derail her work efforts. She steps in to hold the whole family together. 'I'm trying [to get more work] and then something may happen, my mum may get poorly ... and I've got to go and get her some clothes and take her food and ... and I can't look for work at those times.' Sarah is not physically well, but she is not looking for sympathy either. Even after multiple surgeries, "I do still try to keep working afterwards". Sarah has serious ongoing health problems. "I have a lot of trouble with my stomach and my back. Sometimes, it flares up and sometimes [I] end up in hospital because my intestine is blocked. ... I have adhesions ... from being cut open so much, so sometimes ... I have trouble going to the toilet." Then:

'I got a throat and ear infection which then led to Bell's Palsy. I thought I was having a stroke. My mouth drooped, my eye was wide open like Popeye. ... My doctor said it can be caused through stress as well as viral but, at the time, I was going through a lot of stress with evictions and worrying about if my money was coming in on time because I was on a court order from a previous attempt of an eviction. ... Then every month with my Universal Credit up and down, it was constantly a worry. Am I getting paid? Am I going to get evicted?'

Sarah is mired in debt and repeatedly on the brink of eviction because she has incurred multiple sanctions. Universal Credit payments are 'very confusing' with variable working hours. Waiting two months for her first UC payment left Sarah short for food, utilities and rent. An advanced payment helped initially, but she had trouble repaying it alongside other deductions. She called the costly[4] UC helpline and discovered that she owed a total of £2000.

'She [helpline advisor] was on the phone for a long time and she went through all my sanctions. I explained so many, tried to get the evidence that I could from home, I managed to get so many of my sanctions taken off but then there was still so many remaining. ... It was kind of like a realisation then ... "You're going to carry on making me appointments even if I miss one but you're not going to tell me." She was like, "Well, that's your job to phone us and let us know and then we'll tell you that you've got an appointment".'

The 'boss texts' present 'failure to attend' as the 'behavioural problem' being punished by sanctions. However, there are three reasons why applying sanctions was irrational for Sarah. First, the process for informing claimants of appointments was defective – Sarah learned that some sanctions were for missing appointments that she did not know had been arranged and she was given no record of, which was unjust. Other interviewees reported similar experiences. Second, when Sarah was told to attend the Jobcentre at times when she was at work, she was already satisfying the higher purpose that sanctions are designed to serve – to find employment (DWP, 2011b). It was entirely illogical to punish Sarah for not attending a meeting with her work coach during her working hours. Third, the complexity of her UC payment was unfathomable because of multiple deductions (to repay hardship loans, rent arrears and her initial UC advance while waiting for the first payment) alongside variable monthly amounts because of working flexible hours.

This bizarre situation seems to have arisen because without her knowledge or consent, Sarah appears to have been allocated to the 'intensive' group of the DWP in-work conditionality randomised control trial (DWP/GSR, 2018a; see Chapter Three). Sarah is required to maintain fortnightly contact with her work coach, but got repeat sanctions because:

'I've actually been accepted to work and I forgot. So, then I go to work and if I've not got the credit to ring them, I have to wait however long or when I can get to my nan's [to use her phone] and then for them days I'm sanctioned again but even though I've worked.'

Or:

'Sometimes, my mum's been poorly and they [appointments] have just slipped my mind and I've been more trying to get the mental health team to come and assess my mum.'

Sarah felt the system was "very harsh on me":

'£10 odd a day [sanctioned], I think it's a bit brutal, to be honest. … It is a few days and, before you know it, £40, £50 has come off your money. It's just that stopping you either getting gas or your food … because the money that they send you, it's not even enough really.'

Sanctions increased Sarah's rent arrears to the point of a legal action: "The more time the bailiffs came, I didn't want to be at my house. … I've never really been in a debt like that and for it to still carry on now to this day escalating. ... It knocks you down and down and it wears you out." She turned in on herself:

'I don't really go out. Obviously, not got the money to anyway. ... It's stressed me out that much where I don't even feel confident sometimes doing things because I've not got the money or I don't look right or I'm just not how I was where I was always full of life. Trying my best, carrying on, plodding on, doing this, no matter what things threw at me, now I'm not dealing with things so good like when my mum's poorly.'

Sarah's life bears no resemblance to the tidy punitive 'male subtext' of sanctions. The imagined rationality of sanctions as a punishment for non-compliant behaviour collapses in practice. Sarah is embroiled in reciprocal familial-care relationships, the give and take of which constrains and empowers her. The reasons for Sarah's sanctions cannot be understood as individual wilful acts of non-compliance. She had a job when she was multiply sanctioned and her own ill-health and care commitments were delegitimised. The relationship between Sarah's health problems and her experiences of work, welfare and care are multidirectional. Financial problems contribute to ill-health and reduce her ability to engage in work, which is in any case unreliable. She received no support from Jobcentre Plus: "We're not all robots and people have lives and situations and ... do need a bit of a help." Sarah's experiences of multiple Universal Credit sanctions were in 2014–15 at the peak of the 'great sanctions drive' (Webster, 2016), when a quarter of all Jobseeker's Allowance claimants were sanctioned (NAO, 2016). Redman and Fletcher (2021) demonstrate the intense pressure that DWP employees were under at that time to apply sanctions. Next, Helen's experiences show how work conditionality can criminalise women's disability.

Helen's Story: ESA Support Group sanctions on the unstoppable Work Programme merry-go-round

Helen is 38 and has cervical dystonia that twists her head and neck and gives her muscle cramps and spasms. This rare neurological movement condition is 'usually a lifelong condition' (NHS, 2021, 1). The symptoms 'may be triggered by things like stress or certain activities' (NHS, 2021). "When I was really bad, I couldn't wash myself and feed myself or anything." Helen was "in that much pain ... I felt physically sick every day. ... I got to that point where I was going to take my own life." Before becoming disabled, Helen had been to college and "always worked, ever since I left school". The trouble started 15 years ago.

'I was working thirty hours a week doing catering, and my condition got worse. They didn't know what it was. It took 18 months for them to diagnose it. And my condition got worse, and then I had to leave my job because I couldn't physically do it any more.

And of course you're on a waiting list for treatment, so that took another year. And they tried with all these different types of drugs, and it's a process of, you know, "Does this one work? We'll try it for so long. If it doesn't, we'll try something else". So I didn't have any choice: I had to go on benefit.'

Six times in the last five years Helen has been reassessed for eligibility of the Support Group of Employment Support Allowance. Five of the six times, she was deemed capable of work despite evidence from her consultants and physiotherapists.

'I went on appeal through ESA. I waited twelve months to go to court, and when I got there, I was sat in front of a judge for an hour and forty minutes, and it was really stressful, because they asked you all these different questions, and you'd got somebody from benefits sat at the side of you, who wasn't on your side.

I've had no money for so many weeks. I've had to go to the food bank, because ... I didn't have any money for about two months or something like that. They just stopped it. And it wasn't my fault that I was ill, you know. And I had to apply for a hardship fund, just to buy food and heating.'

Her appeals were successful, but the process was harrowing and it takes a long time to repay hardship loans. Helen serves at a charity shop on Friday afternoons. She came to be sanctioned because of her exceptional commitment to job seeking. Despite being in the ESA Support Group (which has no formal job-search expectations), Helen went to the Jobcentre for advice because she wanted to work for a few hours a week: 'They said to me that there was nothing else they could do to me, and, "We'll have to refer to you the Work Programme".' When Helen went to the private provider, she was signed up as a Work Programme participant[5] and unwittingly opened herself up to being sanctioned for non-attendance.

'Well, what I didn't realise is that when you sign a piece of paper [to join the Work Programme], you're signing, like, a contract for two years. And I didn't know about this. And I had to attend these work-focused interviews – I think it was once a month. And I'd expressed that I was looking for permitted work, which is under sixteen hours, because of my illnesses, and I know what I can and can't do. And within those two years I've had about four different advisers, and I think they've offered me one job.'

Helen's Work Programme advisers did not seem to realise that she was in the ESA Support Group. "And they kept saying to me, 'Well, why can't you do more than sixteen hours?' So you're going through – you're like on a merry-go-round. You know, you can't get off it." Helen's experience can be interpreted using Griffith and Smith's (2014b, 14) observation that: 'categories and concepts in the boss text organise selective attention to actualities; the representation of front-line work produced becomes thereby readable and interpretable within the frame established by the boss text'.

The Work Programme was designed mainly as a 'work first' mandatory programme for long-term unemployed and disabled benefit recipients to get them 'off benefits and into work'. Helen's engagement with the service does not fit with the pre-existing categories and concepts, which are designed on the assumption that benefit recipients on the Work Programme will usually be involuntary, motivated by the fear of sanctions to attend. Helen's voluntary engagement as an ESA Support Group claimant (exempt from job-search conditionality and related sanctions) was misread and misinterpreted because it did not fit 'the frame established by the boss text' (Griffith and Smith, 2014b, 14). The advisers she dealt with and the organisational processes that led to her sanctions were selectively attentive to the actualities of her experience, filtering out her genuine motivation to work and her severe bodily limitations.

The first sanction was imposed despite Helen informing her Work Programme provider of good cause for non-attendance.

'I had an appointment for a work-focused interview, and I'd phoned well in advance to tell them that I'd got an appointment at hospital on that day, and I couldn't rearrange that. You know, because it was important for me to go. So they said, "Oh, that's fine. That's all right. We'll rearrange another appointment". So that day came: I got a phone call from [provider] saying, "Why haven't you attended your appointment?" I kept ringing them up, not being able to speak to anybody, leaving a message on their answering machine, and it all came from that. So I got my money stopped.'

Around the time when Helen was repeatedly sanctioned, the harsh design of sanctions for Work Programme participants was criticised in an independent review, which found:

A very high proportion of referrals for sanctions from mandatory back to work schemes are subsequently cancelled or judged to be non-adverse. A potentially large driver of this is that providers of mandatory schemes are unable to make legal decisions regarding good reason. This means that they have to refer all claimants who fail to attend a mandatory interview to a decision maker, even if the claimant has provided them with what would ordinarily count as good reason in Jobcentre Plus. This situation results in confusion as the claimant does not understand why they are being referred for a sanction. (Oakley, 2014, 10)

Helen's private Work Programme provider was investigated for irregularities by the Department for Work and Pensions and the Public Affairs Committee (PAC) (2012). The multimillionaire CEO of the service stepped down over the scandal. In 2015, four employees of the back-to-work company were jailed for fraud because they 'made up files, forged signatures and falsely claimed they had helped people find jobs, enabling them to hit targets and gain government bonuses' (BBC, 2015, 1). After leaving the Work Programme, Helen was not sanctioned again during the three years we were in contact with her.

One year later, Helen is happy about getting a casual job as a school-crossing patrol warden, which is permitted for up to 16 hours per week while claiming ESA Support Group.

> 'I went through all the training and I do feel better in myself for doing that job because I'm part of the community again. I have a sense of pride about doing that job because I know I'm providing that service for them children. ... I felt, you know, I've got a uniform on, I get wage slips; it were all those little things make a big difference to how you feel.' (Wave B)

She manages the short-hours work alongside her disability: 'When you're on the school crossing you're only there for half an hour, then I can come home, I can lay down, take some more medication' (Wave B). Helen is now helping her mobility-limited dad who is 'struggling' with her mum's round-the-clock care – "my mam's been ill ever since I can remember". Helen's dystonia has worsened again and she is having injections every ten weeks.

> 'My body sometimes, when I'm really stressed it can jerk sometimes. ... Last week I had a migraine for nearly three days. I couldn't tilt my head. I couldn't lay down. I was taking all these tablets what they give you and it weren't having any effect. I just had to sit there until it went off.' (Wave B)

Helen now also has endometriosis, which is a painful condition 'where tissue similar to the lining of the womb starts to grow in other places, such as the ovaries and fallopian tubes' (NHS, 2019b, 1). She had surgery to cut away endometriosis tissue, which was partially successful. She is having weekly hospital psychiatry sessions and has medication for anxiety and depression. She is starting a part-time distance-learning degree course.

The third time we speak to Helen, her crossing-patrol job has been made permanent and she does 10 hours a week as permitted work (see DWP, 2020b) while claiming ESA Support Group. "I absolutely love my job. ... It's so rewarding, watching those little kids looking out for me and giving me all these waves. ... I've got one little girl doing cartwheels and [laughing] – and it's community as well which is important to me." She is caring for her brother "as his official appointee". He "got laid off from his job" then got "depression and severe anxiety and then he started self-harming" and is under the care of the mental health crisis team. Helen has stepped in to support him but is not eligible for Carer's Allowance. She manages his conditionality:

'He couldn't deal with anything: letters, phone calls. He managed to get on Universal Credit ... there are conditions with that. So, he's having to send sick notes in and we've got somebody from the Jobcentre ringing him once a month, but he can't even speak to them on the phone so I'm having to do it for him.' (Wave C)

She feels "it is a constant worry" and "sometimes I think the floor's going to open up and just swallow me up".

'When he's stressed he doesn't eat anything, so ... they've told us to keep him busy. So Mondays, we do yoga. ... Tuesdays, it's volunteering. ... Thursdays, it's art group in the afternoon, and Fridays, it's the cafe. ... I don't know how I'm going to keep doing it to be honest.' (Wave C)

Helen is holding the whole family together:

'Where my brother's concerned, it's that difficult and emotionally draining. We've got ... to wait for this phone call, and he's not eaten anything for 24 hours, has he been cutting himself again? And there's lot of stuff of – I've got my mam who's very upset and trying to calm my mam down and my dad just – he's not coping at all.'

Helen's dystonia remains "in my neck and my head and my shoulders it has gone to my arms" and "I've got back problems". She remains determined to do all she can and is excited about passing her first year of university and preparing for the start of the new term. Next, Jo's story shows how kindness and understanding can be more effective than sanctioning.

Jo's story: excessive expectations and the power of listening

Jo is dyslexic. She is 27 years old, White British and single. Jo recently moved into council housing with her cat, after being homeless on and off for five years. Dyslexia is a lifelong learning disability affecting reading, writing and spelling. People with dyslexia[6] find it 'hard to carry out a sequence of directions' and 'struggle with planning and organisation' (NHS, 2018, 1). Jo's Jobseeker's Allowance was sanctioned multiple times because she found it difficult to understand what was required of her.

> 'They weren't clear with me; they just went, "You'll have to do 43 steps". What doing? Then one person goes, "Update your CVs is classed as one step, looking at a job but not applying for it is classed as a step". Applying for jobs and stuff like that was a step and I would go and sign two weeks later, I'd get a different woman to the one I've just seen who told me, "Oh, that was the steps". "This isn't a step, this isn't a step, this isn't a step". I went, "Well, she said it was. What?" "No, they're not steps; you haven't done your job search, sanctioned."'

Jo found it difficult to know what she was required to do – "I'm a bit slow when it comes to understanding things". She was sanctioned repeatedly for insufficient job search but still had to attend appointments at the Jobcentre and look for work. 'I just got really confused. It's like, "Well, tell me exactly what you are expecting from me because I have no idea what you're wanting". 'All they seemed to want to do is get someone out of the door and sanction them. It was like they didn't hear that I need help.'
Then Jo was sanctioned again:

> 'I lost my little job book thing [Jobseeker's Diary]. I wrote it down on paper, "Oh, it's not an official book so we have to sanction you". But the woman said as long as I'd done it, I'm all right and then, "Oh yes, but it doesn't look like you've done a decent job anyway".'

During many months of being sanctioned, Jo survived on hardship payments and help from her sister, but was then suspected of fraud and doubly delegitimised:

> '"Have you got a job because no-one can live on £40 every two weeks?" So they're basically saying you're not meant to survive on hardship. Right, well, you see, I have places where I go and I go to

[support centre]. I get a free meal there and, "Oh, do you work at [support centre]? You spend a lot of time there". I was like, "Well, they do a lot of courses I like to do. It gets me out, it stops me being depressed". It was like, "Well, we think you're working". Well, it doesn't really matter; you've stopped my benefit anyway.'

Being repeatedly sanctioned pushed Jo to the limit:

'I was ready to jump in front of a train because I got so sick of it. I wanted a job for years. I don't want to be on my benefits; I don't like it. I've always wanted to work but no-one will employ me. So that is one of the reasons I'm depressed but at the time they just started messing about on benefits, I came in here [support agency] and went, "I've given up. They can take my benefit, they can have the flat. I'll find someone to look after the cat. I'm done; I've given up".'

Next time Jo lost her benefit completely because she "totally forgot when I was to sign on" at a time when "I had two bouts of depression where I was really bad". Jo got a "fresh start" when a local charity encouraged her and helped her to reapply for benefit. Her new work coach "[listened]" with empathy: 'More understanding ... because he was disabled himself; he had problems walking. ... I think it's because he knows the challenges that he's going, "Yes, I understand".' Jo felt empowered to request a more manageable set of expectations. Her new work coach "cleared it all up for me" and explained "plain and simple, no grey areas".

'When I was signing to say I understand everything I went, "Can I do one little thing first?" He went, "What?" I went, "Can I reduce my steps?" He went, "Why, how many?" I said 43. He was like, "What?!" I was like, "Yes, I have to do 43 steps" and this guy is like, "That doesn't sound right. Can you get online every day?" I went, "No, I'm lucky if I get half hour at this [support] place I go". He was like ... "Well, okay, do Universal Jobmatch ... twice a week, any other internet twice a week and the papers once a week so it's ten every two weeks". Right, that sounds more doable.' (Wave A)

After these reasonable adjustments were made, Jo was never sanctioned again during the three years we spoke to her. At Wave B, she was worried about her cat, who had disappeared. She was repaying hardship loans and rent arrears from her JSA, leaving her short on the other essentials. She had done two days of work experience and was still having trouble evidencing her ID because she couldn't afford a replacement birth certificate "I haven't actually got the money because this tenner needs to go on food". Her depression is "not as bad as it was".

At Wave C, Jo has two new kittens, got her birth certificate and is in a choir. She now earns a bit extra as a support worker. She does 4.5 hours per week on a temporary contract as 'permitted work' while still receiving JSA. Voluntary work also "helped me realise that I'm not useless". Jo is excited about realising her long-term goal to qualify for security work. Her work coach arranged free training and ensured learning materials were suitable for her dyslexia: 'I've got everything on blue paper, I have pre-learned as much as I can without having someone explain things to me, so I'm getting as much info as I can, a nice head start.' Jo feels like the stumbling blocks are "slowly being kicked aside" and "everything is working out". Jo began to thrive after the threat of sanctions lifted, when her work coach listened to her and reduced her job-search expectations, and she got the support she needed. The Jobcentre and a local charity "made it a bit easier to understand that it's [dyslexia] not my fault. I can read and write; it's just the paper doesn't want to play nice." Next, Mira's story shows some of the difficulties of parenting alone under the duress of heavy sanctions.

Mira's story: lone parenting, workplace racism and heavy sanctions

Mira is a 36-year-old lone parent. She was born in the Middle East and moved to the UK as a baby. Her experiences of work and welfare conditionality demonstrate the compound disadvantages at the intersection of gender and race. When her son, Ali, turned five years old (eight months before he started school), Mira lost her Income Support (with no behavioural conditionality) and moved onto Jobseeker's Allowance (with harsh penalties). She is part of a large cohort of lone parents who were required to switch benefits because of the policy decision to apply conditionality to mothers of young children (see Chapter Three). Within the study, most (eight) of the multiply-sanctioned women were in this position, meaning long periods of low or no income. Mira was sanctioned unexpectedly when she believed she was complying with her Jobseeker expectations.

'I was signing on and the people there were very nice. ... The first man I saw ... understood that I was looking for work within the hours when my son was at nursery. One day I had a different woman at the Jobcentre who I hadn't had before and she didn't seem to know much about me. I had to explain to her that I had a child, I was studying and looking for work to fit with his hours and she had just decided that I hadn't applied for enough jobs and without explaining the details she told me that they're going to stop my benefits. ... I asked her: "what can I do to make it better, to help?" But there was nothing.

There was no eye contact even. It was just looking into her computer and processing me like a number. ... It seems just like a punishment rather than help. I left in tears on my way to pick up my son from school thinking 'what am I going to do I have no income now? I just felt it was very wrong. ... I assumed everything I was doing was fine and then suddenly the money was stopped without any warning at all. ... It's very stressful to be in a position like that, especially if you don't like going there and it's so intimidating.'

Mira "hurried up to find a job, anything" and got a job that "it was the wrong hours, but I took it anyway because I thought I had to" and encountered racism.

'I wanted to find something related to what I'm doing to further my career development, something with children basically. I wasn't fussy what it would be – and something that would fit into my hours so I wouldn't have to pay childcare. I was working in this material shop with a woman who was really not nice to me at all and she would talk about things in a very racist way and I really felt uncomfortable working there.'

Rather than tackle workplace racism, Mira's boss agreed for her to quit. This could be considered as constructive dismissal (GOV.UK, 2023,1).

'It got to the point where one day she [colleague] was just fighting with me, arguing with me and I just had to leave. I called up the boss on the phone and she said to me "I can see that this is a very uncomfortable situation for you to be in. It's okay for you to leave".

I tried to sign on again – but because I had left my work voluntarily they wouldn't give me any benefits for three months, and like I said if I didn't have my family, really what would I have done if I have a kid to feed? It was really upsetting. I'm very lucky I do have a family to help me, but I know there are plenty of single mums out there who don't and it just felt awful. What a system. ... It ended up with a very bitter feeling.'

Mira feels that parents should not be 'forced' to put their children into full-time care.

'My son is only five still and I think at that age they need their parents and to be in care full-time is just exhausting for them. He doesn't even want to go to an after-school club. He's just tired at the end of the day and wants to come home. ... It's a long day for him.'

Mira did not find the Jobcentre at all helpful for finding work.

'The atmosphere in the Jobcentre is so horrible. You go in and there are security guards everywhere and you feel like you're going to a high security prison or that you've done something wrong by being there. It's just such an awful depressing place.

There was never anyone who sat and looked at my qualifications or who gave me any advice. I thought it should be a place that's supposed to help you to find work and I never received any help to find work. There was never anyone that could give me any advice or recommend something. It wasn't a helpful place at all. It was a horrible place to go to. People are very much on their own to find work.'

After her bad experiences, Mira took a 25-hour-a-week job as a trainee nursery assistant for low wages (£7.50 an hour and no holiday pay) and got Working Tax Credit. Her income doesn't cover her living costs but she avoids the food bank by getting regular money from her dad. The second time we meet her, Mira still works at the same nursery and has increased her hours to 26 per week. She is disappointed with her low pay (£7.88 an hour) since she has 'a degree and two teaching qualifications' but now at least gets paid holidays and has finished her training. She still gets regular money from her parents, now also gets child maintenance from her ex-partner and has come off Working Tax Credit. At the final interview, Mira has a new job 21 hours a week as a family support co-ordinator for a charity. She is happy in her new job, which is 'better money and a bit more rewarding' and it is a three-year contract. Mira works Monday to Thursday during school hours, which saves money. "Before I had to pay someone to take Ali to school every day, because my work started before his school. So now I don't have to do that." Mira would like additional hours but cannot afford the childcare. She has started studying part-time for a counselling diploma, which her parents fund. She thinks there needs to be "more understanding and a bit more compassion" in the benefits system.

Similarly, another lone parent, 27-year-old Shaneta (Black Caribbean) was also sanctioned for leaving work voluntarily, even though the job she left was not compatible with her mothering duties. Shaneta's experience also seems to fit the definition of constructive dismissal (GOV.UK, 2023), reinforced by punitive sanctions.

'They were making me work every weekend. So I was dropping my daughter off at school on the Friday and I'm not seeing her until the Sunday. And I've got to do washing, help her with her homework. I just didn't think it was fair and I couldn't do it anymore. ... Can you imagine not seeing your child from Friday morning, about half eight in a morning until Sunday about five o'clock? Oh no, it was awful.

Sanctioning is just a waste of time. They just need to re-assess and actually think in the real world instead of thinking in this special world.'

Conclusion

This chapter reveals an enormous void between women's real lives and the fake story told in policy texts about what sanctions are and how they operate. The focus on the 16 most sanctioned women shows that repeat sanctions did not happen because of deliberate and sustained rule-breaking or work avoidance, but because of hostile changes to the social security system that perpetuate 'avoidable diswelfares' (Grover, 2018), administrative mistakes, misunderstandings and perverse incentives for work coaches to meet 'benefit off-flow targets' (Redman and Fletcher, 2021). Multiple sanctions expose gendered relations of ruling that rig the system against lone mothers, women from minoritised ethnic groups and disabled women.

Sarah, Helen and Jo were sanctioned six times or more while living through extremely difficult personal circumstances including distressing long-term health conditions, severe mental health problems and emergency kin care that sometimes made it impossible to comply with impersonal welfare-conditionality rules. Sarah's sanctions made very little sense since she was actually working as a security guard at the time. Her experience demonstrates three fundamental policy-design failures. The first policy failure is that Sarah's family caring duties were explicitly disregarded by multiple work coaches. This is not just an implementation gap that can be pinned on discretion or overzealous target-chasing. It is a fault line that runs right through the middle of the UK's work-first welfare reform strategy. Universal Credit is structurally unsound because it does not reflect women's real caring activities in terms of time, energy or affective significance. Caring for family is not an optional extra for most women – it is an obligation. Imposing multiple sanctions on women for fulfilling family duties is incredibly problematic given the strength of enduring expectations that women will provide informal care. The second policy failure is that Universal Credit in-work conditionality is nonsensical, demotivating and harmful. The third policy failure is the diminishment of Sarah's own ill-health, which connects directly with Helen's experience. Helen is in the Support Group of Employment Support Allowance because of her cervical dystonia, depression and endometriosis. Although her cervical dystonia is likely to be a lifelong condition, its legitimacy is constantly cast in doubt by work-capability reassessments. She volunteered to join the Work Programme because it was the only way to get help looking for 'permitted work' (DWP, 2020b) of under 16 hours. Despite the name, there is no support in the ESA Support Group. Unwittingly, Helen stepped onto an unstoppable merry-go-round of sanctions. Helen's experiences reveal that welfare conditionality does not recognise women's bodily realities. Women are treated as disembodied genderless sanctionable objects. Jo is dyslexic and was sanctioned while homeless on Jobseeker's Allowance with excessive job-search requirements. It was an empathetic work coach and the help of a support organisation that got her back on track with manageable conditionality expectations.

The 12 women sanctioned two to five times had similarly complex stories. Mira's experiences of being transferred from Income Support to Jobseeker's Allowance were like eight other women, who were sanctioned between two and five times while lone parenting. This distinct cohort of lone parents were hammered by sanctions during a major policy change. Racism at work was instrumental in Mira needing to claim benefits again and she was denied JSA because she was deemed to have left work voluntarily. Mira was doubly disadvantaged as an Arab and as a woman. She lost her employment because of a hostile work environment and then lost out on social security because of a hostile policy environment. These women's stories illustrate the full range of working-age benefits, including UC, ESA and JSA. Across the benefits, there is a common disjuncture between women's lived realities and objectified job search and work-related requirements. Women's complex and interdependent family and working lives were reduced to 'stripped-down institutional categories' (Stanley, 2018, 51) that rigidly applied financial penalties without regard for the consequences. The next chapter examines the long shadow of sanctioning – in threat and one-off application – including female-specific sanctioning and the impacts on children of sanctions on their mothers.

In the shadow of sanctions: disciplining women and children for violating male-defined work norms

'My little girl, she got bit by a dog and she got 56 stitches in her face. … I'd phoned the Jobcentre because I was due to sign on and I told them what happened and they told me I'd still have to look for work.' (Angela)

It's 2014 and blowing a hoolie.[1] I rush into an echoey old church. It's cold but the single mums are friendly. A steel urn puffs steam up to the ornate rafters. I relent and accept a smiley face biscuit. Angela is taut as she rattles out her story. She doesn't mind looking for jobs – it's what she's doing anyway. It's the near miss with a sanction she's angry about. The injustice burns. It was six months ago but still fresh in her mind.

On the day, Angela phoned and told her work coach that she couldn't come in because she had to stay at home with her 11-year-old daughter who was recovering from a bull-terrier attack outside their door the night before. Angela wasn't sanctioned but she felt scarred by it. She needed flexibility and empathy from her work coach. What she actually got was a stern warning that if something like that happened again her benefits would get cut.

Angela is 34.[2] She's a lone parent with three kids, 6, 11 and 13. Her narrow escape from sanctions is intensely emotive. The bottom line for women in her position is that "you can't always [work] as a mother, you've got to make sure your little one's fine".

Angela used to work at a call centre but finds it difficult to balance a job with looking after her kids. The second time we speak to her, Angela is working part-time for a call centre but on a self-employed basis. A year later, she has moved off Jobseeker's Allowance onto Employment and Support Allowance Support Group because the stress worsened her asthma and depression. She now volunteers as 'permitted work' in a charity shop two days per week.

Introduction

Angela's brush with the sanctions system came at a traumatic time and had long-lasting negative impacts. Many women in the study feared or experienced sanctions during very difficult times in their lives. Being unfairly branded as rule-breakers while feeling vulnerable was a common experience. The aim of this third and final empirical chapter is to explore this most prevalent form of conditionality experience – the background knowledge of punitive conditionality, empty sanctions threats and one-off sanctions. Warnings and solitary penalties may seem like lesser versions of the crushing experience of repeat sanctions (explored in Chapter Five), but the menacing ubiquity of conditionality (Dwyer and Wright, 2014) was insidious and deeply harmful. First, widespread fear of sanctions is explored in the context of infrequent sanctions and their explanations. Second, mothers' increased risks of sanctions because of children's illnesses are explored, alongside the amplified impact of sanctions on children. Third, the connections between domestic violence, financial abuse and survival sex are highlighted.

Widespread fear of sanctions among those never or rarely sanctioned

Sanctions cast a long shadow. Two-thirds (146) of the women participants had never been sanctioned, but most were afraid of being sanctioned. Many women said that sanctions were mentioned during the claiming process and they were very aware the financial consequences were possible for minor infringements, like missing an appointment. Fear of sanctions was persistent, sometimes intense, and framed women's engagement with the social security system from the outset (Wright and Patrick, 2019). Twenty-seven[3] women (13 per cent) were sanctioned only once in total and that was a recent[4] experience, within 12 months leading up to their first research interview (see Appendix 2, Table A2.3). Just under half of those were disabled. It is clear from Table 6.1 (following) that more than half of the women who experienced sanctions as a one-off had definite good cause for their 'rule-breaking'. Javeria, for example, is a 31-year-old Bangladeshi woman who is unemployed and getting Jobseeker's Allowance. She was sanctioned for missing a Work Programme appointment because her translator was not available to explain a letter to her. Only one woman, Lisette, seemed to have been sanctioned legitimately – because she voluntarily moved to a different area. Most one-off sanctions were applied for missing appointments at the Jobcentre or with a Work Programme provider. Nationally, such 'Did Not Attend' sanctions were statistically the most applied during this period (2013–14, see NAO, 2016; Webster, 2016). Many women, but not all, appealed their unfair sanctions (several were successful, but usually were not fully reimbursed for the income wrongly removed). Insufficient job search was the next most common reason for women in the study being sanctioned, disproportionately experienced by minoritised ethnic women (like Anja, Grace and Amira) who believed they were fully compliant. In some cases, the reason for a sanction was not clear. Bilyana, for example,

Table 6.1: Overview of one-off sanctions reasons and good cause

Reason for sanction	Total applied	Definite good cause
Missed appointment	14	9
Insufficient job search	7	1
Paperwork problem	3	3
Other/unknown	3	2
Total	**27**	**15**

is a 44-year-old Bulgarian woman who is very fearful of the Jobcentre and has no idea why she was sanctioned.

The rarely-sanctioned women included mothers, particularly lone mothers. Women described a range of reasons surrounding their 'non-compliance'. There was a lot of confusion around sanctioning processes and some explanations given in official correspondence seemed flimsy, given the grave consequences. Mostly the grounds for sanctions were trivial, often there had just been a mix-up or miscommunication. Sanctioned women usually felt that while, in principle, it was necessary to have a system of penalties, its application in their own case was erroneous and the consequences far outweighed the 'offence'. Most felt a strong sense of injustice and embarrassment about having been sanctioned. The next section explores the connections between motherhood, risks of sanctions and the amplified impact of sanctions on children.

Children: increasing mothers' sanctions risk and at risk of impacts from sanctions

Mothering roles increased the risk of being sanctioned for three interrelated reasons. First, mothers are less able to protect themselves from poverty via paid work because of career gaps, the need for part-time working hours compatible with nursery/school hours and unequal pay, meaning they are more likely to have to rely on social security at some point in their lives than men or childless women (see Chapters One to Three). Second, working-class women find it difficult to command wages equal to or higher than the UK's exceptionally high childcare costs, meaning they are likely to be worse off financially, or no better off, in employment than on benefits. This has not been adequately accounted for even in the design of the newest benefit, Universal Credit, which has financial disincentives for second earners (usually women) that keep partnered mothers out of the labour market. Third, mothers receiving working-age benefits are increasingly required to look for and take up paid work regardless of irreducible caring obligations for their children. This section explores two important aspects of mothers' experiences: getting sanctioned because of their child's illness; and, sanctions having an amplified impact on children.

Sanctioning mothers for child illness and disability

Mothers were usually the default carers for their children. Enduring societal and family expectations expose mothers to the risk of being sanctioned for their child's ill-health. This was the case for three women who had recently had a one-off sanction and others, like Angela (beginning of this chapter), who were threatened with sanctions that were never applied. Because sanctions are so easily triggered, some fully-compliant mothers were sanctioned the first time they were ever late or made an honest mistake over a Jobcentre appointment. The financial and well-being consequences were potentially devasting. Child illness is a commonplace occurrence, yet the sanctions system cannot accommodate it without plunging families into financial crisis and debt. The mothers in the study talked about how different forms of ill health affected their children: from short-term viruses to chronic or life-threatening conditions and disability. For example, Anastasia, a 34-year-old White Polish lone parent on Jobseeker's Allowance, was sanctioned when she missed her appointment because her eight-year-old daughter had a tummy bug with diarrhoea and 'she was so much sick I didn't know what to do'. Without a partner or any family in the country to rely on, there was no alternative but to stay with her sick child, who needed her. The reason that Anastasia is out of work is that there are no part-time financial-controller jobs that pay well enough for her to manage her rent and cover the cost of living in London. The main barrier, acknowledged by her work coach, is finding a position compatible with her daughter's school hours and school holidays because "there's nothing [childcare] available in this area at all for my child if I work, nothing at all". Anastasia says:

> 'My child is my first priority and I just couldn't in that situation do anything else. I explained this in the letter. ... They wrote to me asking me "can you provide the reason why you didn't attend this appointment with Work Programme". I wrote them back saying look, "I had this situation, my daughter was really sick". I explained everything in detail but regardless of my explanation Jobcentre Plus sent me back a letter that I'm sanctioned for four weeks. ... It was really scary because it's complete uncertainty. I just realised "my god, I'm not going to pay rent".'

The textual realities collide. Anastasia writes that her sick child must be her only concern in the minutes when she is vomiting. Jobcentre Plus overwrite her daughter's bodily realities and Anastasia's mothering obligation, insisting that her only duty at the appointed time was to appear before a work coach. Just as Smith observed in other institutional contexts 'everything that contextualises her has been rendered invisible' (Smith, 1990a, 92) and only 'readable and interpretable within the frame established by the boss text' (Griffith and Smith, 2014b, 14). The system is so harsh, and Anastasia's finances already so tight, that being evicted was immediately a foreseeable reality. Anastasia felt it was "really unfair because I really had a good reason". Anastasia had no choice about caring for her daughter, like the other mothers who were sanctioned or threatened with a sanction while their child needed them.

Kerry was also sanctioned when her daughter needed her. Kerry is a 39-year-old White British lone parent on Jobseeker's Allowance. She changed from full-time to part-time work when her daughter was diagnosed with cancer and she had to take her "back and forward to the hospital". Kerry became unemployed when the contract ended and has full work conditionality. She was sanctioned for four weeks because:

> 'I was late for an appointment [at the Jobcentre], "why are you late?" I said, "I was at the hospital". They said, "well your daughter turned 18 three weeks ago, she's all right to go herself". I said, "it's still my child, she's going through that"; but no they sanctioned me anyway. ... I feel it's too black and white with them. You're not there, you're getting sanctioned. Doesn't matter that your daughter was at hospital and she's got cancer. ... They're punishing me for my daughter being ill. It was only like fifteen minutes difference that I went in late. That's all it was. She's just a kid, she's my kid, she's battled with cancer, I want to be there with her. You can't live if you're getting sanctioned, you're just not getting any money to live on and you can't keep turning to other people for food and oh I'll sit in your house all day today because my house is freezing, you know what I mean?'

Terri was also sanctioned while her mind was on her child's health. Terri is a 26-year-old White British lone parent on Income Support with three children aged 4, 5 and 7. She became a lone parent when her partner left her. "You're obviously in a relationship and you've got kids, you're a family and then when it all changes and you're on your own with kids it's like your whole world falls apart and you think that's the end." Even though Terri's youngest son is below the age for her to have full conditionality, she has to attend work preparation meetings at the Jobcentre and she gets "a lot of grief off them". She wants to work but there are obstacles out of her control.

'Childcare is a big problem. ... I'd even scrub toilets honestly, I don't care, so long as it's paying me money. But it's the childcare, do you know what I mean? ... The Jobcentre would say things like, "Why aren't you going to work?" ... Well you're not going to be any better off, you're going to be worse off. Because by the time I'd paid like the nursery fees and this and that. And what hours are you going to work? Because you might need somebody in the morning because you might need to work a set time so you need somebody for a couple of hours in the morning, an hour earlier than what you'd be getting the kids out of the door.'

Terri was sanctioned for missing a work-focussed interview on the day she discovered her oldest son, Ryan, had been diagnosed with Asperger's Syndrome. The diagnosis was "a big blow", realising that "there's actually something there, there's something. He's not doing all these things for nothing". Terri's "head was messed up properly" over the huge significance of the diagnosis.

'I wasn't expecting it [the diagnosis] that day. It hit me like a ton of bricks, even though I knew it could have been something. I knew what it could have been but to see the fact of somebody telling you that's that – that, that's what's wrong with him and knowing that all the time he hits me and has his meltdowns and all the things that he does, and how hard life is with him. ... He'll throw really bad tantrums like a baby, but he's seven and a half. ... He bites when he gets wound up. ... My house will be trashed and he covers his ears and just, he just cannot understand any of it so it just gets too much for him.

It [work-focussed interview] just went out my head and I was going through my paperwork and I'm like, oh my God I missed that. So I phoned them up, it was the next day then I phoned them up and I was like, "Listen, I've missed my appointment, I'm so sorry". And I explained my circumstances and I explained like it was a big thing. ... She [work coach] was like "That isn't a good enough reason".

That's my Ryan, that's my son that she's saying isn't a good enough reason. But how can somebody say that?

I got a letter through and I had been sanctioned. ... I didn't think I would get sanctioned because I hadn't done anything wrong.'

The sanction caused a huge amount of unnecessary stress. Ryan sensed something was up with his mum but could not understand what. He felt frustrated and had "a lot more meltdowns during the day". Being sanctioned caused financial hardship and Terri's mobile phone – her lifeline – was cut off: "That's my only contact, if the kids are unwell at night then I can phone their dad to come and take me to hospital and my sister can stay with the kids. So anything, emergencies, anything at all I just can't." Anastasia, Kerry and Terry's experiences show how children's illness increased the risk of mothers being sanctioned, within a highly punitive system that is designed to filter out children's needs as irrelevant to their mother's capacity to comply with abstract regulations to attend empty bureaucratic meetings. Many mothers agreed with Kerry that: "I really don't think you get any support from the Jobcentres, absolutely don't". The next section shows the other side of the situation – that when mothers were sanctioned, the impacts were amplified for children.

Sanctions on mothers and impacts on children

Sanctioning had a large-scale and excessive impact on children in this study. More than double the number of children (58) were impacted by recent sanctions than mothers (25). Forty-five of the children (including one who turned 18 years old around the time of the sanction) were impacted by one-off sanctions applied to 16 women. Sanctioning women therefore has an amplified impact on children. Thirty-five of the children impacted by one-off sanctions were in lone parent families (14 of the mothers). A further 13 children (including one who turned 18 years old around the time of a sanction) were impacted by their mother's sanctions in the recently multiply-sanctioned group. All nine of these mothers were lone parents, one of whom was in the most-sanctioned group (six or more sanctions). For comparison, a total of 66 women were sanctioned in the whole study. Looking only at the subset of 44 women who were sanctioned recently revealed that a quarter more children, 58, were impacted by those sanctions. This assumes that household budgets are commonly used to meet all household costs. Forty-eight children were in lone parent households. Although lone parent sanctions only apply a percentage reduction to the adult element, rather than removal of the full amount (DWP, 2011b, 14), the very low rates of UK benefits mean that seemingly small reductions can have major impacts on the possibility of meeting household needs. Substantial deductions also erode the value of inadequate benefits, leaving miniscule sums for children to survive on. Since 1997, lone parents have been a primary target group for increasingly demanding and punitive conditionality requirements. It is deeply concerning that there is no effective route to protect children from sanctions applied to their mothers.

Seventy per cent of the people affected by sanctions applied to mothers were children (see Table 6.2). Of 83 people affected by 25 mother's sanctions, 58 were children. The perversity of applying financial penalties to mothers because of their children's ill health is shocking. The unwarranted impact on children, especially in lone parent households where there is

Table 6.2: Numbers of mothers and children impacted by recent sanctions

Number of sanctions	Number of mothers	Number of children
1	16 (14 lone parents)	45 (35 in lone parent households)
2–5	8 (8 lone parents)	12 (12 in lone parent households)
6 or more	1 (lone parent)	1 (lone parent household)
Total	**25** (23 lone parents)	**58** (48 in lone parent households)

no other potential earner is inhumane. Unfortunately, this was not the only aspect of sanctions threats and one-off sanctions that connected with gendered 'relations of ruling'. The next section outlines the parallels and connections between domestic violence and coercion in the social security system.

Domestic abuse and violence

Benefit sanctions can be seen as a form of state-perpetrated financial abuse. Thirteen women in the study disclosed domestic abuse. Their accounts of behavioural control and financial abuse via the social security system mirrored their experiences of domestic abuse. Most domestic abuse is perpetrated by men on women and economic abuse often accompanies other forms of coercive control, including physical violence (Sharp, 2008). 'Financial abuse is an aspect of "coercive control" – a pattern of controlling, threatening and degrading behaviour that restricts a victim's freedom' (Women's Aid, 2021). In this sense, sanctioning can be understood as a form of degrading control that limits the basic economic freedom of those who experience it, to control their current and future behaviour. Violent and abusive partners contributed to Jordan and Amy's sanctions.

Sanctioning imposed two months of state-endorsed financial abuse on Amy, during a crisis point in her life when she fled domestic violence. Amy is a 36-year-old White British woman, who was sanctioned as a lone parent living on Income Support. She has six children, five of whom live with her (her sixth child is 16 and lives with his father, after drug-related violence towards his siblings). Her nine-year-old son is autistic and has high support needs, for which she receives family support. The family have social work support. Amy was made redundant because her ill-health meant she could not manage her long shifts as a care worker. She is also a qualified nursery nurse. She was sanctioned for not attending work-focused interviews, at the Jobcentre, that she had no knowledge of because the appointment letters were sent to her old address. She left her home as an emergency response to physical danger from her partner:

'We had clothes, but we had none of our belongings with us, so it was sort of get up and go out. The police and social care moved me for safety, got put into temporary accommodation, that was horrendous … because I ended up missing Jobcentre appointments because I didn't have a permanent address, so obviously correspondence wasn't getting to me. They ended up suspending my benefits. I then had to take letters from the social worker and the police and the council to say that obviously I was in temporary accommodation, but yes, I went about eight weeks without any Income Support because I didn't attend … my interview.' (Amy, Wave A)

When Amy explained her circumstances to the Jobcentre, they did not accept it as good cause. Her family experiences are complex, with multiple vulnerabilities:

'Quite a few times they threatened to stop my benefits because they thought I could work apparently. … There was a relationship breakdown, there was domestic violence, there was drug abuse with my son. So, there was a lot going on that sort of meant that she [two-year-old daughter] had her [funded] nursery time. So, it was a bit of stability, but also like for me to go to hospital appointments, meet up with social services, drug counsellors. So, where they'd expect me to work in between sort of hospital appointments and everything, it was, yes, it was quite a funny one. In the real world it wasn't going to be an option that I could go to work.

'The Jobcentre weren't seeing it that I had … two children under a specialist at hospital, and drug counsellors, and meetings at school, and there was a lot going on and I was a single parent, but in their eyes it was I had no children at home for 15 hours a week.

'One [Jobcentre] advisor I had, she was really nice … but like she said, her hands are tied, she can only do what she's told from above her. The impression I got, they were trying to phase the Income Support out so you could get back to work as soon as possible. … Once she [daughter] turned two they were really badgering me.' (Amy)

Amy finds the Jobcentre environment menacing and unsupportive:

'Two big butch security men just as you walk in and I find that's really, really intimidating because it's a Jobcentre. I also find now, because when I went onto ESA, the Jobcentres don't do anything, because I went in and said, "I need to make a claim for ESA". "Oh, well there's the phone number." "Okay", but I can't do – because the doctor is in the process of diagnosing me with ME, I can't do telephone conversations, I will get confused, so I can't do it over the phone. I had to go through a panel, I had social care involvement, there was a lot going on and I was a single mum with six kids. So, yes, I would have loved to go back to work, but run a house and hospital appointments.' (Amy)

At the time of the sanction, Amy and five of her children were dispossessed and in a heightened state of distress. They spent the whole summer school holiday in emergency bed and breakfast accommodation, without cooking facilities, having to eat out, and with few of their belongings.

'I had to get a letter from my social worker, I got a letter from the police officers that were dealing with the case. I had a letter from the council saying that the house had been sort of boarded up, but it took me about eight to ten weeks, and then I obviously had to go to the Jobcentre with all my letters and sort of fight my case, but they wouldn't backdate my money, I had to do a new claim.' (Amy)

Jordan was sanctioned because of her ex-partner's non-compliance and after leaving him discovered that benefits enforced financial and behavioural constraints in familiar ways. Jordan is a 24-year-old homeless single White British woman on Jobseeker's Allowance. She is out of work for the first time since she was 17 after leaving her hospital-cleaning job, which she had for three years, to move to another area with her abusive ex-partner, Craig. Their joint benefit income was paid into his bank account and Jordan did not have access to it.

'He took control of it; he never ever let me have any of the money. … He was too controlling. It was always like when I spoke to him about it he'd be like "It's my money. I deal with the money". … Even in that whole time I was with him I never went and got my hair cut, I never was able to go out and buy shower gel or anything like that. It was always him.'

Their joint claim was sanctioned for four weeks because the Jobcentre said he had not done enough to find work.

'He was on the Construction Skills Certification Scheme. … He couldn't do his job search because it was nine until four and because we didn't have the internet … the library was closed at that time. … So we both got sanctioned for it. But I did mine but that still didn't count.'

The sanction had financial and emotional impacts. "It annoyed me and hurt us because it put me in loads of debt. We didn't have any food. Nothing. … I went to a food bank. … There's one food bank and they'd let you go there twice and that was it." The sanction made Jordan's ex-partner more violent. "It made it worse. The whole time he beat me up more than what he'd done before." Eventually, Jordan left Craig and came to a homeless hostel "for my own safety because I had nowhere else to go".

> 'They [Jobcentre] paid him all the money and when I told them that I'd moved out and I'm not with him anymore they still paid all the money into his account instead of doing it half and half for the first two weeks. … They said we can't do anything until we get your form but because they didn't get it straightaway the money went straight through to his account. … I didn't cope at all. I was so upset and down and depressed because of obviously what's been going on and like when I went to my advisor … she said I'd have to go and talk to him about it. I was like, "how can I go and talk to him about it?; I've just told you what's been going on". The police told me to stay away from him. … I feel like they just don't help or give me any support because when I asked her to try and help me get the money back she was just like "oh you'll just have to talk to him". Which I don't think is fair.'

Now Jordan has no other source of financial support, no family or friends to help her out. Her JSA income is not enough to cover her basic costs and she carries debt from her partner's economic abuse. Jordan's experience of domestic economic abuse was mirrored and compounded by social security practices that left her without enough money for necessities.

Jordan: £60 to £70 goes on rent and then obviously girls' problems and shower gel, things like that I can't go out and get. … Here you get breakfast and dinner, and dinner is at half five so what are we meant to do between eight and half five? So instead of not having any food try and go out and buy some food, just try and keep myself going, I can't.

Interviewer: So how do you manage?

Jordan: I don't. I just get on with it.

Interviewer: What would you say are the main things day-to-day that you have to go without?

Jordan: Just food during the day but I'm used to not having much food anyway.

Interviewer: Do you have any debts at the moment?

Jordan:	Yes. I'm in loads of debt. That's through being with my ex-partner.
Interviewer:	Is that in terms of rent arrears or is that to banks or credit cards?
Jordan:	Bank, my phone bill. I've got loads of bills coming from the flat that he's living in. He's meant to be moving out soon but my deposit that's obviously going to my old landlord because he hasn't been paying the rent so that's got to come out of my pocket that I've saved up for when I used to work.
Interviewer:	Because it was a joint tenancy?
Jordan:	Yes.

For Jordan, the sanction reinforced her partner's domestic abuse by penalising her financially. Even after extricating herself from an abusive relationship, Jordan is kept in a highly vulnerable and subordinate position by the state. Job-search conditionality is coercive and controlled her behaviour in dehumanising and humiliating ways:

'I find it that they [Jobcentre] see us all as targets and not individual people. They say we've got to see this amount of people today, if we don't obviously we get in trouble by the bosses. We've got to send these amount of people on programmes that won't even benefit us, like when I went to this two-day course where they help you find a job and improve on your interviews. Even the woman turned round and said to me ... "you're good enough to be at an interview, you don't need help. You just need help with trying to find the right job for you". She was like "you don't need to be on this course", but still I had to do it. ... I had to go or I would get sanctioned.

I feel like if you don't do a job search for just one day they come hard on you and they will sanction you. It's like even if there are no jobs you still should go out there and just walk around and hand CVs out in shops and at least then that way you can write it down on the website that that's what you've done. But if you don't then you'll easily get sanctioned. ... Basically you follow the Jobcentre's rules or you get sanctioned.'

When Jordan had a joint claim with her ex-partner, she disclosed her domestic violence to one of the series of different work coaches she was seeing but was offered no empathy or flexibility.

Jordan:	When I was dealing with the problems with my ex I went up to my advisor and I was like 'I've been having a bit of trouble, I'm suffering with domestic violence

so I'm a bit low, a bit depressed, I feel like I can't do a job search at the moment, I'm not in the right state of mind.' She was like, 'well you either do your job search or we sign you off'. I was like 'but surely you can put me on sick just for two weeks to just let me clear my head for two weeks?' 'No, no, you'll be sanctioned straightaway.' I feel like they don't give me any support they literally just see me as a target to try and ...

Interviewer: So they didn't offer you any flexibility?

Jordan: No. ... I felt a bit like pushed out sort of thing and alone because they wouldn't help me.

The sanction system reinforced Jordan's vulnerability.

'I hate being out of work, I hate it. The more I'm being out of work and pushed around and going to this place and going to that place and going to this place I feel like I'm just not getting the help at all and I feel like it's unfair. They should be helping.

I always feel like they're trying to victimise us and they'll come hard on us if we haven't done our job search and they will come hard on us and quicker to sanction us than to help us.'

The next section tells Yastika's story to show how income gaps can leave women vulnerable to gender-based violence.

Yastika's story: from a missed appointment to survival sex and rape

One of the most extreme and distressing experiences that emerged from the interviews was Yastika's story. Yastika is a 36-year-old British Asian woman with severe mental health problems, including chronic anxiety – which began when she was 11 years old – and agoraphobia. She lives in temporary accommodation because she was homeless after fleeing domestic violence. She was informed that she had missed an appointment for a Work Capability Assessment that she never knew about and her Employment and Support Allowance claim was ended. The situation escalated quickly and with no source of income at all, Yastika was close to destitution. In a state of desperation, she resorted to survival sex and was raped.

'I was on zero income. Zero Housing Benefit, zero Council Tax Benefit. ... I had nil income for four and a half months. ... I turned to prostitution. It was the most horrific time of my life. I got raped. I got raped. I got [hesitates] beaten up, raped and buggered, trying to [hesitates] earn money via prostitution. I was working with [two support organisations]. They were liaising with the benefits as well. It made no difference.'

Technically speaking, Yastika was not sanctioned, she lost her disability entitlement and had a huge gap in income that meant she was unable to cover her rent and faced imminent eviction. Her experience demonstrates how a set of punitive social security reforms combine to remove financial protection from gender-based violence.

Seven months later, after nearly being evicted, Yastika won her appeal, but only got half of her lost benefit reinstated. Years on, she lives with rape trauma and is still repaying government crisis loans from her below-poverty benefit income. Yastika was the only woman in the Welfare Conditionality study who disclosed rape in connection with losing benefit income, but she is certainly not alone. In 2019, the House of Commons Work and Pensions Committee investigated reports from multiple support organisations of women turning to 'survival sex' for income to meet needs during long delays for the first payment of Universal Credit (WPC, 2019). Yastika's post-traumatic stress disorder is worsened by reliving her trauma during mandatory work capability reassessments:

'I've had four of the medicals now. They sort of – they ask you a lot of questions through and they open up a lot of wounds. I've always left in tears and heartbroken, really sobbing, and they're not interested in making sure you're all right or anything. ... I do find it difficult. I've got one coming up again.'

The social security system, which should function as a social safety net to protect women in highly vulnerable situations like Yastika's, can instead retraumatise (Roberts et al, 2022):

'I think they should just be a bit more sympathetic and sort of help people compose themselves. Because I'm highly critical on myself, and, you know, my anxiety and agoraphobia comes from a place of people judging me, and me more bothered about what people think about me. I don't like people seeing me crying and stuff like that, so I get really embarrassed, and I feel like I'm being belittled when I'm in those interviews. ... Intense. Upsetting. And an ordeal. It's an ordeal, to me, I hate.'

Even just the anticipation of social security appointments triggers Yastika:

'I'm always a nervous wreck when I go there. I'm shaking and, you know, I've spent half the day crying. I don't sleep. I suffer with serious insomnia as well. ... Then waiting for that letter, which they say can take up to two weeks, and you're lucky if you've got it a month later. It's generally about six weeks, six, seven weeks.'

The fear of destitution, inherent in punitive welfare conditionality and the aggressive disentitlement strategy behind unfavourable disability benefit assessments, does not motivate Yastika to find work, it debilitates her. As a result, she is less able to cope with everyday activities and a long way from getting a sustainable job. 'You're just sat in fear, thinking you're going to get sanctioned, you know, because that's the worst thing.' Constant fear was a shared feature of claiming social security benefits for many women in the study, but it held enormous significance for Yastika, who learned in the hardest possible way how traumatic the consequences of a minor administrative slip-up (missing an appointment) can be. 'My mental state got worse. I've had suicide attempts.' Three other women in the study talked about how they had been raped. Although rape was not directly related to the loss of benefit income, as it was for Yastika, the possibility of gender-based violence needs to be prevented and mitigated by restoring social security as a reliable and regular income source for women who need it.

Conclusion

This final empirical chapter reflected the majority experience of conditional social security policies. It told the stories of women who were minimally or never sanctioned. This chapter showed how women experienced the background knowledge that they could be sanctioned for not complying with work-based conditionality. Even the gentlest form of sanctioning could be deeply harmful in long-lasting ways because of the stark disjuncture between the male subtext of punitive policies and women's everyday lives in their local areas. Widespread dread of sanctions is accompanied with a strong sense of injustice and many of the interviewees felt that the system conspired against them, because they had not been informed of appointments that they were punished severely for missing. Sanctions were often triggered by situations that involved the actions or experiences of other household members, children who needed care, as well as abusive partners whose non-compliance impacted on others. The consequences, as well as the causes, of sanctions were interdependent. Sanctions impacted heavily on other household members, including young children, and rippled out to close family and community networks, for example if removal of essential income meant having to rely on others for cash, food, utilities or shelter.

Many of the women we spoke to were disabled or had long-term illnesses. Although we consciously recruited a subsample of disabled people receiving benefit like Employment and Support Allowance, we discovered that health problems were rife among those claiming Jobseeker's Allowance, Income Support and Universal Credit too. The prevalence of ill-health among women subject to full work-related conditionality is an outcome of the UK Conservative government's strategy (DWP, 2013) to slash the numbers of people claiming disability benefits and shunt lone parents off Income Support (IS) and onto Jobseeker's Allowance. The widespread detrimental impacts of conditionality on women and children cannot be ignored. Seemingly unproblematic one-off sanctions and the unrealistic work expectations they reinforce can have devastating consequences for women, that are amplified for children, particularly in lone parent households. The underlying power dynamics of gendered relations of ruling mean that working-class women and their children are positioned to lose most, financially. Losing essential income creates new scope for domestic abuse and sexual violence. Economic independence is crucial for women to protect themselves from male control and violence. Decades of work-based welfare reforms and deep cuts across all aspect of social security have seriously undermined women's economic independence and autonomy. The situation is worsened by the growth of precarious work and policy changes that have weakened worker's rights.

Compared with traditional work and care roles, post-2010 welfare conditionality positions women with equal job-search expectations to men, but with different care obligations. Care is denigrated. Time-consuming family obligations that would once have unquestioningly outweighed earnings expectations are now devalued or ignored. Women raising children are punished financially for breaching male-defined work expectations. In a minority of extreme cases, female survivors of male-perpetrated violence were punished once by the men they knew or were in physical proximity to and then for a second time by the state via financial deprivation – a girl bitten in the face by a dog, a domestic abuse survivor going without food because of her partner's non-compliance. It is clear from the sanctioning stories related previously that DWP reassurances about ensuring 'safeguards for vulnerable people' and to 'ensure that mental health conditions are taken into consideration' (DWP, 2011b, 14) are not effective. State injustice mirrors personal injustice and together they mutually reinforce female subjugation. In these worst examples, structures – the state, the labour market and the family/community – abandon or attack women, rather than support or enable them. Without income, without work and without nurture, women were hungry, scared and angry. To women in these sorts of circumstances, 21st-century social security has become antisocial and insecure.

SEVEN

Conclusions

Introduction

This book reveals the hidden male subtext of punitive UK welfare conditionality for working-age benefit claimants. It begins, as Dorothy Smith suggests, by viewing the social security system from the perspective of women whose lives are shaped by it every day. This creates a 'way of seeing' that is grounded in 'where we actually live' (Smith, 1987, 13). From this position the underlying gendered 'relations and powers of the world we live in become visible from the sites of people's actual experience' (Smith, 1987, 165). For the 138 women claiming working-age benefits who took part in the Welfare Conditionality study between 2014 and 2018, welfare reforms, in a range of guises, had highly gendered impacts. The seemingly neutral design of Universal Credit, Jobseeker's Allowance and Employment and Support Allowance policies are rooted in 'relations of ruling [that] have a strongly gendered character' (Smith, 1987, 165). Multiple layers of texts reveal the power relations of work and welfare. 'Male subtexts' within social security law, guidance documents and policy instruments have, for women, rewritten the parameters of paid work and unpaid caring. This textual mediation of women's lives is 'curious in its capacity to reproduce its order in the same way in an infinite variety of actual local contexts' (Smith, 1990a, 2). Conditional welfare reforms, involving harsh punitive sanctions, are constructed in political discourses, policy design and practice norms *as if* women were unhampered by intersectional labour market disadvantages that combine gender, race, disability, age and class penalties to constrain employment opportunities, restrict pay and impede retention and advancement. Women are subordinated to a false version of their reality, which they must contort themselves and their intersubjective and interconnected lives to fit. Failure to fit is punished severely by potentially life-changing sanctions.

Despite the global rise of precarious working conditions (Standing, 2009), 21st-century social security reasserts an outdated full-time standard model of paid work and extends it far beyond the traditional targets of intervention – unemployed people. Disabled women and lone parents are required by default, on threat of sanctions, to comply with the same intensive 35-hour-per-week job-search expectations as unemployed people. Women already in paid work and claiming Universal Credit must

117

increase their hours of work, negotiate pay rises or take on multiple jobs to fulfil full-time work expectations. Women are required to make special efforts to negotiate conditionality reductions for medically recognised health impairments and care responsibilities. In this sense there is an echo of the past – repeating the mistakes of the Victorian Poor Laws, which were designed to deter able-bodied men from seeking support, but often became the last resort for women and children (Fraser, 2009). This book breaks out of the narrow confines of assessing conditional welfare reforms in their own terms. Instead of assessing whether policies meet their stated objective, this book asks how are conditional-welfare policies experienced by women over time?

The study on which this book is based was conducted during a decade of severe cuts to social security provision, during and in the aftermath of the 'great sanction drive' (Webster, 2016), when a quarter of all Jobseeker's Allowance claimants were sanctioned (NAO, 2016). Much of the focus for discussion has been on the relationship between women's work and their welfare entitlements. It is important to recognise that housing policy also impacted many of the women and housing insecurity was rife among the sample (also see Hardie, 2021). This is a unique period in British history, when fear of destitution is used to discipline working-class women. The magnitude of the ideologically-driven disentitlement project defines the whole 'spirit of the age' (Williams, 1961; also see Wright and Patrick, 2019). First, this chapter outlines how each chapter of the book has demonstrated what benefit sanctions and conditional support mean for women living through them. Second, changes to conditionality since 2018 are outlined, including emergency COVID-19 measures in 2020. Third, recommendations for policy and practice are outlined.

Chapter contributions

Chapter One explained that a gendered analysis of welfare conditionality is necessary because assumptions about the role of men and women in relation to paid work and unpaid care have changed radically since the post-war welfare state was established in the 1950s. The original system of social security was divided neatly into a dual system of social insurance and social assistance. Conditionality was categorical and workers were distinct from those whose health impaired paid employment, who were supported by statutory sick pay and disability benefits. Dedicated maternity benefits and social assistance were the domain of women in the classic welfare state. These were conceived as financial support for those who did not have a close connection with the labour market. Over time this picture has changed and there have been two sets of parallel transformations – one in the world of work and the other in the social security system that supports those who are out of work, either because of unemployment or because they are economically inactive.

Chapter Two set out the book's theoretical framework, which interprets welfare reform policies in situated practice and lived experience (McIntosh and Wright, 2019) by combining interdisciplinary insights from feminist literature, primarily Dorothy Smith (1987; 2005) and the study of street-level bureaucracy (Lipsky, 1980/2010; van Berkel et al, 2017; Zacka, 2017). Dominant academic understandings of welfare conditionality have largely mirrored policy developments by de-emphasising gender. On the surface, adopting a neutral stance towards benefit recipients may seem attractively objective, but that only allows for telling a detached and dehumanised story about what policy means to those who live through it. The reality is that despite decades of equal opportunities legislation, women do not have equal earning potential to men and men do not engage equally with care activities in the private sphere. To better appreciate what welfare conditionality means to women, it is essential to recognise that moral rationalities around motherhood and care (Duncan and Edwards, 1999; Anderson, 2003) continue to exert a strong influence that often comes into tension with the work ethic on which social security policy is based.

Chapter Three shows how the policy context has developed over the course of the 20th century and in the early 21st century. The first radical change came in the late 1990s when the New Labour government first introduced conditionality for lone parents and disabled people. They established the expectation that workers who were previously considered to be inactive because of disability or caring responsibilities were to be potential workers. That fundamental change in the organisation of the system began a process that has developed under Conservative-led governments from 2010 onwards. Conservative-led social security reforms have encapsulated a punitive orientation towards all benefit recipients. In effect what this change means is that women have become redefined as unemployed workers according to broadly the same assumptions that have traditionally applied to unemployed men. The special protection that was envisaged by Beveridge in the post-war system – to take account of women's caring roles in relation to childbirth and early-years child rearing – has been turned on its head. Now women face much the same expectations, as earners, as men. Feminist and street-level bureaucracy perspectives reveal how welfare conditionality operates in practice. Rather than being a gender-neutral approach that is beneficial in terms of employment outcomes and poverty protection, the book identifies ways in which welfare conditionality impacts detrimentally on women and children.

Chapter Four explored older women's gendered encounters with the work ethic to show how women's lives are rewritten by social security and employment policy over time. It demonstrated how women lived through receiving conditional social security benefits. Universal Credit rewrites the citizenship rights and responsibilities for women (Andersen, 2020). There is a generation of women who were born in the 1950s and entered the labour market in the 1970s. One of the women, Karen, faced contrasting gender expectations about paid work and care, at the start and end of her working life. When she first went to work for the British armed forces, she lost her job when she became pregnant and she lost the occupational-pension entitlement that she'd accrued during her working years. The practice of firing pregnant women and denying them their occupational pensions was perfectly legal at the time. It happened in the early 1970s, before equal-opportunities legislation was implemented. Then, at the end of her working life, when Karen had expected to retire aged 60 and receive her state pension, she instead needed to claim Universal Credit because her lifetime earnings and pensions related to work were inadequate to protect her from poverty. On claiming Universal Credit she was subject to 35-hours-per-week mandatory job-search requirements. At the start of her working life, she had been excluded from the labour market because of her gender and her fertility. Yet at the end of her career, that discrimination was entirely unacknowledged. She was subject to the same labour market expectations as a young single childless man would be. There is a strong sense of injustice for that generation of women, exemplified by the Women Against State Pension Inequality campaign, calling for the reinstatement of pensions for women caught out by the increase in pension age.

Welfare conditionality impacts on women with caring responsibilities, including those in the 'sandwich generation' who care for children and for older adults. Many women in the study had caring responsibilities at both ends of the age spectrum, including their own parents and other relatives or extended family. Another important dimension of understanding women's experiences of welfare conditionality is the interdependency between female family members. Older women were required to look for paid work instead of providing grandmother care for their grandchildren, which facilitates mother's employment. Many women also contribute unpaid to their wider communities. Social security legislation has been degendered to the extent that these varied, interdependent and ongoing experiences of care are ignored, denied and overwritten by the male definition of productivity, which prioritises individual paid employment over all other interconnected societal contributions – primarily unpaid care.

The official narrative of sanctioning is to spur individual behaviour change among claimants, based on the assumption that 'wrong choices' explain 'worklessness'. This rationale is deeply flawed in its 'male sub-text' (Smith, 1987), which constructs 35-hours-per-week of paid employment as the standard model of citizen behaviour – to be attained or mimicked via job-search activities. The realities of women's lives, particularly as carers and part-time workers, are largely discounted and held as deviant. The degendering of welfare reform documentary narratives allows space for traditional assumptions of male expectations to dominate. The implicit male-orientated assumptions of sanctioning policy are irreconcilable with the lives of women in the study. Sanctioning operates on an individual rationale, but interdependency is central to human life, particularly for women who are engaged in care activities. Chapter Four shows that conditionality compliance involves *interdependent* processes, rather than independent (for instance in the examples of older women like Karen and Jane, who relied on their family members to apply online for Universal Credit and to perform their job searches). Similarly, sanctions were experienced by many women in the study as interdependent in their causes and consequences. Making sense of conditionality requirements was time-consuming and psychologically demanding. Some complexities were illogical and irrationalities of the punitive system design took a great toll on claimants and their support networks.

Women's accounts of their lived experiences of sanctioning (in threat and application) demonstrate how the 'boss text' of welfare reform filters down to street-level action. Their complex and interconnected lives are translated organisationally in a highly selective way. Attention is given only to pinpoints of time, to determine binary categories of attendance or non-attendance. There was little or no evidence of reasonable margins for lateness and some women were sanctioned even when they attended the Jobcentre or Work Programme just a few minutes late and with good cause. Much of the actuality of life as a woman was deemed irrelevant to the textual representations of social security. In most of the women's accounts of their sanctioning experiences, their lived experiences of caring for sick children, or missing appointments for other legitimate reasons, were discredited by the official sanctioning protocols. Women's accounts were overwritten by the male-defined boss texts of official sanctioning policy and practice, including the requirement[1] for sanctioning of compliant Work Programme participants who are known to be in contact with their Work Programme provider. In many examples, the sanctioned women were treated as unreliable narrators of their own lives.

There is a large disjuncture between the textual representations of welfare conditionality within legislation, guidance and policy instruments and women's interconnected lived experiences of work, care and sanctions. A major feature of the disjuncture for many women is the ongoing and repeated dispute over the veracity of disability and mental health problems. The boss welfare reform text seeks to disqualify women from benefit receipt on health grounds. The actualities of women's lived experiences of disability and health problems, like pain, fatigue and incapacity are nullified by the textual realities of welfare conditionality. Health conditions are deselected in preference for insistence on job-search activities and employment. Women's lives are readable institutionally as 'job-able' or 'sanctionable' without attention to managing ill-health or providing care. Objectified knowledge (Smith, 1990a, 84) makes objects of welfare subjects. Women become 'sanctionable objects' for the organisation. 'If it cannot be resolved into appropriate terminology, it cannot gain currency within the system' (Smith, 1990a, 100).

Sanctions stories are 'structured by the particulars' and become 'a product' of Jobcentre Plus's 'practises of observing and reporting' (Smith, 1990a, 95). Sanctions were used as a first resort, even for vulnerable women with recent and ongoing experience of domestic abuse and those with dependent children in the household. The process of applying sanctions chimes with Smith's accounts of how organisations textually-mediate service users to make them fit into predefined categories. Sanctioning procedures did not seem to allow space to create textual accounts based on women's lived experiences, of childcare constraints or hospital appointments. Women were seen institutionally as sanctionable objects, to meet organisational targets, instead of being understood as mothers and humans in need. Women's accounts of their lives were 'abstracted':

> taken from that context ... into a process that progressively cleaned her up and detaches her from the actualities and the particular contexts of her living ... [She is] constituted as the object of its work, not as a participant to it. ... What she does appears as a behaviour attached to her and detached from her situation. Everything that contextualises her has been rendered invisible. (Smith, 1990a, 92)

Women encounter the work ethic and how they adapt in relation to the new conditionality demands. One group of particular significance is older women workers. Many of those who we interviewed in the study had operated according to traditional gender expectations during their working lives. These are women in their late 50s and early 60s and have cared for their families during what policy constructs as 'working age', which for older women was primarily constructed in their lived experience as prime 'caring age'. After seeing their children to adulthood, many of the women then went on during their 50s to care for their own parents or other older relatives. Lives lived according to traditional gender norms are then re-evaluated by contemporary conditional welfare policies. At a late stage in life, these older women were confronted by a completely different set of expectations about the value of work and care. For working-class women this is particularly difficult because life expectancy is shorter in comparison with wealthier women and changes to retirement age and pension provision create financial vulnerability. Universal Credit has important implications for older workers generally but these have special significance for women workers who cannot turn back the clock, to live their lives to avoid poverty in later life. The financial protection they expected from male breadwinners was often absent because of relationship breakdown. Their own capacity for lifetime earnings is limited by gendered labour market inequalities that influenced the type of job and amount of pay women could command in eras with different domain assumptions about the role of women. Lengthy breaks from employment for child rearing, or part-time earnings to make unpaid care possible, further reduce lifetime earnings. The outcome of these processes is a new period of later working life where Universal Credit is the only option for financial survival. This illustrates Dorothy Smith's argument that policy documents textually misrepresent women's lives, presenting them as 'objectified, impersonal, claiming universality' – disguising a 'gender subtext [that] is unsuitable' (Smith, 1987, 10). Here the new welfare-conditionality text overwrites women's lifetime roles. Older women in these circumstances were shocked to be threatened with or receive benefit sanctions and usually felt that the reasons were unjust and the financial penalties far too harsh.

Chapter Five demonstrated how women were crushed by heavily enforced work-related conditionality. Multiple sanctions were experienced by one in ten of the women in the study. Sixteen women had been sanctioned twice or more in the year leading up to their first research interview. Sanctioning experiences were more prevalent at the start of the study in 2014 and sanctions were rarely experienced in Wave B or Wave C. This fits with national sanctions rates (Webster, 2016). In-depth analysis of recent sanctions revealed substantial barriers to work because of disability and/or childcare responsibilities. Their circumstances varied widely, including migrants, asylum seekers, homeless women, ex-offenders, lone parents, Employment Support Allowance, Universal Credit and Jobseeker's Allowance claimants. Four of the multiply-sanctioned women had been sanctioned six times or more. Their stories were harrowing. All were disabled or had long-term health conditions and most were also holding their families together – caring for children, siblings or parents – while dealing with their own extreme challenges. Sanctions were like a kind of torture for these women, who struggled to make sense of repeat penalties, for example, for missing meetings that they didn't know about. Two of the women (Bridget and Jo) were only able to start thinking about work after the sanctions stopped and they were freed from conditionality. 'Permitted work' was an essential protection for many women, which allowed them to volunteer or work short-hours, mini-jobs or part-time without the risk of losing benefit income. Support, mainly from charities, was far more effective than sanctions.

The long shadow of the sanctions system is considered in Chapter Six. Drawing on accounts from a range of women in the study, we can see that the current sanction system is far too harsh and that it fails to provide a minimum degree of financial security for vulnerable women and children. This is a complete change from the post-war welfare system, which was established with the core aim of preventing poverty and to provide an adequate support for all citizens. Over half of the women were never sanctioned, but many still felt at risk of being sanctioned throughout the duration of the study. During the study years, Jobcentre Plus had an organisational priority to apply sanctions that displaced its earlier function of helping people to find jobs. Women reported being processed at street level primarily as sanctionable, not as 'job-able'. Those who claimed UC, JSA, IS and Employment and Support Allowance in the Work-Related Activity Group (ESA WRAG) were at risk of being sanctioned. This shows that the threat of sanctions applies psychological pressure unnecessarily to most interviewees, who never broke the rules and were never sanctioned.

Twenty-seven of the women had one-off recent sanctions, usually because of a single missed appointment at the Jobcentre or a Work Programme provider, with insufficient job-search the next most common reason. Only one of these sanctions seemed to be entirely legitimate – a migrant woman who left her job to move to a different area of the UK. All the other women either had specific good cause or challenging circumstances that made compliance difficult. Sanctioning was overtly gendered in the cases of those women, like Angela, Anastasia, Kerry and Terri, who were caring for their ill, disabled or vulnerable children at the time they were meant to attend a Jobcentre appointment. For Amy, Jordan and Yastika, sanctioning was related to domestic abuse or violence, for example, because of a male partner's behaviour or because DWP letters were sent to an abandoned address. Women's time commitments to unpaid care work are not acknowledged in the text of the core policy documents that govern welfare conditionality and sanctions policy (DWP, 2010a; 2010b; 2011a; 2011b; 2012). Female research participants reported that care duties were often discounted when they set their weekly hours for job searching in their claimant commitment.

Sanctioning women has an amplified effect on children. 58 children of 25 mothers in total were affected by recent[2] sanctions. Of these, 48 children were impacted by sanctions applied to 13 lone mothers. Lone mothers are the sole carers and sole potential earners in the household, with no alternative source of income while sanctioned. Sanctions were applied for very minor rule infringements, like missing appointments or submitting paperwork late, usually when mothers had good cause for 'non-compliance'. In such circumstances, sanctioning was experienced as unjust, disproportionate and cruel. Although deductions are formally made to the adult personal-allowance of the benefit, the overall amount of money coming into the family during the sanction period is reduced. The practicalities of budgeting on a below-poverty level of income mean that children's lives are affected by sanctions, even when their needs are prioritised by their mothers.

Welfare conditionality changes since 2018

Since the Welfare Conditionality data collection concluded in 2018, there have been important changes to policy and practice.

Changes to conditionality

In 2017, after participants had been recruited to the study, full job-search requirements were placed on lone parents whose youngest child was three years old. This applies to mothers claiming Income Support, Jobseeker's Allowance, Universal Credit and Employment and Support Allowance (in the Work-Related Activity Group). Mothers with younger children are expected to engage with 'work preparation' activities. This restricts the period of unconditional motherhood to the early years of child development.

In 2018, the comprehensive Universal Credit In-Work Conditionality Randomised Control Trial ended (DWP/GSR, 2018a/b). Since then, there has been ambiguity about the job-search requirements for Universal Credit claimants while working. The 'mainstream offer' (DWP, 2013) remains in place, with the expectation that all Universal Credit claimants – including many disabled claimants and those with long-term health conditions – will work or look for a job full-time, 35 hours per week. At the time of writing (2023), in-work conditionality is being revived.

Changes to sanctions

One change was made to sanctions law. The harshest three-year sanction for Universal Credit was removed in November 2018. However, three-year sanctions were rarely used in practice (Webster, 2016; Adler, 2018) and the UK sanction regime remains in place, including open-ended sanctions and provision to apply multiple concurrent sanctions. The UK sanction regime remains very harsh by historic and international standards.

Sanctioning practices have been reformed at street-level. Around 2016, an internal DWP decision was made to 'ease back on sanctions' (Webster, 2016). This managerial decision was not publicly announced and the shift occurred largely unnoticed, only coming to light when research (for example, Robertson et al, 2020) evidenced a 'change of culture' within Jobcentre Plus. This welcome U-turn moved away from the performance management of sanctions via 'benefit off-flow' targets, exposed by independent researchers (Kaufman, 2020; Redman and Fletcher, 2021). After this internal managerial change around 2016, the rates of sanctions declined for a period for all working-age benefits (Webster, 2016). This is particularly important for Universal Credit, which had a later peak in sanctioning rates than Jobseeker's Allowance, which was not originally known outside of DWP because the data were withheld.

Temporary COVID-19 changes: labour market, child care, Universal Credit £20 uplift

The UK government made emergency welfare provisions in response to the COVID-19 pandemic. In March 2020, national lockdowns had a major impact on jobs and well-being throughout the UK. An extended period of labour market disruption followed. The UK government introduced a furlough scheme to protect jobs, support employees and workers and mitigate the long-term impacts of the pandemic. Women were disproportionately affected by school and nursery closures, home–based childcare and home-schooling became the norm over repeated periods in 2020 and 2021. There were job losses in female-dominated sectors, like hospitality and retail. Women were also impacted in their roles as essential workers. COVID-19 deaths rates were higher among working-class women doing essential work (Winchester, 2021).

In response to the pandemic, the UK Government introduced a temporary £20 uplift to the personal allowance of Universal Credit. This was extremely important in helping claimants to manage financially, particularly since the rates of Universal Credit are insufficient to afford necessities. However, the value of the uplift was undermined by ongoing deductions, to repay advanced payment for the controversial five-week wait for the first payment, the 'bedroom tax' and other deductions like Working Tax Credit overpayments. Research has also shown that even with the uplift, many claimants continued to struggle to make ends meet (Griffiths et al, 2022; Scullion et al, 2022; Patrick et al, 2022). There was a strong consensus that the £20 uplift needed to be retained, with evidence presented by the third-sector campaigners and experts (Robertson et al, 2020), including the House of Lords Economic Affairs Committee. In September 2021, the Conservative government ignored these calls and removed the £20 uplift. This is likely to have impoverished many claimants. Universal Credit was the only social security benefit to increase in value during the pandemic. This suggests that policy makers may have been primarily concerned with civil unrest from new claimants who lost their jobs because of virus-containment measures, rather than a genuine interest in protecting all vulnerable people from the increased financial risks created by the pandemic (for example, food and medicine shortages). It is telling that disability benefits (like ESA and PIP) and Carer's Allowance were not increased even during the most challenging periods of social isolation, when underlying health conditions may have made these claimants more vulnerable to the virus.

During the pandemic, sanctions were paused from March to July 2020 (Webster, 2021a) while Jobcentre Plus offices were closed and priority shifted to administering payments to the large influx of new claimants. Two changes in DWP policy were involved: only claimant commitments agreed or updated during the pandemic were sanctionable; and a new internal Sanction Assurance Framework 'based on the principles of fairness, compassion, respect and dignity' (DWP, 2021f, 1) was introduced to improve decision-making. This meant an end to new sanctions for claimants of ESA, JSA or IS that continued into spring 2021 after the sanctioning regime was officially reactivated (Webster, 2021b, 2). Importantly, new Universal Credit sanctioning never completely stopped, even during the COVID-19 national lockdowns, when it continued at a very low level (Webster, 2021a, 2). In 2021, with nearly six million UC claimants (41 per cent of whom had conditionality requirements), sanctioning began to creep up again, mainly for non-attendance at Jobcentre Plus appointments (Webster, 2021b, 2). The digital delivery system for Universal Credit was invaluable during the pandemic, when it would have been impossible to process claims using a paper-based system. This was a very welcome move since new job opportunities were scarce, particularly in early 2020.

It seemed initially, at least, that the pandemic opened up fresh awareness of the health and social needs of the British population. Unpredicted expansion of social provision was both welcome and necessary. For example, street homelessness was tackled, using emergency measures to quell the spread of the virus. In some areas, rough sleepers were put up in underoccupied hotels. However, as soon as 2021, many of the necessary provisions were withdrawn. The COVID-19 vaccination programme enabled high rates of protection for the population, but with rates rising, those on lower incomes, particularly in precarious situations, were still vulnerable to the virus and its impacts when emergency housing and income measures were withdrawn.

Key issues for policy and practice

This research shows that 21st-century work-first welfare reforms enshrine inherited male-defined assumptions that demand full-time economic productivity from both men and women, at the expense of paid care. The falsely individualised work ethic fails to recognise that interdependent care is fundamental to human life, social flourishing and planetary survival (The Care Collective, 2020). Social security needs to be reformed in response to the actualities of women's lives, to work with, rather than against the interdependency of family and social networks. There is an urgent need to adjust the sanction system and reset welfare conditionality for women on female-defined terms. Instead of insisting on one narrow individual male definition of productivity as the 'norm' of full-time paid employment, it is important to understand the role of care and the interdependency of families. Claimant commitments should include protected time for unpaid care. There is a need to acknowledge parental care of children but also care of older adults and grandchildren. There should be acknowledgement of the interdependency between mothers and grandmothers.

The impacts of lone-mother sanctions on their children were not identified as a potential risk in the gender-equality analysis conducted by DWP (2011b) and the impacts for couples were described as 'gender neutral' (DWP, 2011b, 5). The findings presented in this book demonstrate that conditionality and sanctions operate in gendered, racialised, ageist, disablist and discriminatory ways. Existing safeguards do not protect women or children from extreme hardship or intense psychological pressure. It is essential that DWP recognise the gendered impacts of conditionality and sanctions on women, Black and minoritised ethnic women and the children of lone parents.

'Permitted work' crucial as an 'unconditional' work activity

'Permitted work' (DWP, 2020b) was incredibly important for women in the study who had positive experiences of voluntary and paid[3] positions of less than 16 hours per week. Permitted work enables claimants of legacy benefits like JSA and ESA, including those who are severely disabled, to engage in small amounts of work without fear of losing their benefit income or their home. The security of predictable regular benefit income, even if it is inadequate to fully protect citizens from poverty, remained important for women in the study. For ESA Support Group claimants, 'permitted work' was the equivalent of a 'conditionality-free' work activity. Of course, receipt of any form of social security involves eligibility conditions and ESA claimants must undergo stringent Work Capability Assessment to access financial support, so ESA Support Group claimants are not fully 'unconditional' or 'conditionality-free'. ESA Support Group claimants are working-age people with access to benefit income free from the types of work-related conditionality (including Jobcentre Plus attendance, job-seeking activities, mandatory training, and so on) that UC and JSA claimants are usually subject to. Women's experiences of being empowered to choose to work for an employer, as self-employed or a volunteer, was invaluable in gaining meaningful higher-quality and sustainable forms of work. This contrasted starkly with the pressure experienced by many women on JSA, UC and ESA WRAG to do any job regardless of its impacts on them and their family. This indicates that tough punitive welfare conditionality was less effective than free choice.

One clear message is that the decisions about capability for work had a big influence on whether women claiming out-of-work benefits (UC, JSA, ESA, IS) were sanctioned. Disabled women and those with long-term health conditions, including mental health problems, were vulnerable to sanctions when they were wrongly assessed as fit for work. Many women in the study had health problems that were not accurately recognised by the social security system. For example, Helen (see Chapter Four) was sanctioned multiple times for missing Work Programme appointments, when she had sought help to get 'permitted work' (up to 16 hours per week) while she was formally recognised as unfit to work and claimed ESA in the Support Group (which should have protected her from risk of sanctions). It is crucially important to ensure that claimants are in the right conditionality group to avoid those who are not capable of working being put under intense psychological and financial pressure. A simple solution would be to remove conditionality from all ill and disabled claimants, to enable 'permitted work' as the default option.

In-work Universal Credit conditionality

In-work conditionality was highly problematic for several women in the study. There is a vicious cycle of labour market disadvantage, sanctions-backed in-work conditionality and low job quality (including low pay, insecurity, lack of progression, powerlessness, lack of autonomy and meaninglessness). Because sanctions-backed conditionality feeds poor job quality it is a self-fulfilling prophesy that women will continue to need to claim in-work earnings top-ups. Under the previous system of tax credits, payments were made based on a 'respectable worker' model of agency, without any need for work-related conditionality (mandatory job search, Jobcentre Plus appointments and the like, see Wright and Dwyer, 2022). Although Universal Credit makes it easier to move in and out of work without losing benefit entitlement, it applies in-work conditionality for the first time. In-work conditionality was experienced negatively by female participants, especially those who were sanctioned for missing appointments or inadequate job-search, *while already in employment*. Treating workers as if they are unemployed is counterproductive. The system creates unnecessary stigma for compliant claimants. Lone mothers are especially vulnerable to poverty (Andrew et al, 2021). DWP (2020b) projections show that most in-work Universal Credit claimants will be women (77 per cent) and parents (70 per cent); over half are expected to be lone parents and almost a third will be disabled. In-work conditionality is likely to compound labour market disadvantage for many working-class mothers, particularly lone mothers (Andersen, 2023).

The new wave of 'work first, then work more' reforms use welfare conditionality to push disadvantaged workers and those traditionally seen as a 'reserve army of labour' (mothers and disabled people) to these same ends, using the same means, as unemployment policies. Women's paid employment is central to the 21st-century workforce, no longer as a 'reserve army of labour' but as 'ideal neoliberal subjects' (Nayak and Kehily, 2008; also see Gerodetti and McNaught-Davis, 2017). Women are ideal 'coerced worker-claimants' (Wright and Dwyer, 2022) only in their textually misrepresented form as genderless sanctionable subjects. Sanctions-backed welfare conditionality continues to frame 'in-work progression' as a key policy priority for DWP, which pushes claimants to take on 'more work' until they are full-time. 'Coerced worker-claimants' (Wright and Dwyer,

2022, 1) are snared in an inescapable vicious cycle where punitive welfare conditionality feeds the poor job quality that creates the need to claim Universal Credit as an earnings top-up. Harsh welfare conditionality is dysfunctional in its own policy terms because it is likely to increase, rather than reduce, public expenditure. A whole section of the labour market is becoming populated by a new 'coerced flexible workforce continually in fear of losing their income and homes' (Wright and Dwyer, 2022, 12).

Rethinking care

Conditional welfare reforms have pushed work obligations onto working-age benefit recipients of all kinds, including disabled people and those with debilitating long-term health conditions, lone parents (who are almost all lone mothers) as well as 'able-bodied' unemployed people and those in paid employment. The all-consuming duty to work has squeezed care out into the margins, where it must be shoehorned around laborious, often futile (Wright et al, 2020) job-search activities and insecure and/or low-paid work. For women, who still deliver most care in all societies, this causes intense and unproductive tensions and avoidable crises. The push towards work regardless of health and care privileges impersonal productivity that is exploited for the profit of others. The design of work-based welfare conditionality and sanctions was influenced by rich White men, whose own elite experiences of childhood and education were likely to have been distant from working-class women's everyday local lived experiences of family care. Punitive policies delegitimise and disrupt care activities that are essential for human survival and flourishing. Social security systems need to be redesigned to protect, support and celebrate care as an essential component of human survival. This book moves beyond the current policy view of women claimants of working-age benefits, including lone parents, as job seekers unencumbered by caring responsibilities and other barriers, to recognise their active agency, variety of circumstances and, in some cases, multiple barriers to engaging in paid work. Conditional welfare reform has emphasised sanctions more heavily than support and there remains substantial scope for the development of services to support mothers returning from labour market breaks to find and retain work, taking into account their differentiation of experience and the extent of multiple barriers.

Policy recommendations

Social security design

- It is essential that the value of social security is set in relation to the actual costs of living. Without this step, women and children face risks of poverty and destitution in all parts of the UK (including Scotland, where devolved benefits mitigate some of the worst impacts).

- Minimum Income Guarantee (MIG) is proposed as a better alternative to conditional social assistance benefits like Universal Credit. Income adequacy is a crucial component of system design. Parallel, so-called 'generous', Universal Basic Income proposals (such as Connolly et al, 2022) are insufficient to cover the costs of living and are lower than existing rates of social security.
  - It is essential that any Minimum Income Guarantee is set at a value that would prevent women and children experiencing poverty and destitution.

Welfare conditionality

- The 2012 British sanction system is far too harsh and causes dangerous harm to women and children in all parts of the UK. The system should be scrapped.
  - It is urgent that maximum sanctions are reduced to pre-2012 levels.
  - Multiple sanctions must be removed completely.
- Social security needs to be reformed to enable and support self- and kin-care, rather than creating anxiety, worsening mental health and squeezing out time and headspace for essential human functioning.
- Social security needs to empower women financially and facilitate autonomy and self-actualisation.
- Physical and mental health problems and the impact they have on capacity for care and paid employment should be recognised accurately by social-security systems.

Children should be protected from poverty and the detrimental impacts of benefit sanctions.

APPENDIX 1

The Welfare Conditionality study

The book is based on qualitative longitudinal research from the '*Sanctions support and behaviour change: understanding the role and impact of welfare conditionality*' project, funded by the Economic and Social Research Council's Centres and Large Grants Scheme Grant (2013–19, grant number ES/K002163/2, www.welfareconditionality.ac.uk). The Welfare Conditionality project aimed to create an international and interdisciplinary focal point for social science research on welfare conditionality and brought together teams of researchers in six universities: York, Glasgow, Heriot-Watt, Salford, Sheffield and Sheffield Hallam. The original research questions were:

- How effective is conditionality in changing the behaviour of those receiving welfare benefits and services?
- Are there any circumstances in which the use of behavioural conditionality may, or may not be, justifiable?

This book presents reanalysis of original data generated in interviews from three rounds of innovative repeat qualitative-longitudinal interviews. The full study involved 481 'welfare service users' (1082 interviews in total) subject to a range of conditionality measures in nine policy fields: Universal Credit, job seekers, disabled people, migrants, lone parents, ex-offenders, family intervention, homeless and social tenants. Many of the participants were subject to work-related conditionality while claiming benefits, especially those who were selected because they claimed Universal Credit or Jobseeker's Allowance. However, other types of behavioural conditionality like antisocial behaviour orders and family intervention projects were included too. This book focuses only on female research participants with experience of social security benefits.

In total, 213 (44 per cent) of the 481 welfare service users who participated in the project self-identified as cisgender women and 268 as cisgender men. Chart A1.1 shows there were higher proportions of women sampled as lone parents (85 per cent) and social tenants (70 per cent). Fewer women were sampled as ex-offenders (21 per cent) and homeless people (27 per cent). The sampling strategy was based on statistical evidence of gender distributions in each of the categories at the start of the study in 2014.

Chart A1.2 shows the age distribution of all 481 men and women at the start of the study. Overall, there were fewer women than men in the older

Chart A1.1: Welfare Conditionality, whole sample classification by gender (n = 481)

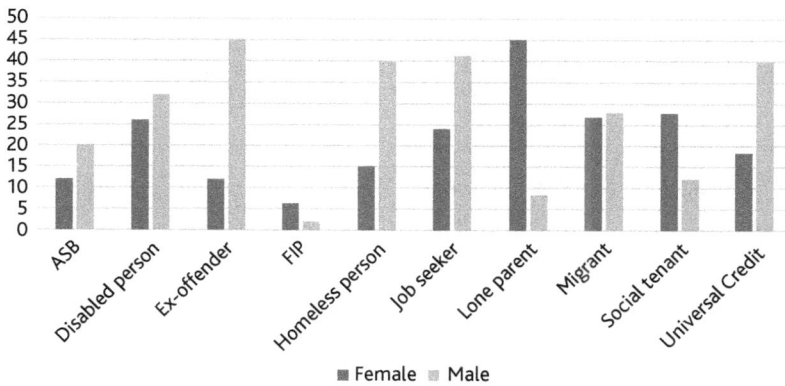

■ Female ▨ Male

Chart A1.2: Welfare Conditionality, whole sample, age group by gender (n = 481)

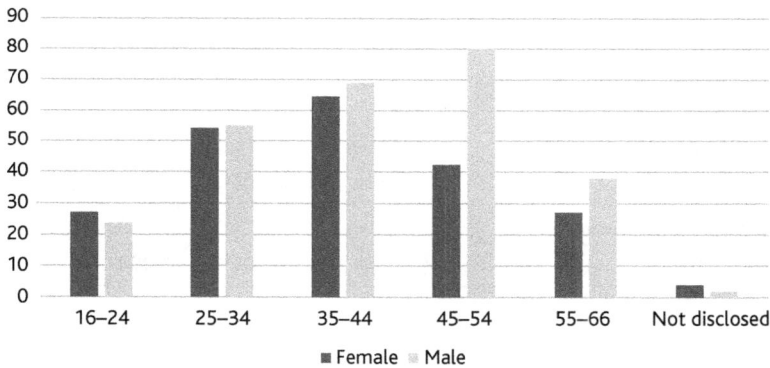

■ Female ▨ Male

age categories, 45–54 and 55–66. This reflects the age profiles of the sampling characteristics (see Table A1.1), since the female-dominated sample of lone parents were young enough to have dependent children in their household, while the male-dominated samples included older age groups.

Table A1.1 shows participants' self-declared ethnicity, based on the categories used by the UK Office for National Statistics. Most participants, 142 women and 207 men, described their ethnicity as White British, English, Northern Irish, Scottish or Welsh. Forty-nine (23 per cent) of the women were from Black or minority ethnic groups and 21 (10 per cent) were White non-British. One woman chose not to define/disclose her ethnicity. Table A1.2 shows female participants in the Welfare Conditionality study by sample group and times sanctioned at Wave A.

Table A1.1: Welfare Conditionality whole sample, participants by ethnicity (nationality) and gender (n = 481)

Ethnicity	Female	Male	Total
African	8	14	22
Any other Asian background	1	2	3
Any other Black/African/Caribbean background	5	3	8
Any other ethnic group	3	7	10
Any other Mixed/Multiple ethnic background	4	3	7
Any other White background	21	14	35
Arab	2	1	3
Bangladeshi	3	1	4
Caribbean	5	7	12
Chinese	1	0	1
White British/English/Northern Irish/Scottish Welsh	142	207	349
Gypsy or Irish Traveller	0	1	1
Indian	2	0	2
Irish	2	2	4
Not Applicable	1	2	3
Pakistani	5	2	7
White and Black African	3	0	3
White and Black Caribbean	5	2	7
Total	**213**	**268**	**481**

Table A1.2: Welfare Conditionality, female whole sample, times sanctioned at Wave A (n = 213)

Sample	Times sanctioned					
	0	1	2–5	6+	Don't know	Total
Antisocial behaviour	9	3				12
Disabled person	16	5	3	2		26
Ex-offender	6	4	2			12
Family Intervention Project	5	1				6
Homeless person	9	4	1	1		15
Job seeker	14	8	2			24
Lone parent	28	11	5		1	45
Migrant	17	5	5			27
Social tenant	28					28
Universal Credit	14	3		1		18
Total	**146**	**44**	**18**	**4**	**1**	**213**

Figure A1.1: Welfare Conditionality, female sample, book subsample and sanctions at any wave (n = 213)

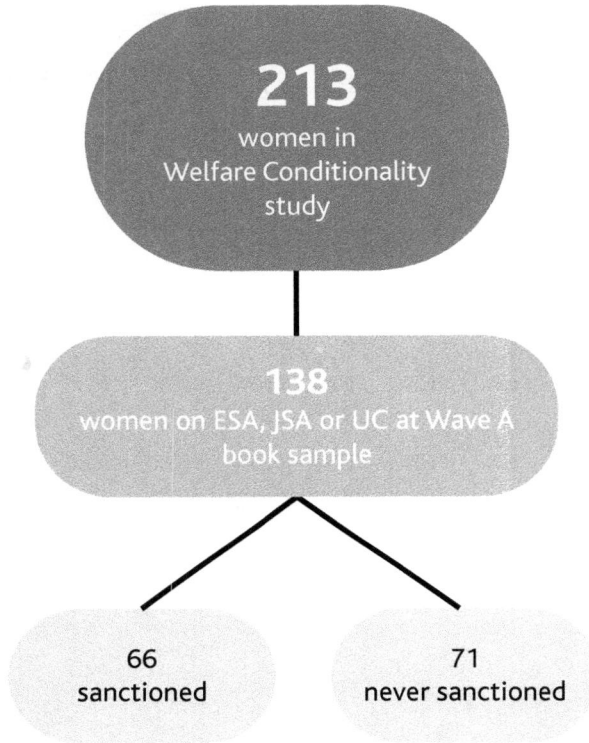

213
women in
Welfare Conditionality
study

138
women on ESA, JSA or UC at Wave A
book sample

66
sanctioned

71
never sanctioned

APPENDIX 2

Sanctions overviews

Table A2.1 overviews the experiences of the four most heavily-sanctioned women in the study (see Chapter 5).

The experiences of 12 women sanctioned between two and five times during the study (see Chapters 4 and 5) are outlined in Table A2.2.

Table A2.1: Women sanctioned ≥6 times, within 12 months prior to first interview and employment status, Waves A–C (n = 4)

Name[1]	Ethnicity/ nationality	Disabled	Lone parent	Number of children at home	Sanctions	Reasons for sanctions	Good cause	Employed any wave
Sarah	White UK[2]	Yes	No	0	UC ≥ 6	Missed appointments	Yes, not notified of appointments; kin care	Yes WA[3] Var
Helen	White UK	Yes	No	0	ESA SG ≥ 6	Missed appointments	Yes, repeated misunderstanding about voluntary Work Programme participation	Yes WB Var WC S–H
Jo	White UK	Yes	No	0	JSA ≥6	Missed appointments; insufficient job search; undocumented job search	Yes, dyslexia	Yes WC S–H
Bridget	White UK	Yes	Yes	1	JSA ≥6	Missed appointments	Yes, mental health problems	Yes WB F–T WC F–T

Table A2.2: Women sanctioned 2–5 times within 12 months prior to Wave A and employment status, Waves A–C (n = 12)

Name[4]	Ethnicity/ nationality	Disabled	Lone parent	Number of children at home	Sanctions	Reasons for sanctions	Good cause	Employed any wave
Latifa	Arab	No	Yes	3	JSA 2–5	Joint claim – her husband's missed appointments and insufficient job search	No	No
Sophia	White European	No	Yes	1	IS/JSA 2–5	Unknown; late for appointment	Unknown	No
Vicky	White UK	Yes	Yes	1	JSA 2–5	Insufficient job search; going on holiday	Expectations unclear; unaware of consequences	No
Lizzie	White UK	No	Yes	1	JSA 2–5	Missed appointments	No; yes, notified of a different appointment time	No
Shaneta	Black Caribbean	Yes	Yes	1	JSA 2–5	Missed appointments; left jobs 'voluntarily'	Yes, ill-health; unknown	No
Lucy	White UK	Yes	Yes	2	JSA 2–5	Missed appointments	Yes, letters sent to old address while homeless	No
Aisling	White European	Yes	No	0	JSA 2–5	Missed appointment(s)	Yes, clashed with support appointment	No
Emma	White UK	Yes	No	0	JSA 2–5	Missed appointments	Yes, mental health problems, no computer or phone	No
June	White UK	Yes	No	0	JSA 2–5	Travelling 300 miles within UK on two occasions	Yes, preparing property for sale/rent, informed work coach in advance	No
Tina	White UK	No	No	0	JSA 2–5	Not bringing evidence of job search	No	Yes WA S-H
Jing	Asian	No	Yes	2	JSA 2–5	Missing appointment(s)	Yes, child unwell; language problems	Yes WA P-T[5] WB P-T WC P-T
Mira	Mixed	No	Yes	1	JSA 2–5	Left work voluntarily; insufficient job search	Yes, left work due to racism; did not understand expectations	Yes WA F-T WB P-T WC P-T

Table A2..3: Women sanctioned only once within 12 months prior to first interview and employment status at Waves A–C[6] (n = 27)

Identifier and pseudonym	Ethnicity/ nationality	Disabled	Lone parent	Number of children at home	Reason for sanction	Good cause	Employed any wave
Lisette	White European	No	No	0	Left job voluntarily	No	Yes WB F-T WC F-T
Javeria	Bangladeshi	No	No	0	Missed appointment	Yes, language problem	Yes WB P-T
Zinhle	Black South African	No	No	0	Missed appointment	Unknown	Yes WB F-T WC F-T
Bilyana	White European	Yes	No	0	Unknown	Yes, complied with all known requirements	No
Lesley	White UK	Yes	Yes	1	Non-submission of form	Yes, did not receive form	No
Amy	White UK	Yes	No	6	Missed appointment	Yes, did not receive appointment notification because fled usual address due to domestic violence	No
Natalie	White UK	Yes	No	0	Insufficient job search	Unknown	No
Charlene	Mixed race UK	No	Yes	6	Missed appointment	Yes, pregnancy-related ill-health	No
Angela	White UK	No, yes by Wave C	Yes	3	Missed appointment	Yes, caring for daughter who had been violently attacked	Yes WB P-T
Terri	White UK	No, yes, by Wave C	Yes	3	Missed appointment	Yes, son's disability	No
Louise	White UK	Yes	Yes	3	Late submission of form	Yes, informed Jobcentre awaiting medical information from GP	No

Table A2.3: Women sanctioned only once within 12 months prior to first interview and employment status at Waves A–C[6] (n = 27) (continued)

Identifier and pseudonym	Ethnicity/ nationality	Disabled	Lone parent	Number of children at home	Reason for sanction	Good cause	Employed any wave
Anastasia	White European	No, Yes at Waves B and C	Yes	1	Missed appointment	Yes, seeking urgent medical help for her seriously ill daughter	No
Claire	White UK	No	Yes	3	Missed appointment	Unknown	No
Carolina	White European	No	Yes	2	Insufficient job search	Unknown	Yes WB F-T
Anja	White European	No	Yes	1	Insufficient job search	Unknown	Yes WB P-T
Leah	White UK	Yes	No	0	Missed appointment	Unknown	No
Dierdre	White European	No	No	0	Missed appointment	Unknown	Yes WB S-E
Karen	White UK	Yes	Yes	2	Missed appointment	Yes, unable to attend due to ill-health, she and her support worker contacted Work Programme in advance by phone and in writing	Yes WB S-E
Ruth	White UK	Yes	Yes	1	Missed appointment	Yes, disability	No
Kayli	White UK	No	No	0	Failure to notify end of training course	Yes, unaware of requirement	No
Amira	Mixed	No	No	0	Insufficient job search	Unknown	Yes WB P-T WC P-T

(continued)

Table A2.3: Women sanctioned only once within 12 months prior to first interview and employment status at Waves A–C[6] (n = 27) (continued)

Identifier and pseudonym	Ethnicity/ nationality	Disabled	Lone parent	Number of children at home	Reason for sanction	Good cause	Employed any wave
Kerry	White UK	Yes	Yes	1	Missed appointment	Yes, taking daughter to hospital for cancer treatment	Yes WB variable
Jordan	White UK	No	No	0	Joint claim – partner's insufficient job search	Yes, domestic abuse survivor who complied with all requirements	No
Anne	White UK	No	No	0	Insufficient job search	Unknown	No
Shamima	Indian	No	No	4	Non-response to DWP letters	Yes, was hospitalised and did not receive letters	No
Ali	White UK	No	Yes	3	Missed appointment	Unknown	Yes WA variable
Grace	African	No	Yes	5	Insufficient job search	Unknown	Yes WA P-T WC P-T

Notes

one

[1] Removing or reducing income for lengthy periods.

[2] The gender profile of those on Universal Credit changed over time according to eligibility. Under 'Live Service' (2013–June 2018), UC was not available to those with dependent children or those exempt from job-search activity. As 'Full Service' was rolled out (including households with children and those not seeking employment, for example because they are looking after young children or incapable of work due to disability or long-term ill-health) the proportion of female claimants increased. From June 2018, when 'Full Service' was operational throughout England, Scotland and Wales, women outnumbered men. This changed during the 2020 COVID-19 lockdown, but has since reverted. See DWP (2021e) for further detail.

[3] Ninety per cent of lone parents are women (ONS, 2016). While lone fathers face labour-market disadvantage and have distinct experiences of marginalisation (Adams, 1996), welfare reforms for lone parents are mainly aimed at mothers, who confront enduring labour market disadvantages relating to horizontal and vertical gendered occupational segregation, unequal pay and part-time employment (EU, 2016).

[4] Some women dropped out of the study before it finished.

[5] ESA Support Group claimants (39) were included, despite being disabled and exempt from work-related conditionality because many had recent experience of behavioural conditionality on other benefits (JSA or ESA WRAG) due to being wrongly deemed 'fit for work' by a Work Capability Assessment.

[6] Three of these job seekers were not currently claiming JSA but had recent experience of work-related conditionality.

[7] This includes any benefit sanction prior to the research interview. Some sanctions experiences were recent, while others were from many years ago and under different circumstances, for example while claiming Jobseeker's Allowance before becoming disabled.

[8] Three migrant women had recently been sanctioned multiple times but were not currently subject to work-related conditionality.

two

[1] Only seven per cent of the UK population is educated at independent schools, but 39 per cent of the elite were privately educated (TST and SMC, 2019, 3).

[2] About a quarter of private schools in the UK are single-sex, not all are boarding schools and the average size of single-sex schools is 477 students (Independent Schools Council, 2019).

[3] Hall (1993) calls paradigmatic change 'third order' change (that is, resetting the goals of the economy or the labour market), compared with 'second order' change that introduces new policies and 'third order' alteration of policy instruments.

[4] Date range for active policy framework during the fieldwork phase of the Welcond study. Adler (2018, 25–34) overviews the history of welfare conditionality. See Chapter Seven of this volume for recent developments.

three

[1] This peak is related to the rising state pension age for women, which was 60 in 2010, 65 in 2018 and will be 67 by 2028 (for men and women).

[2] 72.4 per cent.

3　Although in part-time work, women earn 3.1 per cent more than men on average.

4　Based on the OECD 2016 Labour Force Statistics, using the definition of 'less than 30 weekly hours of work in main job'.

5　Full Service – greater opportunities existed for face-to-face contact with work coaches under the original Live Service.

6　At the time of fieldwork, there were some differences in sanctioning regulations for IS, ESA, JSA and UC. To avoid confusion, the discussion here is limited to Universal Credit because that is the main benefit replacing the other means-tested working-age benefits going forwards.

7　And Child Tax Credit, which also withholds the family element for those born after 6 April 2017 (DWP, 2020a).

8　There are also exceptions for multiple births, adoption and 'non-parental caring arrangements' (DWP, 2020a; DWP, 2021c).

9　With incomes above the Administrative Earnings Threshold but below the Conditionality Earnings Threshold.

10　Capped at to £646.35 for one child and £1,108.04 for two or more children (DWP, 2021).

11　First introduced by a Labour Government in 1999 within Working Families Tax Credit.

12　DWP defines older workers as those aged 50+ (DWP, 2015).

13　The Social Security Scotland Act (2018).

14　Also referred to as 'flexibilities'.

four

1　White British.

2　Three dropped out by Wave B and a further four dropped out by Wave C, meaning 15 older women completed all three waves of interviews.

3　Eight were sampled as disabled, four of whom were in the ESA Support Group. Three were disabled but contacted because of a different sample characteristic.

4　Those women aged 55–64 at Wave A of the study in 2014 were born between 1950 and 1959.

5　Equal Pay Act 1970.

6　Sex Discrimination Act 1975.

7　This rose to 97 per cent by 2021, but around 15 per cent of out-of-work women and those from low/no skill households were digitally excluded (Ofcom, 2022:8).

8　White British.

9　The '03' number was charged as a national geographical rate.

five

1　White British, living alone; her boyfriend lives in his own tenancy. Sarah participated in one research interview, then dropped out of the study.

2　Detained in hospital due to mental disorder, for the safety of self or others, under the Mental Health Act 1983 (Mind, 2020).

3　A fourth women, Bridget, was also sanctioned more than six times. Bridget's story is outlined at the start of Chapter Two.

4　At the time of the fieldwork, UC 'live service' customers like Sarah paid call charges of up to 45p per minute for the official helpline. The average length of UC helpline phone calls was 7 min. 20 sec. once the call was answered, which cost up to £7.63 per call, including £3.59 spent before speaking to anyone (BBC, 2017). The UK government decided to remove call charges in late November 2017, following evidence from this project and other lobbying.

[5] It is unclear from Helen's account why this happened. It may have been a misunderstanding when the Jobcentre referred Helen to the Work Programme. It was possible to sign up to the Work Programme as a voluntary participant.

[6] One in ten people in the UK are estimated to have dyslexia (NHS, 2018).

six

[1] Windy and rainy.

[2] White British.

[3] One participant was originally categorised as 'sanctioned once' because her boyfriend missed an appointment at the Jobcentre at the start of their claim and was referred to a decision-maker. Although they feared they would be sanctioned at Wave A, it transpired (at Wave B) they were not. Another participant was originally included but it later transpired she was not sanctioned, but did receive an Antisocial Behaviour Order.

[4] A further 16 women reported older sanctions, more than a year before their Wave A interview. Older sanctions experiences have been omitted to ensure sanctions stories relate to the post-2013 policy context. Recent experiences may also be remembered and retold more accurately.

seven

[1] Subsequently removed.

[2] Sanctions applied more than 12 months before the first research interview are excluded because reliable information was not available in all cases about household circumstances and children's ages. This is likely to underestimate the prevalence of childhood impacts within the sample.

[3] Earning up to £143 per week after tax in 2021.

Appendix two

[1] Names have been changed to protect anonymity. Identifying information has been omitted or altered.

[2] Includes White British, English, Scottish, Northern Irish and Welsh.

[3] WA/WB/WC = Wave A/B/C of the study; Var = Variable hours of work, S-H = short-hours work.

[4] Names have been changed to protect identity.

[5] P-T = part-time job; F-T = full-time job; S-H = short-hours job.

[6] Missing data indicates interviewee dropped out of the study.

References

Abbring, J.H., van den Berg, G.J. and van Ours, J.C. (2005) 'The effect of unemployment insurance sanctions on the transition rate from unemployment to employment', *Economic Journal*, 115(505): 602–630.

Adams, J. (1996) 'Lone fatherhood: still a problematic status?', *Practice: Social Work in Action*, 8(1): 15–26.

Adamson, M. and Roper, I. (2019) '"Good" jobs and "bad" jobs: contemplating job quality in different contexts', *Work, Employment and Society*, 33(4): 551–559.

Adler, M. (2016) 'A new leviathan: benefit sanctions in the twenty-first century', *Journal of Law and Society*, 43(2): 195–227.

Adler, M. (2018) *Cruel, Inhuman or Degrading Treatment? Benefit sanctions in the UK*, London: Palgrave.

Altman, R. (2015) *A New Vision for Older Workers: Retain, retrain, recruit*, Report to Government, London: Department for Work and Pensions, https://assets.publishing.service.gov.uk/government/uploads/system/uploads/attachment_data/file/411420/a-new-vision-for-older-workers.pdf [Accessed 27 July 2021].

Andrew, A., Bandiera, O., Costa-Dias, M. and Landais, C. (2021) *Women and Men at Work*, London: Institute for Fiscal Studies https://ifs.org.uk/uploads/IFS-Inequality-Review-women-and-men-at-work.pdf [Accessed 15 December 2021].

Andersen, K. (2020) 'Universal Credit, gender and unpaid childcare: mothers' accounts of the new welfare conditionality regime', *Critical Social Policy*, 40(3): 430–449.

Andersen, K. (2023) *Welfare that Works for Women: Mothers' experiences of the conditionality within Universal Credit*, Bristol: The Policy Press.

Anderson, P.S. (2003) 'Autonomy, vulnerability and gender', *Feminist Theory*, 4(2): 149–164.

Ariss, A., Firmin, C., Meacher, M., Starmer, K. and Urwin, R. (2015) *Where's the Benefit? An independent inquiry into women and Jobseeker's Allowance*, London: Fawcett Society.

Arni, P., Lalive, R. and van Ours, J.C. (2013) 'How effective are unemployment benefit sanctions? Looking beyond unemployment exit', *Journal of Applied Econometrics*, 28(7): 1153–78.

Bacchi, C. (1999) *Women, Policy and Politics: The construction of policy problems*, London: Sage.

Barnes, C. and Mercer, G. (2005) 'Disability, work and welfare: challenging the social exclusion of disabled people', *Work, Employment and Society*, 19(3): 527–545.

Baumberg-Geiger, B. (2017) 'Benefits conditionality for disabled people: stylised facts from a review of international evidence and practice', *Journal of Poverty and Social Justice*, 25(2): 107–128.

BBC (2015) 'A4e staff jailed for DWP back-to-work training fraud', 31 March, https://www.bbc.co.uk/news/uk-england-32139244 [Accessed 8 October 2021].

BBC (2017) 'Universal credit callers face five minutes on hold', https://www.bbc.co.uk/news/uk-politics-41913208 [Accessed 25 August 2021].

Beatty, C. and Fothergill, S. (2018) 'Welfare reform in the United Kingdom 2010–16: expectations, outcomes and local impacts', *Social Policy & Administration*, 52(5): 950–68.

Beatty, C., Foden, M., McCarthy, L. and Reeve, K. (2015) *Benefit Sanctions and Homelessness: A scoping report*, London: Crisis.

Bennett, F. (2011) 'Universal credit: the gender impact', *Poverty (Journal of Child Poverty Action Group)*, 140: 15–18.

Bennett, F. (2012) 'Universal Credit: overview and gender implications', in M. Kilkey, G. Ramia and K. Farnsworth (eds) *Social Policy Review 24: Analysis and Debate in Social Policy*, Bristol: Policy Press, 15–34.

Bennett, F. (2013) 'Researching within-household distribution: overview, developments, debates and methodological challenges', *Journal of Marriage and Family*, 75(3): 582–597.

Bennett, F. and Daly, M. (2014) *Poverty Through a Gender Lens: Evidence and policy review on gender and poverty*, Oxford: University of Oxford, https://www.spi.ox.ac.uk/sites/default/files/Gender_and_poverty_Bennett_and_Daly_final_12_5_14_28_5_14.pdf [Accessed 21 December 2021].

Bennett, F. and Millar, J. (2009) 'Social security reforms and challenges', in J. Millar (ed) *Understanding Social Security: Issues for policy and practice*, 2nd Edition, Bristol: Policy Press, 11–30.

Bennett, F. and Sung, S. (2013a) 'Dimensions of financial autonomy in low-/moderate-income couples from a gender perspective and implications for welfare reform', *Journal of Social Policy*, 42(4): 701–719.

Bennett, F. and Sung, S. (2013b) 'Gender implications of UK welfare reform and government equality duties: evidence from qualitative studies', *Oñati Socio-Legal Series*, 3(7): 1202–1221.

Bennett, F. and Sung, S. (2014) 'Money matters: using qualitative research for policy influencing on gender and welfare reform', *Innovation: The European Journal of Social Science Research*, 27(1): 5–19.

Berthoud, R. (2003) *Multiple Disadvantage in Employment: A quantitative analysis*, York: Joseph Rowntree Foundation.

Berthoud, R. (2008) 'Disability employment penalties in Britain', *Work, Employment and Society*, 22(1): 129–148.

Betzelt, S. and Bothfeld, S. (eds) (2011) *Activation and Labour Market Reforms in Europe: Challenges to social citizenship*, Basingstoke: Palgrave.

Beveridge, W. (1942) *Social Insurance and Allied Services*, London: The Stationery Office, https://www.sochealth.co.uk/national-health-serv ice/public-health-and-wellbeing/beveridge-report/beveridge-married-women-change-6/ [Accessed 2 July 2021].

Beveridge, W. (1944) *Full Employment in a Free Society*, London: Allen & Unwin.

Blackburn, S. (1995) 'How useful are feminist theories of the welfare state?', *Women's History Review*, 4(3): 369–394.

Bonoli, G. (2005) 'The politics of the new social policies: providing coverage against new social risks in mature welfare states', *Policy & Politics*, 33(3): 431–449.

Bonoli, G. (2010) 'The political economy of active labor-market policy', *Politics and Society*, 38(4): 435–457, https://onlinelibrary.wiley.com/toc/14679515/2020/54/2 [Accessed 22 May 2023].

Boockmann, B.L., Thomsen, S. and Walter, T. (2014) 'Intensifying the use of benefit sanctions: an effective tool to increase employment?', *IZA Journal of Labor Policy*, 3(21), https://doi.org/10.1186/2193-9004-3-21.

Bordone, V., Arpino, B. and Aassve, A. (2017) 'Patterns of grandparental child care across Europe: the role of the policy context and working mothers' need', *Ageing and Society*, 37(4): 845–873.

Bosch, G. (2006) 'Working time and the standard employment relationship', in J.Y. Boulin, M. Lallement, F. Messenger and F. Michon (eds) *Decent Working Time: New trends and new issues*, Geneva: ILO, 41–64.

Bothfeld, S. and Betzelt, S. (2011) 'How do activation policies affect social citizenship? The issue of autonomy', in S. Betzelt and S. Bothfeld (eds) *Activation and Labour Market Reforms in Europe*, London: Palgrave Macmillan, 15–34.

Boulin, J.Y., Lallement, M., Messenger, F. and Michon F. (eds) (2006) *Decent Working Time: New trends and new issues*, Geneva: ILO.

Bourquin, P., Cribb, J., Waters, T. and Xu, X. (2019) *Why Has In-Work Poverty Risen in Britain?* Working Paper W19/12, London: Institute for Fiscal Studies.

Bradshaw, J. (2017) 'Why the two-child policy is the worst social security policy ever', Social Policy Association 50th Anniversary Blog Series, No. 3, http://www.social-policy.org.uk/50-for-50/two-child-policy/ [Accessed 17 August 2021].

Bradshaw, J., Finch, N., Kemp, A.P., Mayhew, E. and Williams, J. (2003) *Gender and Poverty in Britain*, York: University of York.

Bradshaw, J., Kennedy, S., Kilkey, M., Hutton, S., Corden, A., Eardley, T. et al (1996) *Policy and the Employment of Lone Parents in 20 Countries*, York: University of York.

Breitenbach, E. (1982) *Women Workers in Scotland: A study of women's employment and trade unionism*, Glasgow: Pressgang.

Brewer, M., Joyce, R., Waters, T. and Woods, J. (2019) *Universal Credit and its Impact on Household Incomes: The long and the short of it*, London: Institute for Fiscal Studies.

Briken, K. and Taylor, P. (2018) 'Fulfilling the 'British way': beyond constrained choice – Amazon workers' lived experiences of workfare', *Industrial Relations Journal*, 49(5–6): 438–458.

Brodkin, E.Z. (2011) 'Policy work: street-level organizations under new managerialism', *Journal of Public Administration Research and Theory*, 21(2): 253–277.

Brodkin, E.Z. (2012) 'Reflections on street-level bureaucracy: past, present, and future', *Public Administration Review*, 72: 940–949.

Brodkin, E.Z. (2013a) 'Commodification, inclusion, or what? Workfare in everyday organizational life', in E.Z. Brodkin and G. Marston (eds) *Work and the Welfare State: Street-level organizations and workfare politics*, Washington, DC: Georgetown University Press.

Brodkin, E.Z. (2013b) 'Work and the welfare state reconsidered: street-level organizations and the global workfare project', in E.Z. Brodkin and G. Marston (eds) *Work and the Welfare State: Street-level organizations and workfare politics*, Washington, DC: Georgetown University Press.

Brodkin, E.Z. and Larsen, F. (2013) 'Changing boundaries: the policies of workfare in the U.S. and Europe', *Poverty & Public Policy*, 5(1): 37–47.

Brodkin, E.Z. and Marston, G. (eds) (2013) *Work and the Welfare State: Street-level organizations and workfare politics*, Washington, DC: Georgetown University Press.

Brower, R.L., Jones, T.B., Osborne-Lampkin, L., Hu, S. and Park-Gaghan, T.J. (2019) 'Big Qual: defining and debating qualitative inquiry for large data sets', *International Journal of Qualitative Methods*, 18, https://doi.org/10.1177/1609406919880692

Buchanan, M. (2018) 'Poverty causing "misery" in UK, and ministers are in denial, says UN official', BBC News, 16 November, https://www.bbc.co.uk/news/uk-46236642 [Accessed 4 October 2021].

Burchardt, T. (2009) 'Inequalities and social security', in J. Millar (ed) *Understanding Social Security: Issues for policy and practice*, 2nd Edition, Bristol: Policy Press, 31–54.

Burchardt, T. and Asghar, Z. (2008) 'Time and money', in J. Strelitz and R. Lister (eds) *Why Money Matters: Family income, poverty and children's lives*, London: Save the Children Fund, 96–106.

Cain, R. (2016) 'Responsibilising recovery: lone and low-paid parents, Universal Credit and the gendered contradictions of UK welfare reform', *British Politics*, 11(4): 488–507.

Campbell, M. (2003) 'Dorothy Smith and knowing the world we live in', *Journal of Sociology and Social Welfare*, 30(1): 3–22.

Campbell, M. (2020) 'Capping motherhood: an equality-based analysis of the UK Benefit Cap Cases ', in M.F. Davis, M. Kjaerum and A. Lyons (eds) *Research Handbook on Poverty and Human Rights*.

The Care Collective (2020) *The Care Manifesto*, London: Verso.

Carling, A.H., Duncan, S. and Edwards, R. (eds) (2002) *Analysing Families: Morality and rationality in policy and practice*, London: Routledge.

Carter, E. and Whitworth, A. (2015) 'Creaming and parking in quasi-marketised welfare-to-work schemes: designed out of or designed in to the UK Work Programme?', *Journal of Social Policy*, 44(02): 277–296.

Caswell, D. and Høybye-Mortensen, M. (2015) 'Responses from the frontline: how organisations and street-level bureaucrats deal with economic sanctions', *European Journal of Social Security*, 17(1): 31–51.

Caswell, D. and Larsen, F. (2017) 'Frontline work in the delivery of Danish activation policies', in R. van Berkel, D. Caswell, P. Kupka and F. Larsen (eds) *Frontline Delivery of Welfare-to-work Policies in Europe: Activating the unemployed*, New York, NY: Routledge, 163–181.

Change (2020) 'Iain Duncan-Smith should not receive a Knighthood', https://www.change.org/p/uk-government-and-parliament-we-object-to-iain-duncan-smith-receiving-a-knighthood [Accessed 12 May 2023].

Cheetham, M., Moffatt, S., Addison, M. and Wiseman, A. (2019) 'Impact of Universal Credit in North East England: a qualitative study of claimants and support staff', *British Medical Journal Open*, 9(7): dx.doi.org/10.1136/bmjopen-2019–029611.

Chzhen, Y. and Bradshaw, J. (2012) 'Lone parents, poverty and policy in the European Union', *Journal of European Social Policy*, 22(5): 487–506.

Ciccia, R. and Sainsbury, D. (2018) 'Gendering welfare state analysis: tensions between care and paid work', *European Journal of Politics and Gender*, 1(1–2): 93–109.

Ciminelli, G., Schwellnus, C. and Stadler, B. (2021) 'Sticky floors or glass ceilings? The role of human capital, working time flexibility and discrimination in the gender wage gap', OECD Economics Department Working Papers, No. 1668, Paris: OECD Publishing, https://doi.org/10.1787/02ef3235-en [Accessed 5 January 2022].

Clasen, J. (2011) 'The United Kingdom: towards a single working-age benefit system', in J. Clasen and D. Clegg (eds) *Regulating the Risk of Unemployment*, Oxford: Oxford University Press.

Clasen, J. and Clegg, D. (2007) 'Levels and levers of conditionality – measuring change in mature welfare states', in J. Clasen and N.A. Siegel (eds) *Investigating Welfare State Change: The dependent variable problem in comparative analysis*, Cheltenham: Edward Elgar, 166–197.

Clasen, J. and Clegg, D. (2011) 'Unemployment protection and labour market change in Europe: towards 'triple integration', in J. Clasen and D. Clegg (eds) *Regulating the Risk of Unemployment*, Oxford: Oxford University Press.

Coffey, C., Espinoza Revollo, P., Harvey, R., Lawson, M., Butt, A., Piaget, K. et al (2020) *Time to Care*, Oxford: Oxfam.

Coleman, L., Dali-Chaouch, M. and Harding, C. (2020) *Childcare Survey 2020*, London: Coram, https://www.familyandchildcaretrust.org/sites/default/files/Resource%20Library/Coram%20Childcare%20Survey%202020_240220.pdf [Accessed 7 July 2021].

Connolly, K., Eiser, D., Kumar, A., McGregor, P.G. and Roy, G. (2022) 'Universal Basic Income as an instrument of regional development policy: a micro-macro economic analysis for Scotland', *Regional Studies*, 56(6): 1043–1055.

Considine, M., Lewis, J., O'Sullivan, S. and Sol, E. (2015) *Getting Welfare to Work: Street-level governance in Australia, the UK, and the Netherlands*, Oxford: Oxford University Press.

Crenshaw, K. (1989) 'Demarginalizing the intersection of race and sex: a black feminist critique of antidiscrimination doctrine, feminist theory and antiracist politics', *University of Chicago Legal Forum*, 1(8): 139–167, https://chicagounbound.uchicago.edu/uclf/vol1989/iss1/8 [Accessed 10 August 2021].

Criado-Perez, C. (2019) *Invisible Women: Data bias in a world designed for men*, New York, NY: Abrams Press.

Crompton, R. (1998) 'Women's employment and state policies', *Innovation: The European Journal of Social Science Research*, 11(2): 129–146.

Crompton, R. and Harris, F. (1998) 'Gender relations and employment: the impact of occupation', *Work, Employment and Society*, 12: 297–315.

Dale, J. and Foster, P. (2012) *Feminists and State Welfare*, London: Routledge.

Daly, M. (2010) 'Families versus State and Market', in F.G. Castles, S. Leibfried, J. Lewis, H. Obinger and C. Pierson, C. (eds) *The Oxford Handbook of The Welfare State*, Oxford: Oxford University Press, 170–182.

Daly, M. and Rake, C. (2003) *Gender and the Welfare State,* Cambridge: Polity.

Davey, C. and Hirsch, D. (2011) 'Childcare in Universal Credit: will work pay for single parents?', *Journal of Poverty and Social Justice*, 19(3): 289–294.

Davies, L. (2015) 'Nudged into employment: lone parents and welfare reform', in M. Harrison and T. Sanders (eds) *Social Policies and Social Control*, Bristol: Policy Press, 151–166.

Davies, L. (2012) 'Lone parents: unemployed or otherwise engaged?', *People, Place & Policy*, 6(1): 16–28.

Davis, M. (2012) 'Women at work', http://www.unionhistory.info/britainatwork/narrativedisplay.php?type=womenatwork [Accessed 8 June 2020].

De Henau, J. (2017) *Austerity is Reducing Social Security for Women*, London: Women's Budget Group, https://wbg.org.uk/wp-content/uploads/2017/11/soc-security-pre-budget-nov-2017-final.pdf [Accessed 22 July 2021].

Department for Education (2019) *30 Hours Free Childcare, England, Summer Term 2019*, London: The Stationery Office, https://assets.publishing.serv ice.gov.uk/government/uploads/system/uploads/attachment_data/ file/ 808862/30_hours_free_childcare_summer_term_2019_Main_Text.pdf [Accessed 22 May 2023].

Department for Work and Pensions (DWP) (2010a) *21st Century Welfare*, London: The Stationery Office.

DWP (2010b) *Universal Credit: Welfare that works,* London: HMSO.

DWP (2011a) *Conditionality Measures in the 2011 Welfare Reform Bill: Impact Assessment,* https://www.parliament.uk/documents/impact-assessments/ IA11-022AI.pdf [Accessed 20 September 2018].

DWP (2011b) *Conditionality, Sanctions and Hardship: Equality impact assessment,* London: DWP, https://assets.publishing.service.gov.uk/government/uplo ads/system/uploads/attachment_data/file/220160/eia-conditionality-wr2 011.pdf [Accessed 12 November 2021].

DWP (2012) *Universal Credit: Impact assessment,* London: DWP.

DWP (2013) *The Disability and Health Employment Strategy: The discussion so far,* London: The Stationery Office.

DWP (2014) 'Universal Credit: increasing the childcare offer', https:// assets.publishing.service.gov.uk/government/uploads/system/uploads/ attachment_data/file/384090/uc-increasing-the-childcare-offer.pdf [Accessed 26 July 2021].

DWP (2015) *Welfare Reform and Work Bill: Impact assessment of the change in conditionality for responsible carers on Universal Credit,* London: DWP.

DWP (2017) 'Lone parent employment rate highest on record', https:// www.gov.uk/government/news/lone-parent-employment-rate-highest- on-record [Accessed 11 June 2020].

DWP/Government Social Research (2018a) *Universal Credit: In-work progression randomised controlled trial: impact assessment,* London: The Stationery Office.

DWP/Government Social Research (2018b) *Universal Credit: In-work progression randomised controlled trial: findings from quantitative survey and qualitative research,* London: The Stationery Office.

DWP (2019) [Withdrawn] *Universal Support 2018/19 Guidance,* https:// www.gov.uk/government/publications/universal-credit-universal-supp ort-201819-guidance/universal-support-201819-guidance [Accessed 18 August 2021].

DWP (2020a) 'Child Tax Credit: exceptions to the 2 Child Limit', https:// www.gov.uk/guidance/child-tax-credit-exceptions-to-the-2-child-limit [Accessed 17 August 2021].

DWP (2020b) 'Permitted work: factsheet', https://www.gov.uk/governm ent/publications/employment-and-support-allowance-permitted-work- form/permitted-work-factsheet [Accessed 15 December 2021].

DWP (2021a) *State Pension Age Timetables*, https://assets.publishing.service. gov.uk/government/uploads/system/uploads/attachment_data/file/310 231/spa-timetable.pdf [Accessed 14 July 2021].

DWP (2021b) 'Universal Credit', https://www.gov.uk/universal-credit/ what-youll-get [Accessed 26 July 2021].

DWP (2021c) 'Universal Credit: support for a maximum of 2 children: information for claimants', https://www.gov.uk/guidance/universal-credit-and-families-with-more-than-2-children-information-for-claimants [Accessed 17 August 2021].

DWP (2021d) 'Universal Credit statistics: background information and methodology', https://www.gov.uk/government/publications/univer sal-credit-statistics-background-information-and-methodology/universal-credit-statistics-background-information-and-methodology#background-information [Accessed 4 October 2021].

DWP (2021e) 'Universal Credit statistics, 29 April 2013 to 8 July 2021', https://www.gov.uk/government/statistics/universal-credit-statistics-29-april-2013-to-8-july-2021/universal-credit-statistics-29-april-2013-to-8-july-2021 [Accessed 4 October 2021].

DWP (2021f) 'Spotlight on Sanctions Assurance Framework', https://www. whatdotheyknow.com/request/covid19_benefit_sanctions_and_co#incom ing-1684665 [Accessed 24 November 2021].

DWP (2021g) 'Universal Credit by Gender', https://stat-xplore.dwp.gov. uk/webapi/jsf/tableView/tableView.xhtml [Accessed 1 May 2021].

DWP/Government Social Research (2018) *Universal Credit: In-work progression randomised controlled trial – findings from quantitative survey and qualitative research*, London: The Stationery Office.

Devine, B.F. and Foley, N. (2020) *Women and the Economy*, London: House of Commons Library.

Dingeldey, I. (2007) 'Between workfare and enablement – the different paths to transformation of the welfare state: a comparative analysis of activating labour market policies', *European Journal of Political Research*, 46(6): 823–885.

Dubois, V. (2009) 'Towards a critical policy ethnography: lessons from fieldwork on welfare control in France', *Critical Policy Studies*, 3(2): 221–239.

Dubois, V. (2012) *The Bureaucrat and the Poor: Encounters in French welfare offices*, Farnham: Ashgate.

Duncan, S. and Edwards, R. (1999) *Lone Parents, Paid Work and Gendered Moral Rationalities*, Basingstoke: Palgrave Macmillan.

Dwyer, P. (2004) 'Creeping conditionality in the UK: from welfare rights to conditional entitlements?', *Canadian Journal of Sociology*, 29(2): 265–287.

Dwyer, P. (2018) 'Punitive and ineffective: benefit sanctions within social security', *Journal of Social Security Law*, 25(3): 142–157.

Dwyer, P. (ed) (2019) *Dealing with Welfare Conditionality: Implementation and effects*, Bristol: The Policy Press.

Dwyer, P. and Wright, S. (2014) 'Universal Credit, ubiquitous conditionality and its implications for social citizenship', *Journal of Poverty and Social Justice*, 22(1): 27–35.

Dwyer, P. and Wright, S. (2020) 'In-work Universal Credit: claimant experiences of conditionality mismatches and counterproductive benefit sanctions', *Journal of Social Policy*, 1(19): doi: 10.1017/S0047279420000562

Dwyer, P.J., Scullion, L., Jones, K., McNeill, J.M. and Stewart, A.B.R. (2020) 'Work, welfare and wellbeing? The impacts of welfare conditionality on people with mental health impairments in the UK', *Social Policy and Administration*, 54(2): 311–326.

Economic Affairs Committee (2020) *Universal Credit Isn't Working: Proposals for reform*, London: House of Lords.

Edmiston, D. (2020) *Welfare, Inequality and Social Citizenship: Deprivation and affluence in austerity Britain*, Bristol: Policy Press.

Edwards, R. and Duncan, S. (1997) 'Supporting the family: lone mothers, paid work and the underclass debate', *Critical Social Policy*, 17(4): 29–49.

Eichhorst, W., Kaufmann, O., Konle-Seidl, R. and Reinhard, H.J. (2008) 'Bringing the jobless into work? An introduction to activation policies', in W. Eichhorst, O. Kaufmann and R. Konle-Seidl (eds) *Bringing the Jobless Into Work?*, Berlin: Springer, 1–16.

Eleveld, A. (2017) 'The sanctions mitigation paradox in welfare to work benefit schemes', *Comparative Labour Law and Policy Journal*, 39: 449.

Elson, D. (2000) *Progress of the World's Women 2000*, UNIFEM Biennial Report, United Nations Development Fund for Women, New York, NY.

Elson, D. (2012) 'The reduction of the UK budget deficit: a human rights perspective', *International Review of Applied Economics*, 26(2): 177–190.

Equality and Human Rights Commission (2018) 'Employers in the dark ages over recruitment of pregnant women and new mothers', 19 February, https://www.equalityhumanrights.com/en/our-work/news/employ ers-dark-ages-over-recruitment-pregnant-women-and-new-mothers [Accessed 7 July 2021].

Esping-Andersen, G. (1990) *The Three Worlds of Welfare Capitalism*, Cambridge: Polity Press.

Etherington, D. (2020) *Austerity, Welfare and Work: Exploring politics, geographies and inequalities*, Bristol: Policy Press.

European Institute for Gender Equality (2021) 'Women's triple role', https:// eige.europa.eu/thesaurus/terms/1442 [Accessed 6 July 2021].

Eurofound (2014) *Work Preferences After 50*, Luxembourg: Publications Office of the European Union, https://www.eurofound.europa.eu/sites/ default/files/ef_files/pubdocs/2014/03/en/1/EF1403EN.pdf [Accessed 22 May 2023].

Eurofound (2021) 'Non-standard employment', https://www.eurofound. europa.eu/topic/non-standard-employment [Accessed 5 August 2021].

European Union (2016) *Report on Equality between Men and Women, 2015*, Luxembourg: European Union.

European Union (2018) *The Future of Work: Implications and responses by the PES Network*, Luxembourg: European Union.

Evans, M., Eyre, J., Millar, J. and Sarre, S. (2003) *New Deal for Lone Parents: Second synthesis report of the National Evaluation*, London: DWP.

Evans, T. (2010) 'Professionals, managers and discretion: critiquing street-level bureaucracy', *The British Journal of Social Work*, 41(2): 368–386.

Fawcett Society (2020) 'Ensure women are not hardest hit by economic downturn', https://www.fawcettsociety.org.uk/ensure-women-not-hard est-hit-economic-downturn [Accessed 22 July 2021].

Ferrant, G., Pesando, L.M. and Nowacka, K. (2014) *Unpaid Care Work: The missing link in the analysis of gender gaps in labour outcomes*, Paris: OECD Development Centre.

Finch, D. (2015) *Making the Most of UC: Final report of the Resolution Foundation review of Universal Credit*, London: Resolution Foundation.

Finch, J. (1989) *Family Obligations and Social Change*, Cambridge: Polity Press.

Finch, J. and Mason, J. (1993) *Negotiating Family Responsibilities*, London: Routledge.

Finch, N. (2006) 'Gender equity and time use: how do mothers and fathers spend their time?', in J. Bradshaw and A. Hatland (eds) *Social Policy, Employment and Family Change in Comparative Perspective*, Cheltenham: Edward Elgar, 255–82.

Finn, D. and Casebourne, J. (2012) *Lone Parent Sanctions: A review of international evidence*, London: Centre for Economic and Social Inclusion.

Finn, D. and Gloster, R. (2010) *Lone Parent Obligations: A review of recent evidence on the work related requirements within the benefit systems of different countries*, London: DWP.

Fisher, L. and Embree, L. (eds) (2000) *Feminist Phenomenology*, Dordrecht: Kluwer.

Fitzpatrick, C. and Chapman, A. (2021) 'From Working Tax Credit to Universal Credit: is the older workforce ready? Perspectives from employees and employers in Northern Ireland', *Journal of Poverty and Social Justice*, online: 1–19, https://doi.org/10.1332/175982721X16231309013027.

Flemmen, M.P., Toft, M., Andersen, P.L., Hansen, M.N. and Ljunggren, J. (2017) 'Forms of capital and modes of closure in upper class reproduction', *Sociology*, 51(6): 1277–1298.

Fletcher, D. (2011) 'Welfare reform, Jobcentre Plus and the street-level bureaucracy: towards inconsistent and discriminatory welfare for severely disadvantaged groups?', *Social Policy and Society*, 10(4): 445–458.

Fletcher, D.R. and Wright, S. (2018) A hand up or a slap down? Criminalising benefit claimants in Britain via strategies of surveillance, sanctions and deterrence, *Critical Social Policy*, 38(2): 323–344.

Flint, J. (2019) 'Encounters with the centaur state: advanced urban marginality and the practices and ethics of welfare sanctions regimes', *Urban Studies*, 56(1): 249–265.

Fraser, D. (2009) *The Evolution of the British Welfare State: A history of social policy since the Industrial Revolution*, Fourth Edition, London: Palgrave.

Fraser, N. (2009) *Scales of Justice*, London: Blackwell.

Frayne, D. (2015) *The Refusal of Work: The theory and practice of resistance to work*, London: Zed Books.

Friedli, L. and Stearn, R. (2015) 'Positive affect as coercive strategy: conditionality, activation and the role of psychology in UK government workfare programmes', *Medical Humanities*, 41(1): 40–47.

Friedman, S. and Laurison, D. (2020) *The Class Ceiling*, Bristol: Policy Press.

Fuertes, V. and Lindsay, C. (2016) 'Personalization and street-level practice in activation: the case of the UK's Work Programme', *Public Administration*, 94(2): 526–541.

Garnham, A. (2018) 'Something needs saying about Universal Credit and women – it is discrimination by design', London: Child Poverty Action Group, https://cpag.org.uk/news-blogs/news-listings/something-needs-saying-about-universal-credit-and-women-%E2%80%93-it-discrimination [Accessed 12 December 2022].

Garthwaite, K. (2011) 'The language of shirkers and scroungers? Talking about illness, disability and coalition welfare reform', *Disability & Society*, 26(3): 369–372.

Garthwaite, K. (2014) 'Fear of the brown envelope: exploring welfare reform with long-term sickness benefits recipients', *Social Policy & Administration*, 48(7): 782–798.

Garthwaite, K., Patrick, R., Power, M., Tarrant, A. and Warnock, R. (2022) *COVID-19 Collaborations Researching Poverty and Low-Income Family Life During the Pandemic*, Bristol: Policy Press.

Government Equalities Office (2019) *Gender Equality Monitor*, London: Government Equalities Office.

GOV.UK (2023) 'Dismissal: your rights', https://www.gov.uk/dismissal/unfair-and-constructive-dismissal [Accessed 7 February 2023].

Gautié, J. and Schmitt, J. (2010) *Low Wage Work in a Wealthy World*, New York, NY: Russell Sage Foundation.

Gerodetti, N. and McNaught-Davis, M. (2017) 'Feminisation of success or successful femininities? Disentangling "new femininities" under neoliberal conditions', *European Journal of Women's Studies*, 24(4): 351–365.

Gilligan, C. (1982) *In a Different Voice*, Cambridge, MA: Harvard University Press.

Ginsburg, N. (1992) *Divisions of Welfare: A critical introduction to comparative social policy*, London: Sage.

Ghelani, D. and Stidle, L. (2014) *Universal Credit: Towards an effective poverty strategy*, *Policy in Practice*, https://policyinpractice.co.uk/wp-content/uploads/2014/09/Universal-Credit-A-Review-by-Policy-in-Practice.pdf [Accessed 22 May 2023].

Glaser, K., Price, D., Montserrat, E.R., di Gessa, G. and Tinker, A. (2013) *Grandparenting in Europe: Family policy and grandparents' role in providing childcare*, London: Grandparenting Plus, https://kinship.org.uk/wp-content/uploads/2020/02/Grandparenting-in-Europe-0313.pdf [Accessed 29 July 2021].

Goode, J., Callender, C. and Lister, R. (1998) *Purse or Wallet?: Gender inequalities and income distribution within families on benefit*, London: Policy Studies Institute.

Goodman, J. (2010) *Global Perspectives on Gender and Work: Readings and interpretations*, Lanham, MD: Rowman and Littlefield.

Goodwin, V. (2008) *The Effects of Sanctions on Lone Parents' Employment Decisions and Moves into Employment. Research report no. 511*, London: DWP.

Goos, M. and Manning, A. (2007) 'Lousy and lovely jobs: the rising polarization of work in Britain', *The Review of Economics and Statistics*, 89(1): 118–133.

Gordon, E. (1987) 'Women, work and collective action: Dundee jute workers 1870–1906', *Journal of Social History*, Autumn, 21(1): 27–47.

Gov.uk (2022) 'Gender Pay Gap Service', https://gender-pay-gap.service.gov.uk/ [Accessed 25 February 2023].

Graham, H. (1991) 'The concept of caring in feminist research: the case of domestic service', *Sociology*, 25(1): 61–78.

Graham, H. and McQuaid, R. (2014) *Exploring the Impacts of the UK Government's Welfare Reforms on Lone Parents Moving into Work: Literature review*, Edinburgh/Stirling: Employment Research Institute/University of Stirling.

Grandia, J., La Grouw, Y. and Kruyen, P. (2019) 'Motivating the unemployed: a full-range model of motivational strategies that caseworkers use to activate clients', *Social Policy & Administration*, https://doi.org/10.1111/spol.12540.

Green, F. and Kynaston, D. (2019) *Engines of Privilege: Britain's private school problem*, London: Bloomsbury Publishing.

Green, M. and Rossall, P. (2013) *Digital Inclusion Evidence Review*, London: AgeUK.

Greer, I. (2016) 'Welfare reform, precarity and the re-commodification of labour', *Work, Employment and Society*, 30(1): 162–173.

Griffith, A. and Smith, D.E. (eds) (2014a) *Under New Public Management: Institutional ethnographies of changing front-line work*, Toronto: University of Toronto Press.

Griffith, A. and Smith, D.E. (2014b) 'Introduction', in A. Griffith and D.E. Smith (eds) *Under New Public Management: Institutional ethnographies of changing front-line work*, Toronto: University of Toronto Press, 3–23.

Griffiths, R., Wood, M., Bennett, F. and Millar, J. (2020) *Uncharted Territory: Universal credit, couples and money*, Bath: Institute for Policy Research/University of Bath.

Griffiths, R., Wood, M., Bennett, F. and Millar, J. (2022) *Couples Navigating Work, Care and Universal Credit*, Bath: Institute for Policy Research/University of Bath.

Grover, C. (2018) 'Violent proletarianisation: social murder, the reserve army of labour and social security "austerity" in Britain', *Critical Social Policy*, 39(3): 1–21.

Gulland, J. (2019a) *Gender, Work and Social Control: A century of disability benefits*, London: Palgrave Macmillan.

Gulland, J. (2019b) 'Conditionality in social security: lessons from the household duties test', *Journal of Social Security Law*, 26(2): 62–78.

Hagelund, A. (2016) 'The activating profession: coaching and coercing in the welfare state', *International Journal of Public Sector Management*, 29(7): 725–739.

Hakim, C. (2000) *Work–Lifestyle Choices in the 21st Century: Preference theory*, Oxford: Oxford University Press.

Hakim, C. (2006) 'Women, careers, and work–life preferences', *British Journal of Guidance & Counselling*, 34: 279–94.

Hall, P. (1993) 'Policy paradigms, social learning and the state: the case of economic policymaking in Britain', *Comparative Politics*, 25(3): 275–96.

Hällsten, M. (2013) 'The class-origin wage gap: heterogeneity in education and variations across market segments', *The British Journal of Sociology*, 64(4): 662–690.

Hanlon, N. (2012) *Masculinities, Care and Equality: Identity and nurture in men's lives*, London: Palgrave Macmillan.

Harari, D., Francis-Devine, B., Bolton, P. and Keep, M. (2022) *Rising Cost of Living in the UK*, London: House of Commons Library.

Hardie, I. (2021) 'The impact of Universal Credit rollout on housing security: an analysis of landlord repossession rates in English local authorities', *Journal of Social Policy*, 50(2): 225–246.

Harding, S. (2020) *The Impact of Universal Credit on Women*, Belfast: Women's Regional Consortium.

Hasenfeld, Y. (2010) 'Organizational responses to social policy: the case of welfare reform', *Administration in Social Work*, 34(2): 148–167.

Haux, T. (2012) 'Activating lone parents: an evidence-based policy appraisal of the 2008 welfare-to-work reform in Britain', *Social Policy and Society*, 11(1): 1–14.

Heaton, J. (2004) *Reworking Qualitative Data*, London: Sage.

Hebson, G., Rubery, J. and Grimshaw, D. (2015) 'Rethinking job satisfaction in care work: looking beyond the care debates', *Work, Employment and Society*, 29(2): 314–330.

Heinämaa, S. and Rodemeyer, L. (2010) 'Introduction to special issue on feminist phenomenologies', *Continental Philosophy Review*, 43(1): 1–11.

Held, V. (2006) *The Ethics of Care: Personal, political, and global*, Oxford: Oxford University Press.

Hills, J. (2017) *Good Times, Bad Times: The welfare myth of them and us*, Bristol: Policy Press.

Himmelweit, S. and Plomien, A. (2014) 'Feminist perspectives on care: theory, practice and policy', in M. Evans, C. Hemmings, M. Henry, H. Johstone, S. Madhok, A. Plomien et al (eds) *The Sage Handbook of Feminist Theory*, London: Sage.

Hines, S. (2006) 'What's the difference? Bringing particularity to queer studies of transgender', *Journal of Gender Studies*, 15(1): 49–66.

Hirsch, D. (2015) *Paying the Price: Childcare in universal credit and implications for single parents*, Loughborough: Loughborough University.

Hobson, F. (2020) *The Aims of Ten Years of Welfare Reform (2010–2020)*, London: House of Commons Library, https://researchbriefings.files.parliament.uk/documents/CBP-9090/CBP-9090.pdf [Accessed 21 December 2021].

House of Commons (2004) *Work and Pensions Committee: Second report, 2003–4*, https://publications.parliament.uk/pa/cm200304/cmselect/cmworpen/85/8502.htm [Accessed 11 June 2020].

House of Commons Work and Pensions Committee (2018) *Universal Credit and Domestic Abuse*, London: House of Commons, https://publications.parliament.uk/pa/cm201719/cmselect/cmworpen/1166/1166.pdf [Accessed 18 August 2021].

Howard, J.A., Risman, B. and Sprague, J. (2005) 'Series editors' foreword', in D.E. Smith (ed) (2005) *Institutional Ethnography: A sociology for people*, Toronto: Altamira Press, ix–xii.

Howard, M. (2018) *Universal Credit and Financial Abuse: Exploring the links*, London: Women's Budget Group, https://wbg.org.uk/wp-content/uploads/2018/09/FINAL-exec-summary-financial-abuse-and-UC.pdf [Accessed 18 August 2021].

Howard, M. and Bennett, F. (2020) 'Payment of Universal Credit for couples in the UK: challenges for reform from a gender perspective', *International Social Security Review*, 73(4): 75–96.

Howard, M. and Skipp, A. (2018) *Unequal, trapped and controlled*, 2015; Letter to the Chair of Work and Pensions Select Committee from PCS regarding Universal Credit and Domestic Abuse, 14 May 2018, Women's Aid and TUC.

Hupe, P., Hill, M. and Buffat, A. (eds) (2015) *Understanding Street-Level Bureaucracy*, Bristol: Policy Press.

Immervoll, H. and Knotz, C. (2018) 'How demanding are activation requirements for jobseekers?', *OECD Social, Employment and Migration working Papers*, 215, Paris: OECD.

Independent Schools Council (2019) *ISC Census and Annual Report, 2019*, London: ISC, https://www.isc.co.uk/media/5479/isc_census_2019_report.pdf [Accessed 23 November 2021].

Ingold, J. (2018) 'Employer engagement in active labour market programmes: the role of boundary spanners', *Public Administration*, 96: 707–720.

Ingold, J. and Etherington, D. (2013) 'Work, welfare and gender inequalities: an analysis of activation strategies for partnered women in the UK, Australia and Denmark', *Work, Employment and Society*, 27(4): 621–638.

Jacobsson, K., Wallinder, Y., Seing, I. (2020) 'Street-level bureaucrats under new managerialism: a comparative study of agency cultures and caseworker role identities in two welfare state bureaucracies', *Journal of Professions and Organization*, 10(1093): 316–333.

Jensen, T. and Tyler, I. (2015) '"Benefits broods": the cultural and political crafting of anti-welfare commonsense', *Critical Social Policy*, 35(4): 470– 491.

Johnsen, S. (2014) *Conditionality Briefing: Lone parents*, York: University of York, http://www.welfareconditionality.ac.uk/wp-content/uploads/2014/09/Briefing_LoneParents_14.09.10_FINAL.pdf [Accessed 22 May 2023].

Johnsen, S. (2016) *First Wave Findings: Lone parents*, York: University of York, http://www.welfareconditionality.ac.uk/wp-content/uploads/2016/05/WelCond-findings-lone-parents-May16.pdf [Accessed 22 May 2023].

Johnsen, S. and Blenkinsopp, J. (2018) *Final Findings: Lone parents*, http://www.welfareconditionality.ac.uk/wp-content/uploads/2018/05/39273-Lone-parents-web.pdf [Accessed 7 July 2023].

Johnson Dias, J. and Maynard-Moody, S. (2007) 'For-profit welfare: contracts, conflicts, and the performance paradox', *Journal of Public Administration Research and Theory*, 17(2): 189–211.

Jones, C. and Novak, T. (1999) *Poverty, Welfare and the Disciplinary State*, London: Routledge.

Jones, O. (2015) *The Establishment: And how they get away with it*, London: Penguin.

Joseph Rowntree Foundation (2017) *UK Poverty 2017: A comprehensive analysis of poverty trends and figures*, York: Joseph Rowntree Foundation.

Joseph Rowntree Foundation (2018) *UK Poverty 2018: A comprehensive analysis of poverty trends and figures*, York: Joseph Rowntree Foundation.

Kaine, S. and Josserand, E. (2019) 'The organisation and experience of work in the gig economy', *Journal of Industrial Relations*, 61(4): 479–501.

Kaufman, J. (2020) 'Intensity, moderation, and the pressures of expectation: calculation and coercion in the street-level practice of welfare conditionality', *Social Policy and Administration*, 54(2): 205–218.

Kennedy, S. and Keen, R. (2018) *Universal Credit Roll-Out: 2018–19*, London: House of Commons Library.

Kessler, S. (2018) *Gigged: The gig economy, the end of the job and the future of work*, London: Random House.

King, B. (2020) 'Make all schools coeducational by law, including Eton', *The Times*, https://www.thetimes.co.uk/article/make-all-schools-coeducational-by-law-including-eton-0jmgz8wx9 [Accessed 23 November 2021].

Kingfisher, C. (1996) *Women in the American Welfare Trap*, Philadelphia, PA: University of Pennsylvania Press.

Klein, E. (2021) 'Unpaid care, welfare conditionality and expropriation', *Gender, Work and Organization*, 28: 1475–1489.

Knijn, T. and Kremer, M. (1997) 'Gender and the caring dimension of welfare states: toward inclusive ctizenship', *Social Politics: International Studies in Gender, State and Society*, 4(3): 328–361.

Knotz, C.M. (2018) 'A rising workfare state? Unemployment benefit conditionality in 21 OECD countries, 1980–2012', *Journal of International and Comparative Social Policy*, 34(2): 91–108.

Kowalewska, H. (2017) 'Beyond the "train-first"/"work-first" dichotomy: how welfare states help or hinder maternal employment', *Journal of European Social Policy*, 27(1): 3–24.

Knijn, T. and Lepianka, D. (eds) (2020) *Justice and Vulnerability in Europe: An interdisciplinary approach*, Cheltenham: Edward Elgar.

Kruks, S. (2001) *Retrieving Experiences: Subjectivity and recognition in feminist politics*, Ithaca, NY: Cornell University Press.

Kruks, S. (2014) 'Women's "lived experience": feminism and phenomenology from Simone de Beauvoir to the present', in M. Evans, C. Hemmings, M. Henry, H. Johnstone, S. Madhok, A. Plomien et al (eds) *The Sage Handbook of Feminist Theory*, London: Sage, 75–92.

Lakhani, B. (2009) 'Lone parents: the move from IS to JSA', *Welfare Rights Bulletin*, Issue 208 (February) London: CPAG, https://cpag.org.uk/welfare-rights/resources/article/lone-parents-move-jsa [Accessed 6 January 2023].

Lalive, R., Zweimuller, J. and van Ours, J. C. (2005) 'The effect of benefit sanctions on the duration of unemployment', *Journal of the European Economic Association*, 3(6): 1386–1417.

Lens, V. (2008) 'Welfare and work sanctions: examining discretion on the front lines', *Social Service Review*, 82(2): 197–222.

Larsen, F. and Wright, S. (2014) 'Interpreting the marketisation of employment services in Great Britain and Denmark', *Journal of European Social Policy*, 24(5): 455–469.

Lepianka, D. and Knijn, T. (2020) 'Introduction', in T. Knijn and D. Lepianka (eds) *Justice and Vulnerability in Europe: An interdisciplinary approach*, Cheltenham: Edward Elgar.

Levin, P. (1997) *Making Public Policy*, Milton Keynes: Open University Press.

Lewenhak, S. (1980) *Women and Work*, Glasgow: Fontana Paperbacks.

Lewis, J. (1992) 'Gender and the development of welfare regimes', *Journal of European Policy*, 2(3): 159–173.

Lewis, J. (1994) 'Gender, the family and women's agency in the building of "welfare states": the British case', *Social History*, 19(1): 37–55.

Lewis, J. (1998) '"Work", "welfare" and lone mothers', *Political Quarterly*, 69(1): 4–13.

Lewis, J. (2001) 'The decline of the male breadwinner model: implications for work and care', *Social Politics: International Studies in Gender, State & Society*, 8(2): 152–169.

Lewis, J. (2002) 'Gender and welfare state change', *European Societies*, 4(4): 331–357.

Lewis, J. (2006) 'Men, women, work, care and policies', *Journal of European Social Policy*, 16(4): 387–392.

Lewis, J. (2009) *Work-Family Balance, Gender and Policy*, Cheltenham: Edward Elgar.

Lewis, J. and Giullari, S. (2005) 'The adult worker model family, gender equality and care: the search for new policy principles and the possibilities and problems of a capabilities approach', *Economy and Society*, 34(1): 76–104.

Lewis, J., Campbell, M. and Huerta, C. (2008) 'Patterns of paid and unpaid work in Western Europe: gender, commodification, preferences and the implications for policy', *Journal of European Social Policy*, 18(1): 21–37.

Lindsay, C. (2007) 'The United Kingdom's "work first" welfare state and activation regimes in Europe', in A. Serrano Pascual and L. Magnusson (eds) *Reshaping Welfare States and Activation Regimes in Europe*, Brussels: Peter Lang, 35–70.

Lipsky, M. (1980/2010) *Street-Level Bureaucracy: Dilemmas of the individual in public service*, London: Russell Sage Foundation.

Lister, R. (1997) *Citizenship: Feminist perspectives*, London: Macmillan Press.

Lister, R. (2003) *Citizenship: Feminist perspectives*, 2nd Edition, Basingstoke: Palgrave Macmillan.

Lødemel, I. and Moreira, A. (2014) *Activation or Workfare? Governance and the neo-Liberal convergence*, Oxford: Oxford University Press.

Lødemel, I. and Trickey, H. (2001) *'An Offer You Can't Refuse': Workfare in international perspective*, Bristol: Policy Press.

Lorber, J. (2022) *The New Gender Paradox*, Cambridge: Polity Press.

Low Pay Commission (2020) *National Minimum Wage Report 2019*, London: The Stationery Office.

Office for National Statistics (2019) *Families and the Labour Market, UK: 2019*, https://www.ons.gov.uk/employmentandlabourmarket/peopleinwork/employmentandemployeetypes/articles/familiesandthelabourmarketengland/2019#:~:text=There%20were%201.8%20million%20lone,to%2018%2Dyear%2Dolds [Accessed 11 June 2020].

Machin, R. (2017) 'The professional and ethical dilemmas of the two-child limit for Child Tax Credit and Universal Credit', *Ethics and Social Welfare*, 11(4): 404–411.

Mackley, A., Foster, D., Gheera, M., Keen, R., Kennedy, S. and Wilson, W. (2018) *Effect of Welfare Reform and Work Act 2016*, London: House of Commons Library, https://commonslibrary.parliament.uk/research-briefings/cdp-2018–0072/ [Accessed 21 December 2021].

MacLeavy, J. (2011) 'A new politics of austerity, workfare and gender? The UK coalition government's welfare reform proposals', *Cambridge Journal of Regions, Economy and Society*, 4(3): 355–367.

Main, G. and Bradshaw, J. (2016) 'Child poverty in the UK: measures, prevalence and intra-household sharing', *Critical Social Policy*, 36 (1): 38–61.

Mandel, H. and Shalev, M. (2009) 'How welfare states shape the gender pay gap: a theoretical and comparative analysis', *Social Forces*, 87(4): 1873–1911.

Marston, G., Larsen, J. and McDonald, C. (2005) 'The active subjects of welfare reform: a street-level comparison of employment services in Australia and Denmark', *Social Work & Society*, 3(2): 141–158.

Matarese, M. and Caswell, D. (2017) '"I'm gonna ask you about yourself so I can put it on paper": analysing street level bureaucracy through form-related talk in social work', *British Journal of Social Work*, 48(3): 714–733.

Mathiesen, T. (2004) *Silently Silenced: Essays on the creation of acquiescence in modern society*, Winchester: Waterside Press.

Maynard-Moody, S.W. and Musheno, M.C. (2003) *Cops, Teachers, Counselors: Stories from the front lines of public service*, Ann Arbor, MI: University of Michigan Press.

McCann, P. and Vorley, T. (eds) (2020) *Productivity Perspectives*, Cheltenham: Edward Elgar Publishing.

McCarthy, H. (2021) *Double Lives: A history of working motherhood*, London: Bloomsbury.

McDonald, C. and Marston, G. (2006) 'Room to move? Professional discretion at the frontline of welfare-to-work', *Australian Journal of Social Issues*, 41(2): 171–182.

McIntosh, I. and Wright, S. (2019) 'Exploring what the notion of lived experience might offer for social policy analysis', *Journal of Social Policy*, 48(3): 449–467.

McNeil, C. and Parkes, H. with Garthwaite, K. and Patrick, R. (2021) *No Longer 'Managing': The rise of working poverty and fixing Britain's broken social settlement*, London: IPPR.

McNeill, F. (2020) 'Penal and welfare conditionality: discipline or degradation?' *Social Policy and Administration*, 54(2): 295–310.

McQuaid, R.W. and Lindsay, C. (2005) 'The concept of employability', *Urban Studies*, 42(2): 197–219.

McRae, S. (2003) 'Constraints and choices in mothers' employment careers: a consideration of Hakim's Preference Theory', *British Journal of Sociology*, 54(3): 317–338.

Meneses, M.P., Araújo, S. and Ferreira, S. (2020) 'Welfare labour and austerity: resistances and alternatives through women's gaze', in T. Knijn, and D. Lepianka (eds) *Justice and Vulnerability in Europe: An interdisciplinary approach*, Cheltenham: Edward Elgar, 178–196.

Meyers, M., Glaser, B. and Donald, K. (1998) 'On the front lines of welfare delivery: are workers implementing policy reforms?', *Journal of Policy Analysis and Management*, 17(1): 1–22.

Millar, J. (2003) 'Gender, poverty and social exclusion', *Social Policy and Society*, 2(3): 181–188.

Millar, J. (2008) 'Making work pay, making tax credits work: an assessment with specific reference to lone parent employment', *International Lone Parent Review*, 61(2): 21–38.

Millar, J. (2019) 'Self-responsibility and activation for lone mothers in the United Kingdom', *The American Behavioral Scientist*, 63(1): 85–99.

Millar, J. and Bennett, F. (2017) 'Universal Credit: assumptions, contradictions and virtual reality', *Social Policy and Society*, 16(2): 169–182.

Millar, J. and Ridge, T. (2008) 'Relationships of care: working lone mothers, their children and employment sustainability', *Journal of Social Policy*, 38(1): 103–121.

Millar, J. and Ridge, T.M. (2011) 'Lone mothers and paid work: the "family-work project"', *International Review of Sociology*, 23(3): 564–577.

Mind (2020) 'About sectioning', https://www.mind.org.uk/informat ion-support/legal-rights/sectioning/about-sectioning/ [Accessed 25 August 2020].

Monaghan, M. and Ingold, J. (2019) 'Policy practitioners' accounts of evidence-based policy making: the case of Universal Credit', *Journal of Social Policy*, 48(2): 351–368.

National Audit Office (2016) *Benefit Sanctions*, London: National Audit Office.

National Audit Office (2018) *Rolling out Universal Credit*, HC 1123, London: National Audit Office.

National Health Service (2018) 'Overview Dyslexia', https://www.nhs.uk/conditions/dyslexia/ [Accessed 13 October 2021].

National Health Service (2019a) 'Overview Fibromyalgia', https://www.nhs.uk/conditions/fibromyalgia/ [Accessed 16 August 2021].

National Health Service (2019b) 'Overview Endometriosis', https://www.nhs.uk/conditions/endometriosis/ [Accessed 11 October 2021].

National Health Service (2021) 'Dystonia', https://www.nhs.uk/conditions/dystonia/ [Accessed 8 October 2021].

Nayak, A. and Kehily, M.J. (2008) *Gender, Youth and Culture: Young masculinities and femininities,* Basingstoke: Palgrave Macmillan.

Neale, B. (2019) *What is Qualitative Longitudinal Research?,* London: Bloomsbury.

Newman, I. (2011) 'Work as a route out of poverty: a critical evaluation of the UK welfare to work policy', *Policy Studies,* 32(2): 91–108.

Newsome, K. and Vorley, T. (2020) 'Contemporary work and employment and the productivity puzzle', in P. McCann and T. Vorley (eds) *Productivity Perspectives,* Cheltenham: Edward Elgar Publishing, 224–242.

Nicolaisen, H., Kavli, H.C. and Steen Jensen, R. (eds) (2019) *Dualisation of Part-Time Work: The development of labour market insiders and outsiders,* Bristol: Policy Press.

Nicolaisen, H., Kavli, H.C. and Steen Jensen, R. (2019) 'Introduction', in H. Nicolaisen, H.C. Kavli, and R. Steen Jensen (eds) *Dualisation of Part-Time Work: The development of labour market insiders and outsiders,* Bristol: Policy Press, 1–31.

Nothdurfter, U. (2016) 'The street-level delivery of activation policies: constraints and possibilities for a practice of citizenship', *European Journal of Social Work,* 19(3): 420–440.

Oakley, M. (2014) *Independent review of the operation of jobseeker's allowance sanctions validated by the Jobseekers Act 2013,* London: Department for Work and Pensions.

O'Connor, J.S., Orloff, A.S. and Shaver, S. (1999) *States, Markets, Families: Gender, liberalism, and social policy in Australia, Canada, Great Britain, and the United States,* Cambridge: Cambridge University Press.

Organisation for Economic Cooperation and Development (OECD) (2018) *Bridging the Digital Gender Divide: Include, upskill, innovate,* Paris: OECD.

OECD (2020) *Is Childcare Affordable? Policy brief on employment, labour and social affairs,* Paris: OECD.

Ofcom (2014) *Adults' Media Use and Attitudes Report 2014,* London: Ofcom.

Ofcom (2022) *Digital exclusion: a review of Ofcom's research on digital exclusion among adults in the UK,* London: Ofcom.

Office for National Statistics (ONS) (2016a) *Families and Households 2016,* London: ONS.

ONS (2016b) 'Women shoulder the responsibility of "unpaid work"', London: Office for National Statistics, https://www.ons.gov.uk/employmentandlabourmarket/peopleinwork/earningsandworkinghours/articles/womenshouldertheresponsibilityofunpaidwork/2016-11-10 [Accessed 6 October 2021].

ONS (2021a) 'Sex and gender identity question development for Census 2021', https://www.ons.gov.uk/census/censustransformationprogramme/questiondevelopment/sexandgenderidentityquestiondevelopmentforcensus2021 [Accessed 23 August 2021].

ONS (2021b) 'Divorces in England and Wales: 2021', https://www.ons.gov.uk/peoplepopulationandcommunity/birthsdeathsandmarriages/divorce/bulletins/divorcesinenglandandwales/2021 [Accessed 28 February 2023].

ONS (2022) 'Families and the labour market, UK', https://www.ons.gov.uk/employmentandlabourmarket/peopleinwork/employmentandemployeetypes/datasets/familiesandthelabourmarketukmaindatasetusingthelabourforcesurveyandannualpopulationsurvey [Accessed 25 February 2023].

Olkowski, D. and Weiss, G. (eds) (2006) *Feminist Interpretations of Merleau-Ponty*, University Park, PA: Pennsylvania State University Press.

O'Reilly, J. and Bothfeld, S. (2002) 'What happens after working part time? Integration, maintenance or exclusionary transitions in Britain and Western Germany', *Cambridge Journal of Economics*, 26: 409–39.

Orloff, A. (1993) 'Gender and the social rights of citizenship: the comparative analysis of gender relations and welfare states', *American Sociological Review*, 58(3): 303–328.

Orloff, A. (2009) 'Gendering the comparative analysis of welfare states: an unfinished agenda', *Sociological Theory*, 27(3): 317–343.

Orloff, A.S. (2010) 'Gender', in F.G. Castles, S. Leibfried, J. Lewis, H. Obinger and C. Pierson (eds) *The Oxford Handbook of The Welfare State*, Oxford: Oxford University Press, 283–295.

Ortiz-Ospina, E. and Tzvetkova, S. (2017) 'Working women: key facts and trends in female labor force participation', October 16, https://ourworldindata.org/female-labor-force-participation-key-facts#licence [Accessed 6 July 2021].

Osterman, P. (2013) 'Introduction to the special issue on job quality: what does it mean and how might we think about it?', *Industrial and Labor Relations Review*, 66(4): 739–752.

Pahl, J. (2002) 'The gendering of spending within households', *Radical Statistics*, 75: np.

Pascall, G. (2012) *Gender Equality in the Welfare State?*, Bristol: Policy Press.

Patrick, R. (2011) 'Disabling or enabling: the extension of work-related conditionality to disabled people', *Social Policy and Society*, 10(3): 309–320.

Patrick, R. (2012) 'Work as the primary "duty" of the responsible citizen: a critique of this work-centric approach', *People, Place and Policy*, 6(1): 5–15.

Patrick, R. (2014) 'Working on welfare: findings from a qualitative longitudinal study into the lived experiences of welfare reform in the UK', *Journal of Social Policy*, 43(4): 705–725.

Patrick, R. (2016) 'Living with and responding to the "scrounger" narrative in the UK: exploring everyday strategies of acceptance, resistance and deflection', *Journal of Poverty and Social Justice*, 24(3): 245–259.

Patrick, R. (2017) *For Whose Benefit?: The everyday realities of welfare reform*, Bristol: Policy Press.

Patrick, R. and Simpson, M. (2020) 'Conceptualising dignity in the context of social security: bottom-up and top-down perspectives', *Social Policy & Administration*, 54(3): 475–490.

Patrick, R., Power, M., Garthwaite, K., Kaufman, J., Page, G. and Pybus, K., in partnership with the Covid Realities Participants (2022) *A Year Like No Other: Life on a low income during COVID-19*, Bristol: Policy Press.

Pattaro, S., Bailey, N., Williams, E., Gibson, M., Wells, V., Tranmer, M. et al (2022) 'The impacts of benefit sanctions: a scoping review of the quantitative research evidence', *Journal of Social Policy*, 51(3): 611–653.

Pfau-Effinger, B. (2008) 'Cultures of childhood and the relationship of care and employment in European welfare states', in J. Lewis (ed) *Children, Changing Families and Welfare States*, Cheltenham: Edward Elgar Publishing, 137–153.

Pfau-Effinger, B. (2012) 'Women's employment in the institutional and cultural context', *International Journal of Sociology and Social Policy*, 32: 530–43.

Pidd, H. (2020) 'Why Iain Duncan Smith knighthood was "slap in the face"', *The Guardian*, 3 January, https://www.theguardian.com/politics/2020/jan/03/why-iain-duncan-smith-knighthood-was-a-slap-in-the-face [Accessed 6 June 2023].

Prus, R. (1996) *Symbolic Interaction and Ethnographic Research*, New York, NY: SUNY Press.

Public Affairs Committee (PAC) (2012) *Fifteenth Report, 2011–2012: Preventing fraud in contracted employment programmes*, London: House of Commons http://www.publications. parliament.uk/pa/cm201213/cmselect/cmpubacc/103/10302.htm [Accessed 8 October 2021].

Quilter-Pinner, H., Patel, P., O'Grady, T. and Collignon, S. (2022) *Closing the Gap: Parliament, representation and the working class*, London: IPPR.

Rabindrakumar, S. (2017) *On the Rise: Single parent sanctions in numbers*, London: Gingerbread.

Raeymaeckers, P. and Dierckx, D. (2012) 'To work or not to work? The role of the organisational context for social workers' perceptions on activation', *British Journal of Social Work*, 43(6): 1170–1189.

Rafferty, A. and Wiggan, J. (2011) 'Choice and welfare reform: lone parents' decision making around paid work and family life', *Journal of Social Policy*, 40(2): 275–293.

Redman, J. and Fletcher, D.R. (2021) 'Violent bureaucracy: a critical analysis of the British public employment service', *Critical Social Policy*, 42(2): 306–326.

Rees, J., Whitworth, A. and Carter, E. (2014) 'Support for all in the UK Work Programme? Differential payments, same old problem', *Social Policy & Administration*, 48(2): 221–239.

Reeve, K. (2017) 'Welfare conditionality, benefit sanctions and homelessness in the UK: ending the "something for nothing culture" or punishing the poor?', *Journal of Poverty and Social Justice*, 25(1): 65–78.

Reis, S. (2018) *The Impact of Austerity on Women in the UK*, London: Women's Budget Group, https://www.ohchr.org/Documents/Issues/Development/IEDebt/WomenAusterity/WBG.pdf [Accessed 22 July 2021].

Resolution Foundation (2018) *Low Pay Britain 2018*, London: Resolution Foundation.

Rice, D., Fuerta, V. and Monticelli, L. (2018) 'Individualized employment support: does it deliver what is promised?', *International Social Security Review*, 71(4): 91–110.

Ridge, T. (2002) *Childhood Poverty and Social Exclusion: From a child's perspective*, Bristol: Policy Press.

Rhodes, R.A.W. (2011) *Everyday Life in the British Government*, Oxford: Oxford University Press.

Roberts, H., Stuart, S., Allan, S. and Gumley, A. (2022) '"It's like the sword of Damocles": a trauma-informed framework analysis of individuals' experiences of assessment for the Personal Independence Payment benefit in the UK', *Journal of Social Policy*, 1–16.

Robertson, L., Wright, S. and Stewart, A.B.R. (2020) *How Well is Universal Credit Supporting People in Glasgow?*, York: Joseph Rowntree Foundation.

Romero, M. (2018) *Introducing Intersectionality*, Cambridge: Polity Press.

Royston, S. (2012) 'Understanding universal credit', *Journal of Poverty and Social Justice*, 20(1): 69–86.

Rubery, J. and Rafferty A. (2013) 'Women and recession revisited', *Work, Employment and Society*, 27(3): 414–432.

Rubery, J., Keizer, A. and Grimshaw, D. (2016) 'Flexibility bites back: the multiple and hidden costs of flexible employment policies', *Human Resource Management Journal*, 26(3): 235–251.

Rubery, J., Grimshaw, D., Keizer, A. and Johnson, M. (2018) 'Challenges and contradictions in the "normalising" of precarious work', *Work, Employment and Society*, 32(3): 509–527.

Sadeghi, T. and Fekjær, S.B. (2018) 'Frontline workers' competency in activation work', *International Journal of Social Welfare*, 28(1): 77–88.

Sadeghi, T. and Terum, L.I. (2020) 'Frontline managers' perceptions and justifications of behavioural conditionality', *Social Policy & Administration*, 54(2): 219–235.

Sainsbury, R. (2008) 'Administrative justice, discretion and the "welfare to work project"', *Journal of Social Welfare and Family Law*, 30(4): 323–338.

Sage, D. (2013) 'Activation, health and well-being: neglected dimensions?', *International Journal of Sociology and Social Policy*, 33(1/2): 4–20.

Sainsbury, D. (1996) *Gender, Equality and Welfare States,* Cambridge: Cambridge University Press.

Scott, J. (1992) 'Experience', in Butler, J. and Scott, J.W. (eds) *Feminists Theorize the Political*, London: Routledge.

Scottish Government (2018a) *Work First Scotland and Work Able Scotland: Statistics 2017–2018*, Edinburgh: Scottish Government, https://www.gov.scot/publications/scotlands-devolved-employment-services-work-first-scotland-work-scotland-2017-9781788519236/pages/2/ [Accessed 22 September 2021].

Scottish Government (2018b) *Scotland's Devolved Employment Services Work First Scotland and Work Able Scotland, 2017/18*, Edinburgh: Scottish Government, https://www.gov.scot/binaries/content/documents/govscot/publications/statistics/2018/05/scotlands-devolved-employment-services-work-first-scotland-work-scotland-2017-9781788519236/documents/00535688-pdf/00535688-pdf/govscot%3Adocument/00535688.pdf [Accessed 22 September 2021].

Scottish Government (2019) *Universal Credit Scottish Choices: Management information to end August 2019*, Edinburgh: Scottish Government, www2.gov.scot/Resource/0054/00548656.pdf [Accessed 7 November 2019].

Scottish Government (2021) *Early Education and Care*, Edinburgh: Scottish Government, https://www.gov.scot/policies/early-education-and-care/ [Accessed 5 January 2022].

Scullion, L., Gibbons, A., Pardoe, J., Connors, C. and Beck, D. (2022) 'Complex lives: exploring experiences of Universal Credit claimants in Salford during Covid-19', in K. Garthwaite, R. Patrick, M. Power, A. Tarrant and R. Warnock (eds) *COVID-19 Collaborations: Researching Poverty and Low-Income Family Life During the Pandemic*, Bristol: Policy Press.

Senghaas, M., Freier, C. and Kupka, P. (2018) 'Practices of activation in frontline interactions: coercion, persuasion, and the role of trust in activation policies in Germany', *Social Policy & Administration*, https://doi.org/10.1111/spol.12443.

Serrano Pascual, A. and Magnusson, L. (eds) (2007) *Reshaping Welfare States and Activation Regimes in Europe*, Brussels: Peter Lang.

Serwotka, M. (2018) 'Universal Credit and domestic abuse', Public and Commercial Services Union letter to Chair of Work and Pensions Committee, 14 May, https://www.parliament.uk/globalassets/documents/commons-committees/work-and-pensions/Correspondence/pcs-chair-uc-domestic-abuse-140518.pdf [Accessed 18 August 2021].

Sevenhuijsen, S. (1998) *Citizenship and the Ethics of Care*, London: Routledge.

Sharp, N. (2008) *"What's Yours is Mine": The different forms of economic abuse and its impact on women and children experiencing domestic violence*, London: Refuge.

Shaw, J. (2017) *The Introduction of UC*, Edinburgh: Scottish Parliament Information Centre, https://www.parliament.scot/ResearchBriefingsAndFactsheets/S5/SB_17-09_The_Introduction_of_Universal_Credit.pdf [Accessed 23 December 2021].

Simpson, M. and Patrick, R. (2019) *Universal Credit in Northern Ireland: Interim report*, https://pure.ulster.ac.uk/ws/portalfiles/portal/76913293/Universal_credit_in_Northern_Ireland_interim_report_public_version.pdf [Accessed 18 August 2021].

Slater, T. (2012) 'The myth of "broken Britain": welfare reform and the production of ignorance', *Antipode*, 45: 1–22.

Slote, M. (2007) *The Ethics of Care and Empathy*, Abingdon: Routledge.

Smart, C. and Shipman, B. (2004) 'Visions in monochrome: families, marriage and the individualization thesis', *The British Journal of Sociology*, 55(4): 491–509.

Smith, A. and McBride, J. (2021) '"Working to live, not living to work": low-paid multiple employment and work–life articulation', *Work, Employment and Society*, 35(2): 256–276.

Smith, D.E. (1987) *The Everyday World as Problematic: A feminist sociology*, Boston, MA: Northeastern University Press.

Smith, D.E. (1990a) *The Conceptual Practises of Power: A feminist sociology of knowledge*, Toronto: University of Toronto Press.

Smith, D.E. (1990b) *Texts, Facts and Femininity: Exploring the relations of ruling*, London: Routledge.

Smith, D.E. (2004) 'Ideology, science and social relations: a reinterpretation of Marx's epistemology', *European Journal of Social Theory*, 7(4): 445–462.

Smith, D.E. (2005) *Institutional Ethnography: A sociology for people*, Toronto: Altamira Press.

Smith, D.E. (2009) 'Categories are not enough', *Gender and Society*, 23(1): 76–80.

Social Security Advisory Committee (2019) *The Effectiveness of the Claimant Commitment in Universal Credit: A study by the Social Security Advisory Committee,* London: Social Security Advisory Committee.

Social Security Scotland (2021) 'Information on benefits', https://www.socialsecurity.gov.scot/benefits [Accessed 20 August 2021].

Sodha, S. (2016) 'Austerity effect hits women "twice as hard as it does men"', *The Guardian*, 19 November, https://www.theguardian.com/society/2016/nov/19/austerity-women-men-low-income [Accessed 12 December 2022].

Soss, J., Fording, R. and Schram, S.F. (2011a) *Disciplining the Poor*, Chicago, IL: University of Chicago Press.

Soss, J., Fording, R. and Schram, S.F. (2011b) 'The organization of discipline: from performance management to perversity and punishment', *Journal of Public Administration Research and Theory*, 21(sup.2): i203–i232.

Soss, J., Fording, R. and Schram, S.F. (2013) 'Performance management as a disciplinary regime: street-level organizations in a neoliberal era of poverty governance', in E.Z. Brodkin, and G. Marston (eds) *Work and the Welfare State: Street-level organizations and workfare politics*, Washington, DC: Georgetown University Press, 125–139.

Speak, S. (2000) 'Barriers to lone parents' employment', *Local Economy*, 15(1): 32–44.

Standing, G. (2009) *The Precariat: The new dangerous class*, London: Bloomsbury.

Stanley, L. (2018) *Dorothy E. Smith, Feminist Sociology and Institutional Ethnography*, Edinburgh: X Press.

Stinson, H. (2019) 'Supporting people? Universal Credit, conditionality and the recalibration of vulnerability', in P. Dwyer (ed) *Dealing with Welfare Conditionality: Implementation and effects*, Bristol: Policy Press, 15–40.

Sung, S. and Bennett, F. (2007) 'Dealing with money in low-moderate income couples: insights from individual interviews', in K. Clarke, T. Maltby and P. Kennett (eds) *Social Policy Review 19: Analysis and debate in social policy*, Bristol: Policy Press, 151–173.

Taylor, P., Earl, C., Brooke, E. and McLoughlin, C. (2021) 'Older women, public policy and work', in P. Taylor, C. Earl, E. Brooke and C. McLoughlin (eds) *Retiring Women: Work and post-work transitions*, Cheltenham: Edward Elgar, 7–45.

Taylor, P., Earl, C., Brooke, E. and McLoughlin, C. (eds) (2021) *Retiring Women: Work and post-work transitions*, Cheltenham: Edward Elgar.

Terum, L.I., Torsvik, G. and Øverbye, E. (2018) 'Discrimination against ethnic minorities in activation programmes? Evidence from a vignette experiment', *Journal of Social Policy*, 47(1): 39–56.

Torche, F. (2011) 'Is a college degree still the great equaliser? Intergenerational mobility across levels of schooling in the United States', *American Journal of Sociology*, 117(3): 763–807.

The Sutton Trust and Social Mobility Commission (2019) *Elitist Britain 2019: The educational backgrounds of Britain's leading people*, London: Sutton Trust and the Social Mobility Commission, https://www.suttontrust.com/wp-content/uploads/2019/12/Elitist-Britain-2019.pdf [Accessed 23 November 2021].

Thurley, D. and McInnes, R. (2020) *State Pension Age Increases for Women Born in the 1950s: Briefing CBP-7405*, London: House of Commons Library.

Tobio, C. and Trifiletti, R. (2005) 'Strategies, everyday practices and social change', in U. Gerhard, T. Knijn and A. Weckwert (eds) *Working Mothers in Europe: A comparison of policies and practices*, Cheltenham: Edward Elgar, 74–96.

Todd, S. (2004) 'Poverty and aspiration: young women's entry into employment in inter-war England', *Twentieth Century British History*, 15(2): 119–142.

Todd, S. (2005) *Young Women, Work, and Family in England, 1918–1950*, Oxford: Oxford University Press.

Toerien, M., Sainsbury, R., Drew, P. and Irvine, A. (2013) 'Putting personalisation into practice: work-focused interviews in Jobcentre Plus', *Journal of Social Policy*, 42(2): 309–327.

Trades Union Congress (2020) *BME Women and Work*, London: TUC, https://www.tuc.org.uk/research-analysis/reports/bme-women-and-work [Accessed 25 July 2022].

Tronto, J.C. (1993) *Moral Boundaries: A political argument for an ethic of care*, London: Routledge.

TUC (2021) *Extending Working Lives: How to support older workers*, London: TUC, https://www.tuc.org.uk/research-analysis/reports/extending-working-lives-how-support-older-workers [Accessed 25 July 2022].

Uberoi, E., Watson, C., Mutebi, N., Danechi, S. and Bolton, P. (2021) *Women in Politics and Public Life*, briefing 01250, London: House of Commons Library.

University of Oxford (2023) 'Sir Robert Devereux: Biography', Oxford: St Johns College, https://www.sjc.ox.ac.uk/discover/people/sir-robert-devereux/ [Accessed 12 May 2023].

van Berkel, R. (2020) 'Making welfare conditional: a street-level perspective', *Social Policy and Administration*, 54(2): 191–204.

van Berkel, R. and Valkenburg, B. (2007) *Making it Personal: Individualising activation services in the EU*, Bristol: Policy Press.

van Berkel, R. and Knies, E. (2017) 'The frontline delivery of activation: workers' preferences and their antecedents', *European Journal of Social Work*, 21(4): 602–615.

van Berkel, R., Caswell, D., Kupka, P. and Larsen, F. (eds) (2017) *Frontline Delivery of Welfare-to-Work Policies in Europe: Activating the unemployed*, London: Routledge.

Veitch, J. with Bennett, F. (2010) *A Gender Perspective on 21st Century Welfare Reform*, London: Oxfam, https://financialhealthexchange.org.uk/wp-content/uploads/2015/11/A-gender-perspective-on-21st-centruy-welfare-reform.pdf [Accessed 27 July 2021].

Vosko, L.F. (2010) *Managing the Margins: Gender, citizenship, and the international regulation of precarious employment*, Oxford: Oxford University Press.

Wacquant, L. (2009) *Punishing the Poor*, Durham, NC: Duke University Press.

Warhurst, C. (2016) 'Accidental tourists: Brexit and its toxic employment underpinnings', *Socio-Economic Review*, 14(4): 819–25.

Watkins-Hayes, C. (2009) *The New Welfare Bureaucrats: Entanglements of race, class, and policy reform*, Chicago, IL: University of Chicago Press.

Watts, B. and Fitzpatrick, S. (2018) *Welfare Conditionality*, London: Routledge.

Webster, D. (2016) 'Explaining the rise and fall of JSA and ESA sanctions 2010–16', https://cpag.org.uk/policy-and-campaigns/briefing/david-webster-university-glasgow-briefings-benefit-sanctions (Accessed 29 May 2023).

Webster, D. (2021a) *Benefit Sanctions Statistics February 2021*, https://cpag.org.uk/policy-and-campaigns/briefing/david-webster-university-glasgow-briefings-benefit-sanctions [Accessed 24 November 2021].

Webster, D. (2021b) *Benefit Sanctions Statistics August 2021*, https://cpag.org.uk/policy-and-campaigns/briefing/david-webster-university-glasgow-briefings-benefit-sanctions [Accessed 24 November 2021].

Welfare Conditionality (2018) *Final Findings Report Welfare Conditionality Project 2013–2018*, York: University of York.

Welfare Reform Act (2012) London: The Stationery Office, https://www.legislation.gov.uk/ukpga/2012/5/contents [Accessed 21 December 2021].

Welfare Reform and Work Act (2016) London: The Stationery Office, https://www.legislation.gov.uk/ukpga/2016/7/contents [Accessed 21 December 2021].

Wellard, S. (2011) *Doing It All? Grandparents, childcare and employment: an analysis of British Social Attitudes Survey data from 1998 and 2009*, London: Grandparents Plus.

Wheelock, J., Oughton, E. and Barris, S. (2003) 'Getting by with a little help from your family: towards a policy-relevant model of the household', *Feminist Economics*, 9(1): 19–45.

Whiteside, N. (1991) *Bad Times: Unemployment in British social and political history*, London: Faber & Faber.

Whittaker, M. and Hurrell, A. (2013) *Low Pay Britain 2013*, London: Resolution Foundation.

Whitworth, A. and Griggs, J. (2013) 'Lone parents and welfare-to-work conditionality: necessary, just, effective?', *Ethics and Social Welfare*, 7(2): 124–140.

Wiggan, J. (2012) 'Telling stories of 21st century welfare: the UK coalition government and the neo-liberal discourse of worklessness and dependency', *Critical Social Policy*, 32(3): 383–405.

Wiggan, J. (2015) 'Reading active labour market policy politically: an autonomist analysis of Britain's Work Programme and mandatory work activity', *Critical Social Policy*, 35(3): 369–392.

Wiggan, J. (2016) 'Austerity politics', in P. Alcock, T. Haux, M. May and S. Wright (eds) *The Student's Companion to Social Policy*, 5th Edition, London: Wiley-Blackwell, 144–150.

Williams, E. (2021a) 'Unemployment, sanctions and mental health: the relationship between benefit sanctions and antidepressant prescribing', *Journal of Social Policy*, 50(1): 1–20.

Williams, E. (2021b) 'Punitive welfare reform and claimant mental health: the impact of benefit sanctions on anxiety and depression', *Social Policy & Administration*, 55(1): 157–172.

Williams, F. (2001) 'In and beyond New Labour: towards a new political ethic of care', *Critical Social Policy*, 21(4): 467–493.

Williams, F. (2018) 'Intersectionality, gender and social policy', in S. Shaver (ed) *Handbook on Gender and Social Policy*, Cheltenham: Edward Elgar.

Williams, F. (2021) *Social Policy: A critical and intersectionality analysis*, Cambridge: Polity Press.

Williams, R. (1961) *The Long Revolution*, London: Chatto & Windus.

Winchester, N. (2021) *Universal Credit: An end to the uplift*, London: House of Lords.

Wodon, Q., Onagoruwa, A., Malé, C., Montenegro, C., Nguyen, H. and de la Brière, B. (2020) *How Large Is the Gender Dividend? Measuring selected impacts and costs of gender inequality*, cost of gender inequality note, Washington, DC: World Bank.

Women's Aid (2017) 'Women's Aid responds to the Department for Work and Pensions' Benefit Cap: number of households capped to May 2017', https://www.womensaid.org.uk/womens-aid-calls-government-scrap-damaging-benefit-cap/ [Accessed 23 December 2021].

Women's Budget Group (2019) 'DWP data reveals: women and children continue to be worst affected by poverty', Blog 29, London: Women's Budget Group, March, https://wbg.org.uk/blog/dwp-data-reveals-women-continue-to-be-worst-affected-by-poverty/ [Accessed 23 December 2021].

Women's Budget Group (2020) *Social security, Gender and Covid-19: Briefings on coronavirus and inequalities*, London: Women's Budget Group.

Work and Pensions Committee (2018) *Benefit Sanctions: Nineteenth report of session 2017–19*, London: House of Commons.

Work and Pensions Committee (2019) 'Universal Credit and "survival sex"', https://publications.parliament.uk/pa/cm201919/cmselect/cmworpen/83/8304.htm [Accessed 22 May 2023].

World Bank (2020) 'The World Bank in Gender', April 10, https://www.worldbank.org/en/topic/gender/overview [Accessed 6 July 2021].

World Bank (2021a) 'Labour force participation rate, female (percentage of female population 15+) modelled ILO estimate', June 15, https://data.worldbank.org/indicator/SL.TLF.CACT.FE.ZS [Accessed 6 July 2021].

World Bank (2021b) 'World Bank country and lending groups', July, https://datahelpdesk.worldbank.org/knowledgebase/articles/906519-world-bank-country-and-lending-groups [Accessed 6 July 2021].

World Bank (2022) *Women, Business and the Law*, Washington, DC: World Bank.

Women's Aid (2018) 'Briefing on Universal Credit', https://www.womensaid.org.uk/wp-content/uploads/2018/12/Womens-Aid-Briefing-on-Universal-Credit-November-2018-Short-Version.pdf [Accessed 18 August 2021].

Women's Aid (2021) 'What is financial abuse?', https://www.womensaid.org.uk/information-support/what-is-domestic-abuse/financial-abuse/ [Accessed 25 November 2021].

Wood, A.J., Graham, M., Lehdonvirta, V. and Hjorth, I. (2019) 'Good gig, bad gig: autonomy and algorithmic control in the global gig economy', *Work, Employment and Society*, 33(1): 56–75.

Work and Pensions Committee (2016) *The Future of Jobcentre Plus: Second report of session 2016–2017*, House of Commons: London.

Worth, E. (2022) *The Welfare State Generation: Women, agency and class in Britain since 1945*, London: Bloomsbury.

Wright, S. (2003) *Confronting Unemployment in a Street-level Bureaucracy: Jobcentre staff and client perspectives*, Stirling: University of Stirling.

Wright, S. (2011) 'Relinquishing rights? The impact of activation on citizenship for lone parents in the UK', in S. Betzelt and S. Bothfeld (eds) *Activation and Labour Market Reforms in Europe: Challenges to social citizenship*, Basingstoke: Palgrave, 59–78.

Wright, S. (2016) 'Conceptualizing the active welfare subject: welfare reform in discourse, policy and lived experience', *Policy & Politics*, 44(2): 235–252.

Wright, S. and Dwyer, P. (2022) 'In-work Universal Credit: claimant experiences of conditionality mismatches and counterproductive benefit sanctions', *Journal of Social Policy*, 51(1): 20–38.

Wright, S. and Patrick, R. (2019) 'Welfare conditionality in lived experience: aggregating qualitative longitudinal research', *Social Policy and Society*, 18(4): 597–613.

Wright, S., Fletcher, D.R. and Stewart, A. (2020) 'Punitive benefit sanctions, welfare conditionality and the social abuse of unemployed people in Britain: transforming claimants into offenders?', *Social Policy and Administration*, 54(2): 278–294.

Yeandle, S. (1984) *Women's Working Lives: Patterns and strategies*, London: Tavistock.

Young, I.M. (2005) *On Female Body Experience: 'Throwing like a girl' and other essays*, Bloomington, IN: Indiana University Press.

Zacka, B. (2017) *When the State Meets the Street: Public service and moral agency*, Cambridge, MA: The Belknap Press of Harvard University Press.

Index

References to figures, tables and charts appear in **bold** type.
References to the Appendices are indicated with an 'A' (132A).

www.ingramcontent.com/pod-product-compliance
Lightning Source LLC
Chambersburg PA
CBHW070931030426
42336CB00014BA/2621